Among the Host of Heaven

Among the Host of Heaven

The Syro-Palestinian Pantheon as Bureaucracy

Lowell K. Handy

Winona Lake, Indiana
Eisenbrauns
1994

Library of Congress Cataloging-in-Publication Data

Handy, Lowell K., 1949–
     Among the host of Heaven : the Syro-Palestinian pantheon as
bureaucracy / Lowell K. Handy
        p.   cm.
     Includes bibliographical references and indexes.
     ISBN 0-931464-84-6 (alk. paper)
     1. Gods, Semitic.   2. Gods, Syrian.   3. Gods, Canaanite.   4. Gods,
Phoenician.   5. Palestine—Religion.   6. Syria—Religion.
7. Lebanon—Religion.   I. Title.
BL1605.G63H36   1994
299′.2—dc20   94-12969
                                                                       CIP

The paper used in this publication meets the minimum requirements of the
American National Standard for Information Sciences—Permanence of Paper
for Printed Library Materials, ANSI Z39.48-1984.♾™

for my parents

Dr. Ora Addison Handy
and
Doris Mary-Alice Leamon Handy

Ἔστιν δὲ πίστις ἐλπιζομένων ὑπόστασις,
πραγμάτων ἔλεγχος οὐ βλεπομένων
[Hebrews 11:1]

Table of Contents

Preface

The primary research that led to the thesis of this work was done in 1982 as a paper written for a course on Canaanite religion supervised by Gösta W. Ahlström at the University of Chicago. During the following two years, that text doubled and became the second chapter of a doctoral dissertation. The 120-page chapter was just completed when Gary Greig, then of the Oriental Institute archives, who graciously had watched for relevant materials in new publications, announced to me the existence of Mark Smith's one-page article on the four-tiered pantheon at Ugarit. Terror set in, as is natural when a doctoral candidate fears that someone else has preceded him in publishing a novel theory. As it turned out, Smith's perceptive article supported my thesis but did not approach the argument or extent of content I was proposing. The chapter remained pretty much as written in the final dissertation, which was accepted in 1987. During the winter of 1988, the thesis of the dissertation chapter was expanded and updated to become the original manuscript of this volume. It was produced in a quaint, archaic manner on a manual portable typewriter. There was only a single clean copy, and whole sections had to be retyped (all to the sounds of Andrew Lloyd Webber's *Phantom of the Opera*, which may or may not explain anything). That summer the finished manuscript was mailed to Jim Eisenbraun as a proposal for this book. The text was in the process of another revision (this time on a computer, to the accompaniment of Mozart's *Requiem*) when Jim's acceptance letter arrived. An attempt has been made to take seriously work that appeared, or came to my attention after the original manuscript was composed, but it should be assumed that any source published after 1988 was incorporated after the thesis was determined.

It is impossible to thank all of the people who deserve recognition for helping in this project. A long list of professors have directly or indirectly contributed to the production of the volume. At the University of Iowa, where I did my undergraduate and master degrees, I should mention the late Fred Bargebuhr, my first Old Testament professor, who urged me not to allow academics (or academicians) to destroy the life of the texts I studied. Jonathan Goldstein not only taught ancient history, but demonstrated that a teacher could be kind as well as demanding. Special thanks are extended to Ken Kuntz, my M.A. professor and one of the nicest men in academics, who maintained an active interest in my studies through all these years. Indeed, when I first mentioned this book project to Ken, he reminded me of my early work on the subject of gods in Israel and Judah. Sure enough, I was able to dig out a dimly remembered 1972 term paper written for him on the topic, though it did not have the same thesis as this book.

I was enabled to attend the University of Chicago through the generosity of my denomination, the Christian Church (Disciples of Christ). Rev. Frank Hoss, Prof. Don S. Browning, and Dean W. Clark Gilpin were largely responsible for aiding me in being accepted into, as well as finishing, the program. The Division of Higher Education granted generous stipends, scholarships, and living quarters for the duration of my studies at Chicago, which allowed me to research this subject. For the funds required of me, thanks are due to The United States Gypsum Company, who employed me "on the line" for five years at their Fort Dodge plant, knowing I would leave when I had funds for doctoral studies.

I owe a great debt, which this volume cannot repay, to my doctoral committee. They were a bit skeptical when I proposed the topic but agreed to oversee the project anyway. Not only did they pressure me to tie up loose ends, use terms properly, and avoid speculation, they also encouraged as much condensation as possible. Thanks go to Frank Reynolds for supplying knowledge of hierarchic mythological structures in comparative religions and continued reminders that history of religions scholars use terms differently from Bible scholars. Walter Michel deserves special commendation for being the most suspicious of the entire endeavor at the outset and ending the dissertation process by being my most enthusiastic supporter. What can one say about Gösta Ahlström? I chose a topic he was not particularly interested in and used an approach he was not too fond of and that required some positions he didn't believe in at the time, but he nevertheless allowed me to "try it." In a field in which recapitulation of an advisor's thesis has become the norm for doctoral work, Professor Ahlström allowed me to investigate on my own, to produce what I wanted, and to argue using my own methods. This is what higher education is supposed to do and he cannot be praised too highly for keeping the process alive.

As those who have been there know, the University of Chicago will grind a student into pulp if possible. Friends keep a student from going under. I cannot mention all who should be named, but I want to list some of the friends who held me together through hard times (and continue to do so). Heartfelt thanks are due to Larry Bouchard, Peter Browning, Elena Chermak, Larry Colvin, Steven Holloway, Mary Patrick, Elaine Ramshaw, Julie Ryan, and Erica Treesh (as mixed a group of saints as one is apt to find this side of heaven). During the time that the manuscript awaited confirmation, three people encouraged me to continue with the project: Shirley Jenke, Tom Thompson, and Diana Edelman, who supplied much-needed enthusiasm for the work when exhaustion set in. They are as responsible for its final appearance in print as anyone. Two people kindly read drafts of the manuscript and made helpful suggestions. Innumerable errors in spelling and grammar were caught in a gracious reading of the manuscript by Erica Treesh, as well as advice about clarity and just plain common sense. Steven Holloway did a careful reading and offered numerous suggestions, which found their way into the final production (including the need for a section on the future possibilities of the Ebla materials).

Finally, my parents, to whom the book is dedicated, cannot be thanked adequately enough. Throughout my life they kept a house stocked with books (to which they may now add one more) and encouraged avid reading by their example. They raised me to take seriously the religious convictions of others (an extension of the ecumenical movement of the Disciples of Christ), which I have attempted to put into practice in this study, even though the Syro-Palestinian devotees have long since departed. They have patiently supported me through all the frustrations of education and the completion of this work. Due to their insistence that serious work entails taking a hard look at reality and telling the truth about what one sees, I have attempted to produce a study of our religious origins. I hope they will be as proud of it as I am of them.

Easter, 1991

I would like to thank Beverly Fields and Jim Eisenbraun for their careful editing of the manuscript and for allowing me to add numerous items to the footnotes when the proofs were otherwise ready.

March 25, 1994

Abbreviations

AB	Anchor Bible
AfO	*Archiv für Orientforschung*
AIPHOS	Annuaire de l'institut de philologie et d'histoire orientales et slaves
AIR	*Ancient Israelite Religion*, ed. Patrick D. Miller Jr., Paul D. Hanson, and S. Dean McBride (Philadelphia: Fortress, 1987)
AJA	*American Journal of Archaeology*
AKM	Abhandlungen für die Kunde des Morgenlands
ANEP	*The Ancient Near East in Pictures Relating to the Old Testament*, ed. James B. Pritchard, 2d ed. with supp. (Princeton: Princeton University Press, 1969)
ANET	*Ancient Near Eastern Texts Relating to the Old Testament*, ed. James B. Pritchard, 3d ed. with supp. (Princeton: Princeton University Press, 1969)
AnOr	Analecta orientalia
ANRW	Aufstieg und Niedergang der römischen Welt
AOAT	Alter Orient und Altes Testament
AOS	American Oriental Series
ARET	Archivi reali di Ebla
ArOr	*Archiv orientální*
ASR	*American Sociological Review*
ASTI	*Annual of the Swedish Theological Institute*
BA	*Biblical Archaeologist*
BARev	*Biblical Archaeology Review*
BASOR	*Bulletin of the American Schools of Oriental Research*
BDB	F. Brown, S. R. Driver, and C. Briggs, *A Hebrew and English Lexicon of the Old Testament with an Appendix Containing the Biblical Aramaic* (Oxford: Oxford University Press, 1906)
BeO	*Bibbia e oriente*
BETL	Bibliotheca ephemeridum theologicarum lovaniensium
BibOr	Biblica et orientali
BibSal	Bibliotheca Salamanticensis
BJRL	*Bulletin of the John Rylands University Library of Manchester*

BJS	Brown Judaic Studies
BO	*Bibliotheca orientalis*
BOH	Bibliotheca orientalis hungarica
BR	*Biblical Research*
BRA	Beitráge zur Religionsgeschichte des Altertums
BSBA	Baker Studies in Biblical Archaeology
BVsAWL	Berichte über die Verhandlungen der sächsischen Akademie der Wissenschaften zu Leipzig
BZAW	Beihefte zur Zeitschrift für die alttestamentliche Wissenschaft
CAD	The Assyrian Dictionary of the Oriental Institute of the University of Chicago
CBCNEB	The Cambridge Bible Commentary on the New English Bible
CBQ	*Catholic Biblical Quarterly*
CBQMS	Catholic Biblical Quarterly Monograph Series
CBSC	Cambridge Bible for Schools and Colleges
ConBOT	Coniectanea biblica, Old Testament
CRB	Cahiers de *Revue biblique*
DMOA	Documenta et monumenta orientalia antiqui
EI	Eretz Israel
EncJud	*Encyclopaedia Judaica* (1971)
EPROER	Études préliminaires aux religions orientales dans l'Empire Romain
ERE	*Encyclopedia of Religion and Ethics*, ed. James Hastings (12 vols.; Edinburgh: T. & T. Clark, 1908–1922)
EstBib	*Estudios bíblicos*
FCB	Fuentes de la ciencia bíblica
FGrH	*Die Fragmente der griechischen Historiker*, ed. Felix Jacoby (Leiden: Brill, 1958)
HdA	Handbuch der Archäologie
HSM	Harvard Semitic Monographs
HSS	Harvard Semitic Studies
HTR	*Harvard Theological Review*
HUCA	*Hebrew Union College Annual*
ICC	International Critical Commentary
IEJ	*Israel Exploration Journal*
Int	*Interpretation*
JAOS	*Journal of the American Oriental Society*
JAOSSup	Supplement to the *Journal of the American Oriental Society*
JBL	*Journal of Biblical Literature*
JCS	*Journal of Cuneiform Studies*
JFSR	*Journal of Feminist Studies in Religion*
JHNES	Johns Hopkins Near Eastern Studies

JJS	*Journal of Jewish Studies*
JNES	*Journal of Near Eastern Studies*
JNSL	*Journal of Northwest Semitic Languages*
JPOS	*Journal of the Palestine Oriental Society*
JPSTC	Jewish Publication Society Torah Commentary
JSOT	*Journal for the Study of the Old Testament*
JSOTSup	Journal for the Study of the Old Testament Supplement Series
JSS	*Journal of Semitic Studies*
JTS	*Journal of Theological Studies*
KAI	*Kanaanäische und aramäische Inschriften*, ed. H. Donner and W. Röllig (Wiesbaden: Harrassowitz, 1969–1973)
KB	L. Koehler and W. Baumgartner, *Lexicon in Veteris Testamenti libros* (Leiden: Brill, 1958)
KC	Kamper Cahiers
KTU	M. Dietrich, O. Loretz, and J. Sanmartín, *Die keilalphabetischen Texte aus ugarit: Einschliesslich der keilalphabetischen Texte ausserhalb Ugarits: Teil 1 Transkription* (AOAT 24; Kevelaer: Butzon & Bercker/Neukirchen-Vluyn: Neukirchener Verlag, 1976)
LAPO	Littératures anciennes du proche-orient
LCL	Loeb Classical Library
LEC	Library of Early Christianity
LSJ	Liddell, Scott, Jones, *Greek-English Lexicon* (Oxford: Oxford University Press, 1979)
MIO	Mitteilungen des Instituts für Orientforschung
MRS	Mission de Ras Shamra
N	Nisaba
NCE	*New Catholic Encyclopedia*
OLP	Orientalia lovaniensia periodica
OP	*The Organization of Power: Aspects of Bureaucracy in the Ancient Near East*, ed. McGuire Gibson and Robert D. Biggs (SAOC 46; Chicago: Oriental Institute of the University of Chicago, 1987)
Or	*Orientalia*
OTL	Old Testament Library
OTS	*Oudtestamentische Studiën*
OTSt	Old Testament Studies
PA	Problème der Ägyptologie
PEQ	*Palestine Exploration Quarterly*
PhHKA	Philosophische-Historische Klasse Abhandlungen new series
POS	Pretoria Oriental Series
RA	*Revue d'assyriologie et d'archéologie orientale*

RAI	Rencontre assyriologique internationale
RB	*Revue biblique*
RHA	*Revue hittite et asianique*
RHR	*Revue de l'histoire des religions*
RM	Die Religionen der Menscheit
RSP III	*Ras Shamra Parallels: The Texts from Ugarit and the Hebrew Bible*, vol. 3, ed. Stan Rummel (AnOr 51; Rome: Pontifical Biblical Institute, 1981)
SAOC	Studies in Ancient Oriental Civilization
SARC	Centro di Studi Semitici: Serie Archeologica
SBLDS	Society of Biblical Literature Dissertation Series
SBLMS	Society of Biblical Literature Monograph Series
SBLTT	Society of Biblical Literature Texts and Translations
SBT	Studies in Biblical Theology
SCL	Sather Classical Lectures
SeD	Studia et documenta
SHANE	Studies in the History of the Ancient Near East
SJOT	*Scandinavian Journal of the Old Testament*
SS	Studia semitici
SSN	Studia semitica nederlandica
SSS	Semitic Studies Series
ST	*Studia theologica*
STEANE	*State and Temple Economy in the Ancient Near East*, ed. Edward Lipiński (Orientalia Lovaniensia Analecta 6; Louvain: Department Oriëntalistiek, 1979)
StudOr	Studia orientali
SupN	Supplementa ad numen, altera sreies
SWBAS	The Social World of Biblical Antiquity Series
TDOT	*Theological Dictionary of the Old Testament*, ed. G. Johannes Botterweck and Helmer Ringgren (Grand Rapids, Mich.: Eerdmans, 1974–1990). 6 vols.
TSH	Le trésor spirituel de l'humanité
TSSI	J. C. L. Gibson, *Textbook of Syrian Semitic Inscriptions* (Oxford: Clarendon Press, 1971–1982). 3 vols.
TUAT	Texte aus der Umwelt des Alten Testaments
TZ	*Theologische Zeitschrift*
UBL	Ugaritisch-Biblische Literatur
UF	*Ugarit Forschungen*
UHDP	L'Univers: Histoire et description des tous les peuples
UT	Cyrus H. Gordon, *Ugaritic Textbook* (AnOr 38; Rome: Pontifical Biblical Institute, 1965)
VAB	Vorderasiatische Bibliothek
VT	*Vetus Testamentum*
VTSup	Vetus Testamentum Supplements

WS	World Spirituality: An Encyclopedic History of the Religious Quest
WUS	J. Aistleitner, *Wörterbuch der ugaritischen Sprache* (Berlin: Akademie, 1974)
YSE	Yale Studies in English
ZA	*Zeitschrift für Assyriologie und Vorderasiatische Archäologie*
ZASA	*Zeitschrift für Ägyptische Sprache und Altertumskunde*
ZAW	*Zeitschrift für die alttestamentliche Wissenschaft*

Among the Host of Heaven

Chapter 1

Introduction

Whenever anything as nebulous as religious thought becomes the object of scholarly study, there is a built-in chasm between those who do the studying and those whose religious beliefs are being studied. It doesn't matter how much objective data may be collected, religious understanding, as it is known to those who hold that understanding, necessarily eludes any scholar who attempts to describe the "faith" from outside the tradition. Much of religious thought comes couched in symbolic terminology intended to be understood as such by the faithful "insider" but left uncertain in the mind of the "outsider." Great numbers of primary sources, while necessary for a satisfactory description of a religious tradition, usually are, in themselves, insufficient for a clear presentation of a religious tradition. Without "insider" aid in the interpretation of sources, either by commentaries or, preferably, by members of the tradition itself, any description of another's religious convictions remains at best theoretical. Even with adequate primary sources and legitimate commentators it is impossible to gauge the variety within a given religious tradition without being able to examine thoroughly all believers adhering to the faith.

It is, then, with some audacity that anyone decides to explain religious traditions for which there is next to nothing in the way of source material and not a single living devotee of the culture to consult. The religious vision of the world held by some of the people of Syria–Palestine living between the middle of the second millennium B.C.E. and the middle of the first millennium C.E. presents just such a problem.[1] The virtual lack of primary source material has not kept

---

1. In this study *Syria–Palestine* refers to an area encompassing the city-states located at the eastern end of the Mediterranean Sea, including the "Phoenician" coastal cities, the western Syrian states, and the hill country often designated in terms of the minor nations of Israel, Judah, Moab, and others. The time frame has been chosen, not

3

scholars from making several attempts to create a coherent religious vision out of the varied but quite fragmented data currently available. There are just enough sources extant from the culture to be tantalizing while being noticeably insufficient for gaining a sure grasp of the beliefs behind them. However, failing major and numerous discoveries of cultic, legendary, and mythological literature from which to reconstruct a Syro-Palestinian religious world view, all such systematic reconstructions will continue to be built on nebulous rather than firm foundations. The following study is no exception.

The thesis of this study is quite simple.[2] Since the continuing governmental system of Syria–Palestine was found in the city-state, it would appear most reasonable to seek for a key to unlocking the nature of the culture's religion in the structure of these city-states. This would appear all the more probable in that all extant primary texts from which these religious beliefs must be constructed derive from members of city-state scribal circles. The view of the world, structure of society, and vision of the ordered cosmos available to the modern world is the view of these scribes and reflects the norms inculcated in them by their city-states, scribal schools, and position in society.[3] Several aspects of the mythological portrayal of their world

---

because either the beginning or ending dates signal the temporal limits of the religious culture of the area, but for the simple reason that the narrative literature upon which a study such as this depends originated during the period between these two admittedly arbitrary dates.

2. A lecture that presented a condensed rendition of the original thesis has been published: Lowell K. Handy, "Dissenting Deities or Obedient Angels: Divine Hierarchies in Ugarit and the Bible," BR 35 (1989) 18–35. It might be well to point out that this investigation is not a "structuralist" study in the manner of Lévi-Strauss, though such attempts have been made: David L. Petersen and Mark Woodward, "Northwest Semitic Religion: A Study of Relational Structures," UF 9 (1977) 233–48; Gregorio del Olmo Lete, "La estructura del panteón ugarítico," in Salvación en la palabra: Targum-Derash-Berith: En memoria del professor Alejandro Diez Macho (ed. Domingo Muñoz Leon; Madrid: Ediciones Cristiandad, 1986) 267–304; and recently, with a Jungian twist, Nicolas Wyatt, "Quaternities in the Mythology of Baᶜal," UF 21 (1989) 451–59; but see caution about such an approach in J. C. L. Gibson, "The Theology of the Ugaritic Baal Cycle," Or 53 (1984) 203.

3. André Caquot and Maurice Sznycer, Ugaritic Religion (Iconography of Religions 15/8; Leiden: Brill, 1980) 6. On the self-contained world view of the scribal schools, see Piotr Michalowski, "Charisma and Control: On Continuity and Change in Early Mesopotamian Bureaucratic Systems," in The Organization of Power: Aspects of Bureaucracy in the Ancient Near East (ed. McGuire Gibson and Robert D. Biggs; SAOC 46; Chicago: Oriental Institute of the University of Chicago, 1987) 62–64; and now see Ronald F. G. Sweet, "The Sage in Mesopotamian Palaces and Royal Courts," in The Sage in Israel and the Ancient Near East (ed. John G. Gammie and Leo G. Perdue; Winona Lake, Ind.: Eisenbrauns, 1990) 101–7; R. N. Whybray, "The Sage in the Israelite Royal Court," in Sage in Israel and the ANE, 137–39; Leo G. Perdue, "Cosmology and the Social Order in the Wisdom Tradition," in Sage in Israel and the ANE, 457–78.

should be explained by taking into consideration the hierarchical and bureaucratic government of a city-state. It is doubtful, however, that a completely satisfactory explanation of Syro-Palestinian religion may be constructed solely from any one model, including governing structures. Yet, certain activities, characteristics, and relationships that have been ascribed to the gods of Syria–Palestine may be intelligible in terms of bureaucratic structure.

RETHINKING THE STRUCTURE OF THE PANTHEON

The ability of existing theories concerned with Syro-Palestinian religious thought to deal adequately with the data in terms of a religious vision of the universe has recently come under increasing criticism.[4] The early facile equation of mythological narratives with cultic ritual, especially the fertility cult, has been questioned for some time. One school of thought had believed that a common mythological and ritual culture had permeated the whole of the ancient Near East and this "Myth and Ritual" scheme was argued to be discernible in the fragmented sources from "Canaan" as well.[5] The possibility of finding such a pattern in the texts of Ugarit was soon observed to be at best dubious, casting doubt on the larger area of Syria–Palestine as well.[6] Since Ugaritic textual material provided the only extensive primary mythological data, these tablets became the center of study for Syro-Palestinian thought. The most popular position taken with regard to the mythological world represented in the texts from Ugarit has been that these stories are related to the natural changes in the seasons.

4. For two recent critiques of popular theories based on the texts from Ugarit, see Robert A. Oden, "Theoretical Assumptions in the Study of Ugaritic Myths," *MAARAV* 2 (1979) 43–63; and Mark S. Smith, "Interpreting the Baal Cycle," *UF* 18 (1986) 313–39. On the purposes of ancient myths in general, it is still worthwhile to consult G. S. Kirk, *Myth: Its Meaning and Functions in Ancient and Other Cultures* (Sather Classical Lectures 40; London: Cambridge University Press/Berkeley: University of California Press, 1970).

5. The pattern of this school is most clearly set forth in two volumes, both edited by S. H. Hooke, *Myth and Ritual: Essays on the Myth and Ritual of the Hebrews in Relation to the Culture Pattern of the Ancient East* (Oxford: Oxford University Press, 1933); *The Labyrinth: Further Studies in the Relation between Myth and Ritual in the Ancient World* (London: SPCK, 1935). That this pattern was to be found in Canaan is argued by S. H. Hooke, "Traces of the Myth and Ritual Pattern in Canaan," in *Myth and Ritual*, 68–86.

6. R. de Lange, "Myth, Ritual, and Kingship in the Ras Shamra Tablets," in *Myth, Ritual, and Kingship: Essays on the Theory and Practice of Kingship in the Ancient Near East and in Israel* (ed. S. H. Hooke; Oxford: Clarendon, 1958) 122–48. A refutation of this standard pattern was made by Henri Frankfort, *Kingship and the Gods: A Study of Ancient Near Eastern Religion as the Integration of Society and Nature* (Chicago: University of Chicago Press, 1978), first published in 1948. However, the same methodology reappears in more modern "structuralist" approaches; see, for example, Stan Rummel, "Narrative Structures in the Ugaritic Texts," in *RSP III*, 221–332.

The myths are to be seen either as ritual drama in which the religious community marked the cycle of the seasons, or as mythological and liturgical narratives explaining how the seasons come about.[7] Yet, while the seasonal theory remains popular, it has fallen prey to the observation that there simply is too little actual data in the texts to sustain it.[8] In these theories an understanding of the pantheon is based squarely on the notion that the gods reflect natural phenomena. Either the gods are representations of natural events, or they are literary portrayals of seasonal changes of the yearly cycle. While it is certainly true that aspects of natural phenomena are included in the characteristics of at least some of the deities, there is no clear sense of a cyclical pattern to the myths that could suggest seasonal periods.[9] For the seasonal theories regarding the mythological religious texts, the assumed center of the Syro-Palestinian religious universe is agriculture; yet, no matter where the deities may have originally arisen, the texts in which they are now portrayed were created by scribes in the urban city-states rather than by rural agriculturalists, and the characters of the deities reflect their literary origin.[10]

Clearly the deities, not only at Ugarit but in all the extant sources for Syria–Palestine, are portrayed not as natural phenomena, but as anthropomorphic beings. Thus, it would be better argued that the basis for the literary portrayal of the gods in religious mythology was the institution of the city-state, in which the authors themselves were living. The scribes present these deities in a manner familiar to their experience within an operational government. It has been suggested that there was a one-to-one correspondence between the way human families functioned in ancient Ugarit and the way the deities of that city-state acted in the myths.[11] The familial model for mythological relationships among the deities in Phoenician city-states has been used to the extent that every major religious cult is assumed to

7. The most famous presentation of the myths as religious drama is that by Theodore H. Gaster, *Thespis: Ritual, Myth, and Drama in the Ancient Near East* (New York: Norton, 1961), first published in 1950. The myths as seasonal narratives have been described by Johannes C. de Moor, *The Seasonal Pattern of the Ugaritic Myth of Baʿlu According to the Version of Ilimilku* (AOAT 16; Kevalaer: Butzon & Bercker/Neukirchen-Vluyn: Neukirchener Verlag, 1971); see also his *New Year with Canaanites and Israelites, Part One: Description* (Kamper Cahiers 21; Kampen: Kok, 1972). Gibson ("Theology," 210–17) notes that there is a heavy cosmological aspect to these tales even if they are seasonal in some respects.

8. Lester L. Grabbe, "The Seasonal Pattern and the 'Baal Cycle,'" *UF* 8 (1976): 57–63; Oden, "Theoretical Assumptions," 46–48; M. S. Smith, "Interpreting," 314–16.

9. Grabbe, "Seasonal Pattern," 57.

10. On the shift from rural to urban renditions of myth, see Kirk, *Myth*, 252–53.

11. Most extensively posited by A. van Selms, *Marriage and Family Life in Ugaritic Literature* (POS 1; London: Luzac, 1954) 10.

have been constructed around a divine nuclear family creating (always) a triad of gods: father, mother, and child. However, it was not necessary for the family structure to be central for the deities to have been presented anthropomorphically.[12] It does not take a great leap of imagination to theorize that the divine method of governing the cosmos must have been analogous to the governing structure among the devotees.[13] Unfortunately, there is no real evidence for such a close correspondence between the actions of human society and the portrayal of the activities of the gods.[14] It may, in fact, be inferred from the actions ascribed to some of the deities in certain of the myths that the authors were not attempting to display an ideal vision of reality.[15] Neither is there anything in the mythological narratives that would support a theory that the authors were attempting through the myths to legitimate the current structure of their human society by idealizing it in a divine realm.[16]

The contrary position has been posited by some scholars, that insofar as the members of the divine pantheon are shown in less than ideal light in the narratives found at Ugarit, the Late Bronze Age must have found itself in a state of religious crisis. De Moor has called the divine population of the Ugaritic religious literature "the pantheon of disillusion."[17] In this vision of the divine government of the cosmos, the human population had passed into a sort of futile pessimism in which there was no hope of escape from the arbitrary whims of the individual gods, which led inevitably to the nothingness of death.[18] In much the same manner, Wyatt sees the final basic content of the Ugaritic mythological narratives to be an acknowledgment that death is the only constant in the universe.[19] It is unlikely,

---

12. The triadic structure of these pantheons has been a popular theory. See Sabatino Moscati, *The World of the Phoenicians* (New York: Praeger, 1968) 36–37; Albert van den Branden, "La Triade phénicienne," *BeO* 23 (1981) 35–63. But the theory has been shown to rest on quite questionable data: see Richard J. Clifford, "Phoenician Religion," *BASOR* 279 (1990) 62. The pantheon of Palmyra has been described on the basis of triads found on the sculptures, yet most of the depictions of deities portray more than three deities: H. J. W. Drijvers, *The Religion of Palmyra* (Iconography of Religions 15/15; Leiden: Brill, 1976) 13.

13. John Macdonald, "An Assembly at Ugarit?" *UF* 11 (1979) 525.

14. Oden, "Theoretical Assumptions," 51–52.

15. See the study by Nicolas Wyatt, "The Hollow Crown: Ambivalent Elements in West Semitic Royal Ideology," *UF* 18 (1986) 421–36.

16. Oden, "Theoretical Assumptions," 55–56.

17. Johannes C. de Moor, "The Crisis of Polytheism in Late Bronze Ugarit," *OTS* 24 (1986) 3.

18. Ibid., 7, 9, 15–16.

19. Nicolas Wyatt, "Cosmic Entropy in Ugaritic Religious Thought," *UF* 17 (1985) 386.

however, that the religion of Syria–Palestine, or even of Ugarit, can be reduced to an embodiment of anxiety.[20] The imperfections of the divine realm that appear in the narratives might better be assumed to reflect the imperfections of the human realm, adapted by the authors of the myths to beings holding more power than mere mortals and, indeed, controlling the universe. It should not be assumed that the presentation of flawed behavior on the part of divine citizens reflects the despair of the authors; rather, these less than ideal behavior patterns among the gods would seem to reflect the less than ideal behavior of bureaucrats who must function within a hierarchy much like the hierarchical structure found in the city-states where the scribal authors were composing these visions of the governing forces of the universe.

THE TENUOUSNESS OF THEORIES

If previous theories of Syro-Palestinian religious thought had major failings, it was due to the fact that the materials from which this religion must be reconstructed are few in the extreme. A proper understanding of the sources was far from certain even where a consensus may have been reached. Whenever more information becomes available, the reconstructed religious tradition changes, often radically. The texts from Ugarit completely modified positions that had been worked out to a general consensus in the nineteenth century. Even such a simple question as whether one is dealing in a given text with the name of a deity or something else generates a kaleidoscope of debate and revision.[21] This continuing debate needs to be pointed out, not so much to show where scholarship has gone wrong in the past, but in order to emphasize again the fact that theories about the religion of Syria–Palestine remain "wrong" and need (and will continue to need) to be reexamined and corrected.

Yet another problem related to the propagation of theories must be noted. It is a well-established fact about religious traditions that they change through time in thought and cult; this is generally known as "evolution." In the study of religious traditions there has often been a tendency to view this change as a universal progression

---

20. Oden, "Theoretical Assumptions," 49–50.

21. Examples of this shifting consensus on the various deities in Syria–Palestine appear in this book as each divinity is introduced. Among the lesser deities the confusion extends even to their existence; see, for a recent example, Donna Freilich, "Is There an Ugaritic Deity *Bbt*?" *JSS* 31 (1986) 119–30. The major deities are not immune to being argued away, as with Mot in Mark S. Smith's "Death in Jeremiah, IX, 20," *UF* 19 (1987) 292–93.

through which all religious traditions must pass.[22] It has also usually been assumed that all religious traditions passed from simple to complex organizations, moving through the same set of steps in their structures and theories.[23] Unfortunately, evolution is not unilinear and cannot be charted for all societies by using a single, universal scheme.[24] Any changes in a society are related to the characteristics and institutions of the individual society, and responses made by a culture to specific problems are limited by unique cultural patterns.[25] For the study of the Syro-Palestinian world these cultural patterns are insufficiently well known, either historically, through time, or geographically, in a particular location (let alone for the entire area), to provide an evolutionary schema of Syro-Palestinian religious thought. It may safely be said that the culture shows development and change,[26] but, unfortunately, it is impossible to demonstrate what that development was. Because the sources are sparse and derive from widely scattered sites, it is likely that the changes may never be adequately charted.

To propose another model for understanding the Syro-Palestinian gods' dealings with each other and with the cosmos is to add yet another tenuous theory to an already large accumulation of dubious work lacking a solid base. My model is as likely to become outdated by future discoveries as any other posited theory. However, it does demand that the mythological world of Syria–Palestine be placed directly in the social structure known and lived by the authors of the myths themselves. The centers from which these texts derive were the city-state scribal schools, and it is to the scribal view of the cosmos that the mythological religious vision must be connected.

22. The modern origins of this type of evolutionary theory may be found in Edward Herbert, *De veritate* (Bristol: Arrowsmith, 1937), first published in 1624; he expanded his theory of the development of religions in *De religione laici* (YSE 98; New Haven, Conn.: Yale University Press, 1944), first published in 1645; and in Auguste Comte, *Cours de philosophie positive* (4th ed.; Paris: Baillière et Fils, 1877), 1st ed. 1930. See Geo Widengren, "Evolutionism and the Problem of the Origin of Religion," *Ethnos* 10 (1945) 57–96.

23. Robert N. Bellah, "Religious Evolution," *ASR* 29 (1964) 358. See also the survey of such theories in Widengren, "Evolutionism," 72–90.

24. S. N. Eisenstadt, "Social Change, Differentiation, and Evolution," *ASR* 29 (1964) 375.

25. Ibid., 376–78. One may note as well the whole problem of understanding the metaphorical meanings, at any given point in time, that a particular culture places on its own religious language and divine "theology." For a survey of some of the problems involved, see Marjo Christina Annette Korpel, *A Rift in the Clouds: Ugaritic and Hebrew Descriptions of the Divine* (UBL 8; Munster: Ugarit, 1990) 1–34.

26. Patrick D. Miller, Jr., "Ugarit and the History of Religion," *JNSL* 9 (1981) 119.

BUREAUCRACY IN THE ANCIENT NEAR EAST

The biggest problem with suggesting that bureaucracy might have been used as a model for understanding the behavior of the divine world in Syria–Palestine is the fact that *bureaucracy* is a rather nebulous notion. What bureaucracy is understood to be in modern sociological studies remains related to what Max Weber said it was in the nineteenth century.[27] However, Weber was describing "ideal types" and not a functioning organization fraught with problems. He defined an ideal bureaucracy by identifying three factors:[28]

1. Legal authority
   - Rules are established by imposition or agreement on grounds of expediency covering all persons in the organization
   - The body of laws that govern the system is consistent, abstract, intentional, and employed in individual cases
   - One "in authority" occupies an "office"
   - Whoever obeys its authority belongs to the organization
   - When one obeys an authority one obeys the impersonal office in the organization, not the individual
2. Hierarchy
   - A continuous organization of official functions bound by rules
   - Those within the organization perform within a sphere of competence, consisting of: (1) obligations to perform as part of the division of labor; (2) authority given to perform the organization's functions; (3) means to perform its function within definite conditions
   - Each lower office is under the control and supervision of a higher one (= hierarchy)
   - There are regulations for each office, ensuring that an individual is competent to hold it
   - Members of the organization do not own the organization
   - Rights of an office are due the office, not the individual holding it
   - All types of corporate action are articulated in writing
   - Legal authority can be exercised in many different forms

27. Max Weber, *The Theory of Social and Economic Organization* (New York: Free Press, 1947) 324–41.

28. Ibid., 329–34. The points listed here have been paraphrased. For a point-by-point discussion of each item as it relates to the mythological world of Syria–Palestine, see Lowell K. Handy, "A Realignment in Heaven: An Investigation into the Ideology of the Josianic Reform" (Ph.D. diss., University of Chicago, 1987) 118–28.

3. Personnel
  • They are personally free, subject to authority only in their impersonal, official obligations
  • Organized in a hierarchy of offices
  • Each office has a clearly defined sphere of competence
  • The office is a free, contractual relationship
  • One who holds an office is selected because of qualifications to hold that office
  • Remuneration is by fixed salary
  • The office is treated as the sole occupation of the person holding it
  • An office is a career, and promotion comes through superiors
  • Officials do not own the means of administration
  • The official is subject to discipline and control

In order for "bureaucracy" to be a useful category for studying Syro-Palestinian thought, it must be considered as a functioning entity and not as "pure type." Various attempts have been made to restructure Weber's ideal with actual organizational practice.[29] A bureaucracy functions rather than exists by means of innumerable relationships that are developed throughout the organization; most of what takes place within the organization is unrelated to ideal functioning and may even subvert the purpose of the organization as much as aid it.[30] Even though these activities may produce a certain amount of turmoil, the various kinds of malfunctioning within an organization are an inseparable part of bureaucracy.[31] It is the functioning bureaucracy, in all its working aspects, that is of importance as a model for this study, since it is unlikely that the ancient writers of mythology were attempting to produce an ideal model reflecting an abstract notion of statecraft; but they did reflect the hierarchy they knew and of which they were an integral part when they described the heavenly realm.

29. Two general critical articles are useful as overviews and correctives: Gerald M. Britan and Ronald Cohen, "Toward an Anthropology of Formal Organizations," in *Hierarchy and Society: Anthropological Perspectives on Bureaucracy* (ed. Gerald M. Britan and Ronald Cohen; Philadelphia: Institute for the Study of Human Issues, 1980) 9–30; and Stanislav Andreski, *Max Weber's Insights and Errors* (London: Routledge & Kegan Paul, 1984) 99–107. Andreski has outlined the definition of bureaucracy with five points: (1) the divisions of spheres of authority are determined by regulations; (2) a hierarchy of offices channels communication through proper hierarchic levels; (3) official activities are completely separate from private affairs; (4) people are thoroughly trained for holding an office; and (5) all official duties are discharged in accordance with general rules (this is a paraphrase of his list, p. 99).

30. Britan and Cohen, "Anthropology of Formal Organizations," 16–17.

31. Andreski, *Max Weber*, 100.

Recently it has become acceptable to assume that some form of bureaucratic structure functioned in the ancient Near Eastern governmental systems. Whether what scholars mean by this term is a hierarchical series of offices, filled by people who are believed to be competent to carry out such work, or just an institution of scribes for the purpose of tallying the economy of the state, there appear to have been bureaucratic offices at the centers of ancient Near Eastern culture.[32] What we now know of the hierarchy in the city-states, of which the bureaucratic offices formed a part, came to us through what was recorded by the scribes trained in scribal schools. They would have had the same scribal school education that the authors of religious narratives did. Therefore the records that presented a structure for the hierarchy of both the human governments and the divine came from the same social milieu.

The information from which the government of city-states is reconstructed allows a multitude of interpretations. It has often been assumed that the ruling force in the Syro-Palestinian city-state was the city assembly.[33] The idea of finding "democratic" rule by public assembly in the cultures of the ancient Near East was sparked by Jacobsen when he argued that the societies that had invented the mythological world of preliterate Mesopotamia must have ruled themselves in democratic assemblies of all free adults.[34] Even if such assembles existed, and the evidence is questionable at best, they clearly had lost ruling authority long before the extant Syro-Palestinian mythological narratives were composed.[35] In the cities of Syria–Palestine, as in most of the ancient Near East, real power was centered in the monarchy of the city-state. In the ideology of the culture, these monarchs served as regents for the gods of the various city-states; thus, while the kings and queens were not viewed as actually owning the land under their control, the picture that we draw from their religious world was that all land was obtained from the

32. E. W. Heaton, *Solomon's New Men: The Emergence of Ancient Israel as a National State* (New York: Pica, 1974) 47–60; Clyde Curry Smith, "The Birth of Bureaucracy," *BA* 40 (1977) 24–28; and Michael G. Morony, " 'In a City without Watchdogs the Fox Is the Overseer': Issues and Problems in the Study of Bureaucracy," in *Organization of Power: Aspects of Bureaucracy in the Ancient Near East* (ed. McGuire Gibson and Robert D. Biggs; SAOC 46; Chicago: Oriental Institute of the University of Chicago, 1987) 7–18.

33. See, for example, John A. Wilson, "The Assembly of a Phoenician City," *JNES* 4 (1945) 245; and Macdonald, "Assembly at Ugarit?" 520–21.

34. Thorkild Jacobsen, "Primitive Democracy in Ancient Mesopotamia," *JNES* 2 (1943) 159–72.

35. Geoffrey Evans, "Ancient Mesopotamian Assemblies: An Addendum," *JAOS* 78 (1958) 114.

ruler, acting on behalf of the gods.[36] The ruler of the city-state actually controlled vast segments of the society under the jurisdiction of the city-state, but his authority was carried out by means of a large bureaucracy that, in theory, was directed by the monarch.[37]

Such a social system produced a hierarchy within the Syro-Palestinian community. Insufficient data remain to describe that social hierarchy adequately; however, it may safely be stated that the system viewed itself as a form of monarchy.[38] Under the authority of the ruler of the city-state were levels of officers, scribes, and other workers who aided in governing both the city and the region ascribed to the central city.[39] The people who served within the system certainly considered themselves to be serving the monarchy. Since the world in which these folk lived and worked was one of kings of city-states and empires governed by rulers wielding power over wider spheres of territory, they naturally viewed royal family control of societal elements such as state, religion, and commerce as the norm in human existence. It would also have been the view of society taught in the scribal schools, one of whose functions was to prepare scribes to fill the bureaucratic offices in the service of the rulers. The monarchs and the scribal schools came together precisely in the area of bureaucratic government; it was necessary for the royal family to place competent members of its own relatives in key positions,

36. On the position of the king/queen with respect to the gods, see Gösta W. Ahlström, *Royal Administration and National Religion in Ancient Palestine* (SHANE 1; Leiden: Brill, 1982) 1–9. And for the way this ideology was played out in land grants, see Clayton Gene Libolt, "Royal Land Grants from Ugarit" (Ph.D. diss., University of Michigan, 1985) 439–40.

37. See Horst Klengel, "Die Palastwirtschaft in Alalah," in *State and Temple Economy in the Ancient Near East* (2 vols.; ed. Edward Lipiński; Orientalia Lovaniensia Analecta 6; Louvain: Department Oriëntalistiek, 1979) 2.448–49; Michael Heltzer, "Royal Economy in Ancient Ugarit," in *State and Temple Economy*, 2.496; and Elisha Linder, "Ugarit: A Canaanite Thalassocracy," in *Ugarit in Retrospect: Fifty Years of Ugarit and Ugaritic* (ed. Gordon D. Young; Winona Lake, Ind.: Eisenbrauns, 1981) 33–34.

38. John Gray, *The Legacy of Canaan: The Ras Shamra Texts and their Relevance to the Old Testament* (2d rev. ed.; VTSup 5; Leiden: Brill, 1965) 218–30; but note the caution on using the word *monarchy* as a description for the government of ancient Syria–Palestine due to the connotations attached to the term from Western European monarchies of the Medieval Era. See Libolt, "Royal Land Grants," 3–4.

39. See Anson F. Rainey, who concludes: "Life at Ugarit was organized under the leadership and control of a hereditary monarchy supported by a class of landed nobles" ("The Social Stratification of Ugarit" [Ph.D. diss., Brandeis University, 1962] 245). This aspect of the society has been confirmed by more thorough studies of the social structure of Ugarit by Michael Heltzer, *The Internal Organization of the Kingdom of Ugarit* (Wiesbaden: Reichert, 1982); and *The Rural Community in Ancient Ugarit* (Wiesbaden: Reichert, 1976).

as well as to find capable persons for myriads of other scribal posts required by the culture. Some positions in royal court offices were held by people outside the kinship circle of the royal family, by reason of knowing family members or inherited privilege.[40] Beyond these traditionally familial posts other services needed by the society were filled from the ranks of the best people available in the scribal schools, placed in their offices because of their knowledge and skills adapted for that particular position.

While it is necessary for ancient Near Eastern cultures to be seen as monarchies with traditions of influential families holding positions of power, it must also be acknowledged that the personnel placed within the system at any level of bureaucratic organization needed to be competent. The need for capable people was constant, whether they were from the royal ruling family, from a family with hereditary rights to a particular vocation, or were simply functionary; it was in placing such people in office that the need for bureaucratic organization and hierarchy came into play. Since competence was required to hold any position of importance, inherited or not, the dependency of the entire structure, at least in theory, upon the decisions of the monarch allowed for the dismissal and replacement of those who did not function sufficiently well in their tasks. Thus the city-state structure was clearly a monarchy, because of the presence of a king or queen, but it was just as clearly a bureaucracy, having the character and personnel of bureaucratic organization.

However, before a bureaucratic structure may be taken as a useful model for mythological thought, a major shift in its application must be considered. Gods are not human, and the divine world, while described in anthropomorphic terms, is also assumed to be beyond the grasp and existence of mortals.[41] In ancient Near Eastern

40. Michalowski, "Charisma and Control," 55–60; and Piotr Steinkeller, "The Administrative and Economic Organization of the Ur III State: The Core and the Periphery," in *The Organization of Power: Aspects of Bureaucracy in the Ancient Near East* (ed. McGuire Gibson and Robert D. Biggs; SAOC 46; Chicago: Oriental Institute of the University of Chicago, 1987) 24–26.

41. The division between humans and deities was drawn at the point of mortality. Tales of the quest for immortality on the part of humans are common in ancient Near Eastern literature. From Adam and Eve with the tree of life in the Judean story (Genesis 2–3) to Adapa in Mesopotamia, few are the humans who manage to make it into heaven (Elijah) or to immortality (Utnapishtim). In this regard, at least, there was a clearly defined break between people and deities. Moreover, it has been noticed that the sexual behavior of deities in the Ugaritic myths differs considerably from what appears to have been acceptable human behavior for the same culture (Korpel, *Rift*, 216–17). Korpel concludes that anthropomorphism was a metaphorical manner of speaking about the divine, and that perhaps the same respect for Yahweh that there is in biblical research should also be given to Ugaritic deities (p. 267).

thought a chasm existed between the mortal and immortal worlds; gods might live forever but not humans. By extension, then, the divine personnel within a bureaucracy might be expected to hold a position forever, but not his or her human counterpart. Moreover, the deities were capable of vastly greater feats and possessed much more power than mortals. These differences aside, the gods were portrayed as corresponding to human behavior, as known to the authors. Some aspects of the human world translated to the divine realm better than others, and perhaps the easiest aspect was the actual behavior of organizational members, with all the etiquette, interrelationships, intrigue, and even corruption that such a bureaucratic hierarchy entails. And this bureaucratic hierarchy is the primary focus of this book.

ANCIENT GODS AND MODERN STUDIES

There is always a problem when modern terminology is used to describe ancient cultures. Therefore, we must note that bureaucracy as it is known now is undoubtedly different from that which was known then. The variables in any culture are many and often both important and unrecorded; because of the miniscule amount of literature available from Syria–Palestine, the culture itself eludes modern understanding. It is unlikely that the authors of Syria–Palestine ever attempted to portray the heavens as an ideal for the human world, and modern readers should avoid putting such an interpretation back into the texts, since this hinders understanding both the authors and their civilization.

It is popular in academic work to look at ancient mythological texts as though they were written not only by modern authors but also for a modern world. When ancient Assyria is presented as a multinational corporation, one questions the scholar's understanding, not only of Assyria, but also of corporations. One questions whether the scholar is more interested in describing the ancient civilization or in describing modern corporate behavior in terms of a nation of less than pristine reputation.[42] In Syro-Palestinian studies, scholars have recently saddled the mythology of the area with notions useful for modern social thought. On the one hand, it has been argued that Syria–Palestine, exclusive of Israel, employed an intense, self-serving hierarchy, promoting the rights of priests, kings, males, and the dead over the rights of the poor and the peasant. Yet

---

42. See, for example, Mario Liverani, "The Ideology of the Assyrian Empire," in *Power and Propaganda: A Symposium on Ancient Empires* (ed. Mogens Trolle Larsen; Mesopotamia 7; Copenhagen: Akademisk, 1979) 297–317.

on the other hand, deities from the area have been defined in terms of modern state philosophy: Baal, Asherah, and Anat having become in fact "political power," "political economy," and "war profit" respectively.[43] It is not impossible that some relation to reality is found in such observations, but the fact remains that most of this type of study arises out of biblical studies in the firm belief, attested or not, that biblical society was superior to any of its neighboring cultures.[44] It is certainly time to return to the texts.

If all theories related to religious thought in Syria–Palestine are tenuous, this study is no exception. The fourfold hierarchy in this study has been independently discerned both on the divine level and on the human level of society in the ancient Near East.[45] Nonetheless, the division into four levels is at best an insubstantial theory. Since the texts in which these levels have been observed are few and incomplete records of their society, it is distinctly possible they are inadequate for seriously reconstructing an entire culture. Moreover, it is questionable that these sources reflect all divisions in society. The perspective is that of the societal hierarchy of the scribes in scribal schools, but it is undoubtedly not the only perspective of the society at the time. The texts themselves suggest that there were other levels even within the recognized fourfold scheme, and probably outside of it, for which there is simply too little information remaining to make an intelligent description.

The use of theories and behavioral studies derived from modern observations of bureaucratic and hierarchic institutions to posit reasons for behavior in the deities of Syria–Palestine stems from the tenuous though popular theory that human behavior does not change radically over time. I assume here that, given similar hierarchical structures and a chain of authority, people would act toward each other in similar fashion, whether in modern corporations or ancient city-states. I acknowledge from the start that this is a leap of faith; it nevertheless provides another perspective from which to view the actions of the divine realm in Syria–Palestine.

---

43. Respectively, Norman K. Gottwald, *The Tribes of Yahweh: A Sociology of the Religion of Liberated Israel 1250–1050 B.C.E.* (Maryknoll, N.Y.: Orbis, 1979) 694–96; and George E. Mendenhall, "The Worship of Baal and Asherah: A Study in the Social Bonding Functions of Religious Systems," in *Biblical and Related Studies Presented to Samuel Iwry* (ed. Ann Kort and Scott Morschauser; Winona Lake, Ind.: Eisenbrauns, 1985) 157–58.

44. Gottwald, *Tribes of Yahweh*, 507.

45. Mark Smith, "Divine Travel as a Token of Divine Rank," *UF* 16 (1984) 359; I. M. Diakonoff, "The Structure of Near Eastern Society before the Middle of the 2nd Millennium B.C.," *Oikumene* 3 (1982) 94–98.

This undertaking is not, then, an attempt to answer all possible questions concerning the interaction among the various deities, but an attempt to base an understanding of the Syro-Palestinian deities on the city-state bureaucracies from which the myths' authors worked. It is not just the bureaucracy, nor yet the family, nor even the monarchy, that will display the characters as their original audience knew them. A combination of many social structures, most of which modern scholars have no way of recovering, interacted to produce the divine figures. It is possible, however, to make use of bureaucratic hierarchies in an attempt to understand the mythological world. This study is a modest start in that direction.

Chapter 2

Tablets and Texts

The presuppositions that are made concerning source materials influence all interpretations later to be derived from them. Therefore, it is necessary to state in general terms what the more important sources of information for religious thought in Syria–Palestine are and how they are related to this study. To be useful, any source must, of course, relate to the religious views of Syria–Palestine in the period from the middle of the second millennium B.C.E. through the middle of the first millennium C.E. Moreover, the source must convey an understanding of the deities' relationships among themselves and/or between the divine and human realms with respect to divine authority. The most informative material demonstrates in narrative form how gods were believed to behave.

Unfortunately, not only is the available source material sparse in the extreme, but only a small fraction of it consists of intelligible mythological narrative. An even more serious problem is the fact that none of the narrative materials is a complete story; what has been discovered are sections of longer narratives, the remainder of which must be reconstructed, while the literature of other cultures provides only retold portions of earlier, and often otherwise unknown, myths. Of the six major sources currently available for study, not one is free of questions related to the origins of the Syro-Palestinian mythological content it provides, either as to date or provenance. In each instance the existing source is open to varied, and sometimes contradictory, interpretations. For this reason, basic views on the meaning and usefulness of the sources need to be set forth before examining the major topic of the study.

THE UGARITIC TEXTS

Without question the most important sources of information on the gods, cult, culture, and religion of Syria–Palestine at the present time are the numerous tablets found at Ras Shamra, the ancient port city of Ugarit in northern Syria. The contents of these tablets, found in 1929, are now available in transliteration in a standardized collection edited by Dietrich, Loretz, and Sanmartín.[1] Plate and handcopy editions for the majority of the tablet texts can be found in the volume prepared by Herdner.[2] These texts suffer from the usual problems inherent in ancient cuneiform clay libraries. It is the tendency of these tablets to break in such a manner that whole sections of stories are lost, even when the narrative has been found preserved on more than one tablet. Random scratches or cracks on the writing surface of the tablets create no end of headaches for those who have to determine whether the marks were part of the script or merely flaws in the clay. When a series of tablets combine to relate one long narrative sequence, it is not uncommon for entire tablets to have crumbled to dust, leaving behind not minor lacunae in an otherwise comprehensible story, but huge gaps in which the literary intentions of the author have been lost altogether. Even when the narratives have been preserved in almost excellent condition, much of the vocabulary is unknown and has been translated by means of guesses, using theoretical relationships with other ancient Near Eastern languages (Hebrew, Akkadian, Egyptian, Hittite) that might have a better attested possible cognate; failing this, an attempt has been made to find a supposed relationship for such a word in the vocabulary of a living Semitic language (Aramaic, Arabic). Yet, even when this comparative method of interpretation is exhausted, much of the vocabulary on the Ugaritic tablets remains uncertain.

Narrative Texts

Two groups of tablets found at Ras Shamra contain information suitable for a study of divine hierarchical rule: narratives and ritual texts. The more significant of these are the texts that relate substan-

---

1. M. Dietrich, O. Loretz, and J. Sanmartín, *Die keilalphabetischen Texte aus Ugarit: Einschliesslich der keilalphabetischen Texte ausserhalb Ugarits: Teil 1, Transkription* (AOAT 24; Kevelaer: Butzon & Bercker/Neukirchen-Vluyn: Neukirchener Verlag, 1976), cited hereafter as *KTU*.

2. Andrée Herdner, *Corpus des tablettes en cunéiformes alphabétiques: Découvertes à Ras Shamra–Ugarit de 1929 à 1939* (2 vols.; MRS 10; Paris: Imprimerie nationale/Paul Geuthner, 1963). Hand copies of several texts are provided in Johannes C. de Moor and Klaus Spronk, *A Cuneiform Anthology of Religious Texts from Ugarit: Autographed Texts and Glossaries* (SSS 6; Leiden: Brill, 1987); however, the texts have been embellished to correct faults and fill in lacunae in a manner that reflects the editors' interpretations of the meaning of the texts.

tial segments of mythological and legendary narratives.[3] There exist portions of perhaps a dozen recognizably distinct tales, but very few of them form narratives of sufficient length and coherence to present understandable relationships among the divine personnel. None of these myths and legends has been recovered in a complete narrative; instead, long sections of mythological material provide extended scenes that were originally a part of stories that are no longer extant. If the existing texts were originally supposed to have formed an interconnected mythological "history" of the cosmos, the order in which they were supposed to have been read is now largely unknown. Certain tablets clearly fit together in such a manner as to present a continuous, related story; however, it is far from certain that all the mythological narratives formed a complete, interrelated cycle. It is just as feasible that the surviving mythical scenes that tell distinct stories were in fact distinct myths without having a necessary relation to a single mythical cycle. Most important, it must be remembered that what remains of this literature, even the material from Ugarit, is an inestimably small portion of the religious tradition from ancient Ugarit and therefore should be treated as an uncharacteristic, limited sample of the religious literature, not the definitive whole of the culture's religious thought.

Since the myths were stored in an adjunct building to the temple of Baal in the city of Ugarit at the time of the destruction of the city, around 1200 B.C.E., the texts were probably a selection of the religious lore of the Baal cult at the time. It may reasonably be questioned whether the stories contained on the tablets originated in the city of

---

3. The myths and legends have been singled out for publication in translation several times since their discovery. Among modern Western language translations of the tales from Ugarit are the following: H. L. Ginsberg, "Ugaritic Myths, Epics, and Legends," in *ANET*, 129–55. J. C. L. Gibson, *Canaanite Myths and Legends* (2d ed.; Edinburgh: T. & T. Clark, 1977); Gregorio del Olmo Lete, *Mitos y leyendas de Canaan segun la tradicion de Ugarit: Textos, versión y estudio* (FCB 1; Madrid: Ediciones cristiandad, 1981). André Caquot and Maurice Sznycer (eds.), "Textes ougaritiques," in *Les Religions du proche-orient asiatique: Textes babyloniens, ougaritiques, hittites* (ed. René Labat et al.; TSH; Paris: Librairie Arthème Fayard et Éditions Denoël, 1970) 351–458; André Caquot, Maurice Sznycer, and Andrée Herdner, *Textes ougaritiques, 1: Mythes et légendes* (LAPO 7; Paris: Cerf, 1974); J. Aistleitner, *Die mythologischen und kultischen Texte aus Ras Schamra* (BOH 8; Budapest: Kiadó, 1959); Paolo Xella, *Gli antenati di Dio: Divinità e miti della tradizione di Canaan* (Verona: Essedue, 1981). There are also two English editions that have reconstructed (and "corrected") the texts to fill in lacunae and make sense of ambiguities in the extant tablets, a practice that tends to make the corrected texts conform to interpretations adopted by the translators, though they are considerably easier to read than the editions just mentioned: Michael David Coogan, *Stories from Ancient Canaan* (Philadelphia: Westminster, 1978); and Johannes C. de Moor, *An Anthology of Religious Texts from Ugarit* (Nisaba 16; Leiden: Brill, 1987), in which selected ritual texts are included.

Ugarit itself; it is a distinct possibility that the narratives may either have been common to the cultures of Syria–Palestine, or that these particular renditions of mythology were imported into Ugarit from some other center of Syro-Palestinian religious thought.[4] Such speculation is worth contemplating, for it raises this central question: did the individual city-state within Syria–Palestine create its own religious culture, or did all city-states subscribe to a common religious tradition? Unfortunately, the question is simply not answerable from the data now available. This particular question to the side, it is probable that the fragments of mythology recovered from Ras Shamra were part of the religious lore of the Baal cult in Ugarit near the close of the second millennium B.C.E.

It is unlikely that the copies of the narratives found at Ras Shamra were the original editions of those stories. This raises a related pair of questions: how much earlier than the fall of Ugarit were these specific renditions of the narratives composed, and how much earlier still were the stories told in the narratives created? At present it is impossible to answer either question. Theories have been proposed suggesting a progression of mythological thought in the narratives, but too little data exists for a reliable theory to be sustained, the progressions are dubious, and the dating is suspect. The most popular rationale for dating myths arises from the theory that the god Baal was a deity who entered Palestine and Phoenicia from outside the area; when the storm god's cult moved in, it replaced the indigenous cult of El and set its own deity as the chief god of the pantheon, replacing El.[5] Unfortunately for the proponents of this theory, the evidence for Baal/Hadad in Syria–Palestine is as ancient as the evidence for El.[6] Some evidence has been interpreted to sug-

---

4. R. A. Oden ("Theoretical Assumptions in the Study of Ugaritic Myths," *MAARAV* 2 [1979] 51–55) asks the relevant questions concerning the possibility of seeing myths in a one-to-one correspondence with Ugarit's institutions. One other question should be asked: whether, in fact, the stories were composed in that particular city.

5. Arvid S. Kapelrud, *Baal in the Ras Shamra Texts* (Copenhagen: Gad, 1952) 92–93; and idem, "The Relationship between El and Baal in the Ras Shamra Texts," in *The Bible World: Essays in Honor of Cyrus H. Gordon* (ed. Gary Rendsburg et al.; New York: KTAV, 1980) 83; Marvin H. Pope, *El in the Ugaritic Texts* (VTSup 2; Leiden: Brill, 1955) 102; Pope later raised doubts about his earlier thesis, "The Status of El at Ugarit," *UF* 19 (1987) 224–28; Ulf Oldenburg, *The Conflict between El and Baᶜal in Canaanite Religion* (Supplementa ad numen, altera series 3; Leiden: Brill, 1969) 206.

6. See Johannes C. de Moor, "Baᶜal," *TDOT* 2:183; René Follet, "Sanchuniaton, personnage mythique ou personne historique?" *Biblica* 34 (1953) 90; and René Dussaud, "Nouveaux reseignments sur la Palestine et la Syrie vers 2000 avent notre ère," *Syria* 8 (1927) 232. Daniel E. Fleming ("Baal and Dagan in Ancient Syria," *ZA* 83 [1993] 93, 97–98) concludes that "Baal" was originally a title of Dagan that came to be treated as a distinct deity.

gest that the narratives may have gone through a tradition of several previous variants before they appeared in the recension excavated.[7] Yet, even if we were certain that the stories had been retold several times prior to the edition that now exists, we would not be better able to date either the original story or the version found at the site of Ugarit. Since it cannot be determined whether there was a shift in the storyline through the supposed renditions, it is also impossible to posit differences in the hierarchy in the various theoretical renditions solely by studying the final form.

Even the date of the final form of the composition cannot be determined. There is neither evidence nor a reason to assume that all the myths and legends discovered were composed at the same time or in the same place. Cassuto selected the fourteenth century B.C.E. as the date of composition for all the narratives on the grounds that he believed that this was the time of the destruction of Ugarit,[8] but this reason obviously does not hold up. Eissfeldt and Gray proposed the same century but on the basis that they believe that the fourteenth century was the peak of Ugaritic culture.[9] Albright posited a much earlier date, well into the first half of the second millennium B.C.E.,[10] a date that has influenced his pupils; however, there is no valid reason to date the documents more than a century prior to their preservation in the ruins of the city. While original composition of the mythological texts cannot be dated with any certainty, it may be assumed that they reflect the thought of Ugaritic religious circles in the thirteenth century B.C.E. Whether the myths and legends reflect a continuing expansion of religious narratives in the culture, broken by the death of Ugaritic civilization, or whether they were the product of one period of flourishing literary activity (within Ugarit or throughout Syria–Palestine), simply cannot be determined from extant data.

Likewise, it is unclear whether religious tradition dictated the content of the myths and thus the behavior of the gods portrayed in them, or whether the author of any particular narrative had freedom to write an individual view of the divine world. How much of the

7. U. Cassuto, *The Goddess Anath: Canaanite Epics of the Patriarchal Age* (Jerusalem: Magnes, 1971) 16.

8. Ibid.

9. Otto Eissfeldt, *Ras Schamra und Sanchunjaton* (Beiträge zur Religionsgeschichte des Altertums 4; Halle: Niemeyer, 1939) 68; John Gray, *Legacy of Canaan: The Ras Shamra Texts and Their Relevance to the Old Testament* (2d rev. ed.; VTSup 5; Leiden: Brill, 1965) 2.

10. William Foxwell Albright, *Yahweh and the Gods of Canaan: A Historical Analysis of Two Contrasting Faiths* (Garden City, N.Y.: Doubleday, 1968; repr. Winona Lake, Ind.: Eisenbrauns, 1979) 4–5.

literary composition was creative license and how much of it was the
product of the culture as a whole is yet another unanswerable question. The one "author" who is known from the tablets is Ilimilku (*il-
mlk*) who was a scribe and priest under King Niqmaddu (*nqmd*) of
Ugarit.[11] How much these tales reflect the literary talents of Ilimilku
is dependent on how the word *spr* is translated and then understood. Simply translating the word as 'scribe' does not solve the puz-
zle about whether Ilimilku was copying a traditional rendition of the
stories or whether he composed them himself. Either option is a possibility. Then the question arises: did Ilimilku have free reign to create mythology, using his own ideas about what divine activity really
is, or was his work a poetic rendition of an already-established
mythological formula, over which he had little or no literary power?
It must be assumed that any author writing for a religious cult was
under some restraint to keep the actions of the deities portrayed in
the myths consistent with the beliefs of the cult and the wider culture. The two works ascribed to Ilimilku are both myths of the Baal
cult; it is therefore likely that he composed or paraphrased in a manner that would portray Baal in a manner not only understandable to
the general populace, but also in conformity to acceptable views of
the deity held by his own cult personnel. It is therefore possible to
accept the presentation of the gods in these tablets as a reflection of
contemporary Syro-Palestinian understanding of the structure of divine control and behavior, regardless of the literary finesse of a particular author.

A much greater problem than literary creativity or rigidity is the
necessity for acknowledging that the extant mythological material
presents what must be a small fraction of the myths of the Baal cult
in Ugarit. These, in turn, would have been a tiny fraction of the
mythological narratives known in the wider Ugaritic religious culture, which, again, must have been a microscopic portion of the literature of the culture of greater Syria–Palestine. The vast majority of
mythological texts that once existed in this civilization are now irre-
trievably lost. The deities who play an active role in the extant
mythological narratives are relatively few in number. If it is true that
the surviving Ugaritic narratives were related to the cult of Baal in
Ugarit, then by extension it should be assumed that the deities appearing in the tales are gods who were considered related to the cult
of Baal. This would mean that the sources of primary information for
the religious thought of Ugarit are restricted to the single cult of
Baal. Yet, of Baal's cult narratives, only a fraction of the stories re-

---

11. *KTU* 1.6.VI.54–58; see also 1.4.VII, where the same name has been restored at
the broken end of the tablet.

main. This being the case, it is far from certain that the deities who do appear in the extant narratives were the most important deities for the cult of Baal. It is impossible to know what myths perished forever or to know the relative importance of the extant myths with regard to any others. The importance of these same deities for other cults to other gods is simply unknown.

To a certain extent, even determining which gods actually are dealt with in the narratives is problematic. When the Ugaritic tablets were first being studied, it was common for scholars to take any name appearing in the narratives to be a designation for a deity. It took quite a bit of time for the recognition of divine titles and the various names of the divinities to be sorted out. Once scholars realized that *b^cl*, *aliyn*, and *hd* represented one deity instead of three, reading of the texts simplified considerably. However, it would certainly be egotistical to assume that the confusion created by the large number of divine names has now been completely dispelled. Moreover, the very names of two of the more important deities provide further confusion. Both *il* and *b^cl* may designate two distinct deities, but they are also used as the generic word for 'god' and the common noun 'lord' respectively. How to know whether the common noun or the proper noun is intended remains, in too many cases, an area of scholarly conjecture.

Ritual Texts

The second group of relevant materials from Ras Shamra consists of liturgical (ritual) texts of various kinds.[12] While these texts do not provide narrative stories for understanding gods' dealings with each other, they do provide some supplementary information regarding other aspects of divine behavior. One type of ritual text sets forth lists of donations for particular deities, demonstrating at least that the gods mentioned in the tablets were in fact worshiped at that time in the cult.[13] However, major problems arise when such texts

---

12. These texts have been collected, with notes: see Paolo Xella, *I testi rituali di Ugarit, I: Testi* (SS 54; Rome: Consiglio nazionale delle richerche, 1981); André Caquot, Jean-Michel de Tarragon, and Jesús-Luis Cunchillos Ylarri, *Textes ougaritiques, 2: Textes religieux et rituels, correspondance* (LAPO 14; Paris: Cerf, 1989). See now the selected collection in Manfried Dietrich and Oswald Loretz, "Ugaritische Rituale und Beschwörungen" in *Rituale und Beschwörungen II* (TUAT 2/3; Gütersloh: Mohn, 1988) 299–357.

13. Jean-Michel de Tarragon attempts to recreate the cult of Ugarit from the available cultic tablets (*Le Culte à Ugarit: D'après les textes de la pratique en cunéiformes alphabétiques* [CRB 19; Paris: Gabalda, 1980]).

are used to argue for more than the mere existence of the various deities. It is not even clear what type of religious material is being recorded on these tablets. Do the lists of sacrifices made to a given deity mean that on a particular day those offerings were made? Or do the lists form a ritual text for priests, to determine how much of each item was supposed to be sacrificed on a given calendar date? Because the date is given on the tablet, it is clear that the list refers to particular ritual days of the cult, and it is also clear that the pre-sentations were made to specific gods, since the animals and other offerings are listed with the name of the receiving divinity. However, these data do not explain exactly why the tablets were inscribed.

Furthermore, the tablets do not give a clear view of the respective importance of the various gods mentioned in them. It is a well-known phenomenon of ancient Near Eastern religions that deities were honored with special attention on their own feast days throughout the year.[14] The few ritual texts that did survive and have been recovered do not tell much about the city's cult practices over the course of a year or about the importance of various deities to each other or to each god's cult. This problem is compounded by the apparent restriction of the ritual cultic texts to the single cult of Baal. As mentioned above, the gods who appear in ritual texts from the Baal temple were presumably related to the cultic life of the Baal devotees. How these texts would compare with similar documents from another temple in the same city (let alone another city) cannot be determined and cannot, with present sources, even be imagined. Though extant texts can hardly be taken as a thorough representation of the religious life of the Baal temple in Ugarit, it is certain that the gods who are mentioned in the tablets were the deities who were active in the Baal cult and its mythology. Lacking a representative sample of ritual texts from this one cult, we are unable to determine on the basis of these tablets alone whether one particular deity was more revered by the general populace than another. One must also keep in mind that, should tablets with ritual texts from other temples suddenly be discovered, the gods who appear on them might be quite different from those found with the Baal temple.

In addition to the donation lists, there are ritual tablets that provide incantations or ritual actions performed at times when particu-

---

14. For general reference to the practice, see Siegfried Morenz, *Egyptian Religion* (Ithaca, N.Y.: Cornell University Press, 1973) 89; and H. W. F. Saggs, *The Greatness that Was Babylon* (New York: New American Library, 1962) 341. In both Egypt and Mesopotamia deities journeyed to the festivals of other gods. For such a ritual journey, see A. J. Ferrara, *Nanna-Suen's Journey to Nippur* (Studia Pohl, Series Maior 2; Rome: Pontifical Biblical Institute, 1973).

lar deities were needed. Perhaps the most dramatic of these texts is the one describing how to call on the god Baal in time of siege, in expectation that he will save the city.[15] Such a text provides a discernible line of authority among the gods that could be set in motion upon request. This type of text does not provide a great deal of information regarding the activities of the various gods, though an incantation might link a specific problem with a particular deity. It is not clear, even when such texts exist, that the deity appearing in an incantation or ritual tablet was the only deity who might be called upon for aid in a particular situation. For example, if a city were besieged, would one be required to call on Baal, or could one call on whatever god was the patron deity of the municipality under attack? From the limited number of ritual texts available from Ugarit it is not possible to determine whether the identified deities were the only ones associated with individual problems. Sometimes, relevant information is available from other sources in Syria–Palestine; in the case of the besieged city, for example, the biblical book of Kings (2 Kgs 3:26–27) provides an example of calling on a god to lift a siege on a city, though unfortunately the deity being petitioned by means of the child sacrifice is not named. Whether the deities referred to in the various Ugaritic incantations would vary by location is also uncertain.

A third type of text found on the ritual tablets has been used to determine the relative importance of the various deities. It is often pointed out that *il*, in some form or another, appears at the beginning of these lists.[16] Great significance has been attributed to the position of the name *il* on these lists. It is argued that this location must mean that El was the acknowledged leader of the Ugaritic pantheon.[17] While this is not an impossible interpretation, the purpose of the god-lists in the cult is unknown, and therefore it seems hazardous merely to assume that the order of the names on the lists was

15. *KTU* 1.119.

16. *KTU* 1.47, 102, 118; see Xella, *Testi rituali*, 325–31.

17. For a summary of this argument based on Ugaritic texts and similar lists from Ebla, see Paolo Xella, "Aspekte religiöser Vorstellungen in Syrien nach den Ebla- und Ugarit-Texten," *UF* 15 (1983) 279–90; Dietrich and Loretz, "Ugaritische Rituale," 300. At least minimal problems with using these lists for this purpose have been noted; see Patrick D. Miller, Jr., "Aspects of the Religion of Ugarit," in *Ancient Israelite Religion* (ed. Patrick D. Miller Jr., Paul D. Hanson, and S. Dean McBride; Philadelphia: Fortress, 1987) 56–57. It should be noted that similar lists from Mesopotamia are not in order of the importance of the deities appearing on the tablets; W. G. Lambert, "Goddesses in the Pantheon: A Reflection of Women in Society?" in *La Femme dans le proche-orient antique* (ed. Jean-Marie Durand; RAI 33; Paris: Éditions recherche sur les civilisations, 1987) 129.

intended by the authors to correspond to the ranking order of the gods. Granted, the tablets do provide a large number of divine names otherwise not appearing in the narrative texts; but even this fact raises questions. Were these deities part of the cult at Ugarit? Were the deities from Syria–Palestine but not necessarily members of the pantheon of Ugarit? Are the lists even names of deities? Are they related to the cult of Baal, some other deity, or no particular cult? Is it possible that there is repetition within the lists, a single deity referred to by more than one of his or her names or titles? Since gods in ancient Near Eastern religions could die, is it even certain that the gods on the lists were assumed to be alive at the time of the compilation of the various lists? Further, is the order of the names on the lists one of authority, of power, of importance, of origin, of the order of some cultic ritual, of mnemonic device, or of something that cannot even be reconstructed from current knowledge? The lists do provide names, but beyond that they cannot be useful until it is known what they were originally intended to be listing.

Despite questions regarding the origins of the tablets, the representative nature of the texts from Ugarit (let alone Syria–Palestine), the degree of individual creativity of particular authors of the texts, and the uncertainty of the meaning of the ritual texts—despite all these things, the tablets still do form the basis for reconstructing the divine realm as seen in Syria–Palestine. They remain the largest corpus of primary literature for the study of the area's religious culture and the only extensive narratives that have not passed through the hands of other civilizations. Therefore these are the texts, particularly the narrative texts, that must form the core literature to which the other sources may be compared.

SYRO-PALESTINIAN INSCRIPTIONS

A relatively small number of inscriptions have been recovered from the area of Syria–Palestine.[18] An even smaller number mention deities. The inscriptions that do deal with the gods usually present the relationship between a human ruler and his deities in a succinct fashion. In fact, fairly often, inscriptions do not supply much more information about the deities than their names. Most of the inscriptions bearing divine names are not directly related to the cult; they record treaties between rulers on earth who listed the gods standing

---

18. Collections of inscriptions from the area during this period include those by H. Donner and W. Röllig, *Kanaanäische und aramäische Inschriften* (3 vols.; Wiesbaden: Harrassowitz, 1969–1973), cited hereafter as *KAI*; and J. C. L. Gibson, *Textbook of Syrian Semitic Inscriptions* (3 vols.; Oxford: Clarendon, 1971–1982), cited here as *TSSI*.

as witnesses to the treaty, or the inscriptions were made to record for posterity the names of rulers who were chosen by the deities to rule for them on earth.[19] Other inscriptions record deities who protected sarcophagi for the deceased within. These inscriptions do present material on divine authority and interaction among ruling beings in the universe, but it is restricted primarily to the intersection of the divine and human realms. Only in a very few inscriptions do extensive descriptions of divine activity appear.

The traditional formulations for inscriptions remain fairly consistent. The right of any given monarch to rule the city-state or empire was dependent on the gods who controlled the area; these gods chose the ruler and established him on the throne under divine protection. Thus, it is common to encounter a royal inscription documenting the deities who confirmed the right of the ruler to reign: "And Hadad and El and Rakkabel and Shemesh and Resheph gave into my hand the scepter of authority."[20] It is documented in these treaty inscriptions that the authors believed that breaking the clauses of the treaty signified rebellion on the part of the offender against the gods themselves: "If not (done) thus, you will betray all the gods of this treaty on this document."[21] The realm of a given ruler was presumed to be divinely protected as long as the monarch was in good favor with the area's patron deity. If the ruler did what was found to be good in the god's eyes, prosperity was insured for the ruler's kingdom: "And so in my days every goodness was to the Danunians, and satiety, and well-being, and I (have been) filling the silos of Pahar, and I (have been) making horse over horse, and shield over shield, and army over army, because of Baal and the gods."[22]

After the ruler's death, the patron deity was assumed to continue protecting the ruler by guarding the "eternal" resting place of the mortal remains:

> Whoever you are, ruler or man, do not open over me and do not arouse yourself against me and do not carry me from this repose and do not lift the sarcophagus from my repose, lest these holy gods deliver them and cut off that ruler or those men and their seed forever! (*KAI* 14.20–22 = *TSSI* 2.108).

The wording of the various inscriptions is not a fully set formula; however, the sentiment occurs in very similar patterns in many of

---

19. This is not to say that inscriptions are not found on statues that have been dedicated to the deities, only that the contents of the inscriptions themselves are neither cultic nor mythological narrative.

20. *KAI* 214.2–3 (= *TSSI* 2.64).

21. *KAI* 224.4 (= *TSSI* 2.46).

22. *KAI* 26.A.I.5–8 (= *TSSI* 3.46).

the extant examples. The standardized nature of these inscriptions may suggest that the sympathies expressed therein were more formal than felt. Even so, the inscriptions evidence a long-standing official proclamation concerning divine control of the human political realm.

Perhaps the most useful data to be gleaned from the series of inscriptions discovered in Syria–Palestine are the names of deities recognized at the time of the composition of the individual texts. It is probably reasonable to assume that at the time any given inscription was written, the gods mentioned in that inscription were believed to exist. If this is true, a certain amount of information about which gods were worshiped and when they were worshiped may be derived from these names. However, it would be more useful if we could assume that a representative sampling of the religious views of the pantheon at a particular site during a particular time period had been recovered. Such an assumption, based on currently available data, would be at best ludicrous. It cannot be assumed that the inscriptions of a particular period from a single site included all the deities known or even worshiped at that site. It is even less likely that the texts that were discovered can be used to reconstruct anything near a complete pantheon for any particular community. This caution is as true for a site such as Palmyra, with its many inscriptions, as it is for random inscriptions that may be the only religious information about a site at the time to which the inscription dates.[23]

The mere appearance of names of deities on an inscription is not evidence that they were worshiped during the time or in the place from which the inscription originated. Three major problems continue to plague the study of these documents. First, some of the deities mentioned on inscriptions are totally unknown aside from one example on one text. It is impossible in such cases to determine whether the name in the inscription refers to a local deity, a god of wider importance who has not yet been discovered in texts elsewhere, a god who is known from elsewhere by another name, or whether the name does not even refer to a god at all. Second, some deity names occur frequently, but it is uncertain to which god the name refers. Perhaps the most-debated example is the name Baal Shamem. Though occurring fairly often in inscriptions (and in Philo

---

23. For the inscriptions found at Palmyra and an attempt to identify the pantheon represented there, see Javier Teixidor, *The Pantheon of Palmyra* (Études preliminaires aux religions orientales dans l'Empire Romain 79; Leiden: Brill, 1979); H. Drijvers, *Religion of Palmyra* (Iconography of Religions 15/15; Leiden: Brill, 1976) 9–21; and M. Gawlikowski, "Les Dieux Palmyre," in *ANRW* 2.18.4:2605–58, with an excellent bibliography.

of Byblos) and thereby appearing to have been a rather important deity, he is currently assumed by some to be Baal and by others to be El, though there appears to be agreement that the name is a divine title.[24] Such enigmas remain unsolved because of the amount of information currently available. Third, when Syro-Palestinian deity names are translated into other languages, it is often unclear which of the Syro-Palestinian gods is meant by the translated name; this is a particularly acute problem in the later periods when Greek and Latin divine names were used for divine beings in cultures stretching from the British Isles to Mesopotamia. There seems to have been no standardized formula for equating a Syro-Palestinian deity with a classical god.[25] Suffice it here to point out that unless the object of study happens to be a bilingual text, Greek or Latin inscriptions concerned with Syro-Palestinian deities remain less-than-certain sources for determining the identity of deities the devotees actually revered. Moreover, it is unfortunately true that any single bilingual text cannot be assumed to provide accurate intercultural equations for deities mentioned in other inscriptions composed by the authors of other bilingual texts.

If one wished to determine which gods have moved in and out of prominence in the religious thought of Syria–Palestine throughout a period, the dating of all the inscriptions would be of foremost importance. While some of the texts may be dated with a fair amount of accuracy from the content—usually inscriptions by rulers otherwise already known from datable contemporary sources—other texts contain nothing by which the inscription can be dated reliably. If the inscription has been excavated *in situ*, a rough idea of the date of the material can sometimes be determined from the level of the excavation and the artifacts found around it. However, when the dating of the excavation site is inconclusive, as unfortunately it often is, or when the text was removed from its original position without careful attention to its archaeological level, the text of an otherwise unknown ruler is undatable except within large and amorphous temporal boundaries.

24. Frank Moore Cross, *Canaanite Myth and Hebrew Epic: Essays in the History of the Religion of Israel* (Cambridge: Harvard University Press, 1973) 7 n. 13; Javier Teixidor, *The Pagan God: Popular Religion in the Greco-Roman Near East* (Princeton: Princeton University Press, 1977) 26–34; Robert A. Oden, "Baᶜal Samem and ꭓEl," *CBQ* 39 (1977) 470–73; the problem is one of long standing: Otto Eissfeldt, "Baᶜalšamēn und Jahwe," *ZAW* 57 (1939) 1–31.

25. Teixidor (*Pagan God*, 19–60) presents the problems of this identification process but is much too optimistic about the solutions. See also Clifford, "Phoenician Religion," *BASOR* 279 (1990) 55–64.

It has become popular in certain scholarly circles to date problem texts, sometimes with incredible accuracy, by means of paleography. This procedure became popular in the work of Frank Moore Cross and continues with some of his students.[26] While it is unquestionably true that writing styles change over time and that, in broad terms, these changes may be used to show progression in script styles, arguments have been raised against the detailed use of this method in dating documents to specific time periods. These arguments must be taken seriously.[27] The inscriptions available for forming the theories of progression in script style are few in number, come from widely scattered sites, and leave long periods of time without examples. This means that any progression proposed from the use of these inscriptions is at best suspect. Scholars subscribing to this theory of dating have tended to ignore local variations in the form of writing, which means that unsupportable assumptions have been made about the evolution of script formulations. To posit that there was a generally employed writing style over all of Syria–Palestine that changed at a uniform pace, so that any site may be dated by consulting a standardized chart of script forms, is untenable. It is much more likely that there were several trajectories of script development, each changing in its own fashion and at its own pace, determined by the instructors of various local scribal schools. At the same time, the date at which Greek scribes took over the alphabet from the Phoenicians is quite irrelevant for the dating of Syro-Palestinian inscriptions, since at present it is impossible to determine at which of the myriad of sites the Greeks adapted their own form of the alphabet. At this time, therefore, the use of epigraphic style as a tool for dating texts is an uncertain business and should not be used to argue for precise dates, but can only provide broad approximations.

Of the few inscriptions that deal with divine activities beyond the human sphere, none is free from problems of interpretation, date, or relevance. Two such texts are the inscriptions on the votive statue from Tell Fekheriyeh and the "constructions" recreated from plaster paint fragments found at Deir ʿAllā. While both of these texts

26. See, for example, Frank Moore Cross, "The Evolution of the Proto-Canaanite Alphabet," *BASOR* 134 (1954) 15–24; and "The Origin and Early Evolution of the Alphabet," *EI* 8 (1967) 8*–24*. Then see P. Kyle McCarter, "The Early Diffusion of the Alphabet," *BA* 37 (1974) 54–68; and Joseph Naveh, *The Early History of the Alphabet: An Introduction to West Semitic Epigraphy and Palaeography* (Jerusalem: Magnes/Leiden: Brill, 1982).

27. For a systematic critique of the use of epigraphic dating for specific dates, see Stephen A. Kaufman, "The Pitfalls of Typology: On the Early History of the Alphabet," *HUCA* 57 (1986) 1–14. The following section on problems with exact dating based on epigraphy was written before Kaufman's article became available to me.

have been dated with some specificity by followers of the epigraphic dating school, other scholars, who are less certain of the utility of epigraphic dating, have seriously questioned those dates.[28] While the exact dates for these compositions are not of major immediate concern for this study, the contents of the inscriptions are. The text on the votive statue is more certain than most ancient inscriptions for the simple reason that it appears as a bilingual composition. Both languages, Aramaic and Akkadian, are fairly well known. What is more important is that both renditions have been preserved in a very good state. None of these advantages may be claimed for the Deir ᶜAllā Balaam texts. The "constructions" referred to by the scholars who work with the Deir ᶜAllā compositions are just that: reconstructed, hypothetical renditions of a text built out of numerous small bits of fragmented wall plaster slurry. The very content of these "constructions" must be viewed with suspicion. A unified perspective seems to be forming in some scholarly circles regarding the content of the texts and, by extension, the content of the missing sections within the texts as well.[29] Even though a consensus has been

28. Alan R. Millard and Pierre Bordreuil ("A Statue from Syria with Assyrian and Aramaic Inscriptions," *BA* 45 [1982] 136–37, 140) conclude from the textual content and supposed parallel texts that the inscriptions from Tell Fekheriyeh are mid–ninth century B.C.E., while Joseph Naveh ("Proto-Canaanite, Archaic Greek, and the Script of the Aramaic Text on the Tell Fakhariyah Statue," in *Ancient Israelite Religion* [ed. Patrick D. Miller Jr., Paul D. Hanson, and S. Dean McBride; Philadelphia: Fortress, 1987] 109) insists that the epigraphic style would place the text in the eleventh century B.C.E.; Kaufman ("Pitfalls of Typology," 9) suggests that the ninth century is the earliest possible date but that the inscription could just as well be from the eighth century B.C.E. JoAnn Hackett (*The Balaam Text from Deir ᶜAllā* [HSM 31; Chico, Cal.: Scholars Press, 1980] 18–19) argues for a date between the eighth and seventh centuries B.C.E. for the Balaam "constructions," though the debate over the age of the content itself spans four centuries; see Michael David Coogan, "Canaanite Origins and Lineage: Reflections on the Religion of Ancient Israel" (*Ancient Israelite Religion* [ed. Patrick D. Miller Jr., Paul D. Hanson, and S. Dean McBride; Philadelphia: Fortress, 1987] 116–18). See now André Lemaire, "Les Inscriptions sur plâtre de Deir ᶜAlla et leur signification historique et culturelle," in *The Balaam Text from Deir ᶜAlla Re-evaluated: Proceedings of the International Symposium Held at Leiden 21–24 August 1989* (ed. Jacob Hoftijzer and G. van der Kooij; Leiden: Brill, 1991) 34–36. There has also been increasing agreement that the texts derive from Judean or Israelite sources; Baruch Halpern, "Dialect Distribution in Canaan and the Deir Alla Inscriptions," in *"Working with No Data": Semitic and Egyptian Studies Presented to Thomas O. Lambdin* (ed. David M. Golomb; Winona Lake, Ind.: Eisenbrauns, 1987) 121; JoAnn Hackett, "Response to Baruch Levine and André Lemaire," in *The Balaam Text from Deir ᶜAlla Re-evaluated*, 82–84.

29. The consensus is based on the reconstruction of the plaster shreds by P. Kyle McCarter ("The Balaam Texts from Deir ᶜAllā: The First Combination," *BASOR* 239 [1980] 49–60), as adapted by JoAnn Hackett (*Balaam Text*, 25–28). Manfred Weippert ("The Balaam Text from Deir ᶜAllā and the Study of the Old Testament" in *The Balaam Text from Deir ᶜAlla Re-evaluated*, 169–74) comments on the understanding of the texts from "parallel" narratives.

achieved by reading the reconstructed text through the "lenses" of other ancient Near Eastern texts, the final proposed reading must not be used to bolster any argument regarding other texts. Such theorizing would, in fact, merely become the tightest of circular arguments. Neither of these inscriptions was written primarily with a focus on divine activity, and in both the material on the divine world is less than clear. Some sense of divine authority may be found in the texts, but to a certain extent it must be read into the works. This is true to a certain extent of any inscription dealing with the deities.

For the most part, the inscriptions are a primary source of information about the rule of the gods as it was seen to overlap with the human world. The texts are official documents and therefore should be regarded as serious statements of official religious positions taken by the state concerning divine rule in the universe. The authors displayed in these inscriptions a recognition of the fact that the gods acted on behalf of the humans who worshiped them. At least on the official level, humans were depicted as being dependent on the divine populace and were subject to a hierarchy among the gods that was superior to any form of human government. Human rulers served under the will of the deities and became part of a larger cosmic hierarchy. Beyond these generalized characteristics, the inscriptions do not provide much information about divine hierarchy.

THE "ELKUNIRSHA MYTH"

A much less important source than either the Ugaritic tablets or the Syro-Palestinian inscriptions is the narrative fragment of Hittite origin based, apparently, on Syro-Palestinian deities.[30] The main character in this fragment of narrative was named Elkunirsha, who probably was the Syro-Palestinian god El, with one of his more familiar appelatives. Unfortunately, the very short sections of this narrative that have survived are so broken that only two extended portions of the work remain. Moreover, what remains was pieced together from still smaller fragments in order to create the two short sections. Since most of the story is missing, as well as the central action, and since only two segments remain, this narrative source material is without a context.

---

30. The narrative fragments were reconstructed into this continuous story and published as a unit by Heinrich Otten, "Ein kanaanäischer Mythus aus Boğazköy," *MIO* 1 (1953) 125–50. English translations of the reconstructed narrative are available in H. A. Hoffner, "The Elkunirsa Myth Reconsidered," *RHA* 23 (1965) 6–10; and Albrecht Goetze, "Hittite Myths, Epics, and Legends," in *ANET*, 519. See now H. A. Hoffner, *Hittite Myths* (SBLWAW 2; Atlanta: Scholars Press, 1990) 69–70.

The Hittite form of this story appears to date from sometime within the thirteenth century B.C.E.[31] It is not clear whether the mythological narrative to which the fragments belong came originally from Syro-Palestinian culture or was a literary creation of the highly eclectic Hittite Empire. It is possible that the story is a Hittite composition that used foreign deities in the roles of the major characters, since the Hittite pantheon is renowned for incorporating the gods of its neighboring states.[32] If the story was indeed the creation of the Hittite religious community, it must be assumed that the author chose the particular deities for the story because they were proper characters for the plot of the tale. This would mean that the Hittite author thought that the deity El would have acted in this fashion; whether the Hittites thought El acted in the same manner that the Syro-Palestinians thought he behaved cannot be determined from extant materials. On the other hand, if the narrative was taken directly from a Syro-Palestinian myth, it would be a primary source, though in translation; however, one cannot make such an assumption. There is no known myth from Syria–Palestine that corresponds to the story created out of these fragments.

The very continuity of the fragments, as they have been reconstructed, is open to question. Two reconstructed sections of narrative have been posited. It is generally assumed that, together with the missing material, the two sections formed one longer mythological narrative. It is also possible that the two sections derived originally from two distinct myths. Moreover, the interpretation of the "text" as it was reconstructed, and the rationale for the reconstruction itself, were dependent on Ugaritic texts, even though the tablets from Ugarit contain no similar stories. It was, in fact, on a particular understanding of the mythological world of Ugarit, which itself has passed out of favor, that the Hittite reconstruction and interpretation were based.[33] All of this casts doubt on the entire process of reinventing this particular source and should be kept in mind when dealing with information derived from the story fragments as they are now translated.

It is not clear whether the gods appearing in these two reconstructed fragments were understood to be deities of Syria–Palestine. While it would seem that the central god, the one called Elkunirsha in this cuneiform rendition, should be taken as the Syro-Palestinian

31. Hans Gustav Güterbock, "The Hittite Version of the Hurrian Kumarbi Myths: Oriental Forerunners of Hesiod," *AJA* 52 (1948) 123.

32. O. R. Gurney, *Some Aspects of Hittite Religion* (Schweich Lectures 1976; Oxford: Oxford University Press, 1977) 4–23.

33. Hoffner notes the tenuous nature of the text's reconstructed form ("Elkunirsa," 9).

El, the other divinities are less clearly defined. For El, the Hittite tradition has combined the name El and the title "owner of the earth," which is also known from sources in Syria–Palestine.[34] Since both the name and the title used for this particular deity are witnessed in the Syro-Palestinian sources, it seems to be reasonable to take this Elkunirsha as the god El from Syria–Palestine.

Unfortunately, none of the other characters in the narrative is as easily identified. The consort of the god Elkunirsha is called Asherdu in the cuneiform fragments. Because this name is quite similar to the West-Semitic Asherah, it may have been a form of her name, and the pairing of Elkunirsha and Asherdu would also compare with the sources from Ugarit. So the equation, while not a certainty, is reasonable as a suggestion and is an acceptable working hypothesis.

Trying to relate the other two deities appearing in the Hittite textual fragments to known deities of Syria–Palestine, however, is nothing more than guesswork. The deity who is often taken to be Baal is never given a name other than "storm-god." Since many cultures surrounding the Hittite Empire, and the Hittites themselves, had storm gods, it would be stretching credulity a bit to assume that the West-Semitic Baal must be the one intended. This is especially true because neither of the more familiar proper names for him, Baal or Hadad, appears in the fragment to confirm this identification. In the second instance, the cuneiform ideogram for Ishtar designates a goddess in these fragments. It has been customary to equate her with Anat, or sometimes Astarte, but since all that is available by which to identify her is the ideogram, it is not possible to know for certain which goddess was actually intended.[35] By using deities from Syria–Palestine to define the two "unnamed" Hittite gods, one presupposes that the narrative recovered from the Hittite tablets originated in Syria–Palestine. This makes very good sense if one assumes that all the deities referred to above were taken from the pantheon of the same cult. However, if the story was a product of Hittite scribes and not a tale from Syria–Palestine, the gods may have their origin in various religious cultures. Any storm-god from the surrounding civilizations might have been intended, and the lack of a proper name may simply mean that the precise identity of the storm-god in the narrative was nonessential. The same is true of the

34. Patrick D. Miller, Jr., "El, the Creator of Earth," *BASOR* 239 (1980) 43–45; and Bruce Vawter, "Yahweh: Lord of the Heavens and the Earth," *CBQ* 48 (1986) 465.

35. Note that Hoffner, *Hittite Myths*, 70, simply "translates" the ideogram as "Anat-Astarte," which is one way around the problem he had noted in "Elkunirsa," 6 n. 6; Gurney notes that Ishtar of Nineveh herself had attained a place in the Hittite pantheon (*Aspects of Hittite Religion*, 15).

ideogram for Ishtar: any goddess from any culture might have been intended, as long as she was associated in some way with the goddess Ishtar. It is even within the realm of possibility that the goddess intended by the use of this ideogram for Ishtar *was* Ishtar. She was widely known and a popular character for whom any author could have created various plot lines. The religion of the Hittites surely could have absorbed eclectic mythological narratives as easily as it tolerated an eclectic pantheon.

To sum up, the information that the Elkunirsha fragments provide, small though it is, may be important primary data; it may also be secondary material on Syro-Palestinian deities that was used by a foreign writer. Since a decision cannot be made based on the material at hand, this source will be considered a secondary source describing the gods of Syria–Palestine through Hittite scribal eyes. The presentation of the god El is more reliable, perhaps, than the portrayal of the other deities, since, the identity of the other divinities is less than clear.

THE BIBLE

For centuries the "Old Testament" was considered the foremost authority on the subject of "Canaanite" religion. Scholars centered much attention on the descriptions of the horrid native religious practices, which included a great deal of sex and child sacrifice.[36] The biblical texts portray the religious culture of the "Canaanites" as evil; in contrast, the Judean and certain Israelite religious practices are moral and good. The biblical value judgment on the native religious world has usually been accepted in scholarly studies of the biblical texts. This has shaded the understanding of the religion itself.

Throughout most of the history of biblical scholarship, it has been assumed that the Israelite tribes came to the area of Syria–Palestine from outside and there confronted an alien culture. This means that the descriptions of the native culture presented in the biblical texts

36. Sex, nature, and orgy have long been seen as the central aspects of non-Judean religious life in Syria–Palestine. Georg Fohrer (*Geschichte der israelitischen Religion* [Berlin: de Gruyter, 1969] 52) defines this religion with the common designation *Fruchtbarkeitskult*; see also T. C. Vriezen, *The Religion of Ancient Israel* (Philadelphia: Westminster, 1967) 52, 55–56; and Mircea Eliade, *A History of Religious Ideas* (3 vols.; Chicago: University of Chicago Press, 1978–85) 1.159–60. For a survey of child sacrifice in scholarship, see George C. Heider, *The Cult of Molek: A Reassessment* (JSOTSup 43; Sheffield: JSOT, 1985) 1–92; John Day, *Molech: A God of Human Sacrifice in the Old Testament* (University of Cambridge Oriental Publications 41; Cambridge: Cambridge University Press, 1989); and for a modern twist on the theories, see Lawrence E. Stager and Samuel R. Wolff, "Child Sacrifice at Carthage: Religious Rite or Population Control?" *BAR* 10 (January-February 1984) 30–51.

were written by people who had no part in that culture. Through comparative studies of biblical and Syro-Palestinian texts and cultural remains, it has become increasingly clear that the culture of the biblical texts must itself have been part of the Syro-Palestinian world.[37] The various texts that make up the Bible are products of the religious world of Syria–Palestine, but provide evidence of one variant of the Syro-Palestinian tradition, one which clearly had moved away from the vision of a heavenly pantheon.

The biblical material contains a wide variety of form and content. For this reason, it is difficult to make general statements about the usefulness of the Bible as a source for Syro-Palestinian religious traditions. Almost any passage that might be cited to describe Syro-Palestinian religion has to be examined by itself. A few general comments, however, may be made about the Bible as a resource for knowledge about the pantheon of Syria–Palestine.

The material now contained in the Bible that is relevant to the study at hand is found primarily in the texts that make up the Protestant Old Testament; these are basically the same as those for the Hebrew Bible, though the Hebrew Bible is somewhat shorter than the collection in most Christian Bibles. These books, as the individual texts are called, form what is known as the canon of the Bible. This means, in practical terms, that all biblical texts conform to a greater or lesser extent to beliefs espoused by those who collected the canon. The oldest core of the collection is the Torah, the first five books of the Bible. The exact date of the organization of this selection of texts is unknown, but the date for the Torah becoming sacred scripture was after the Babylonian Exile (538 B.C.E.) and before the final separation between the Jews and the Samaritans (which unfortunately is still uncertain). Material that now appears in the Torah was edited to conform to the religious realities of the Persian Period in Judea or to realities in Babylon experienced by people from Judah. Whatever material remains in the Bible from the culture prior to the Exile must be considered to have undergone serious religious redaction by a particular group within the postexilic community.[38] All

37. See, for example, Adolphe Lods, *Israël des origines au milieu du VIIIe siècle* (Paris: Renaissance du livre, 1930) 465–67, 526; Albrecht Alt, *Essays on Old Testament History and Religion* (Garden City, New York: Doubleday, 1966); Albright, *Yahweh and the Gods*; Gösta W. Ahlström, *Aspects of Syncretism in Israelite Religion* (Horae Soederblomianae 5; Lund: C. W. K. Gleerup, 1963), and *Royal Administration and National Religion in Ancient Palestine* (SHANE 1; Leiden: Brill, 1982). See now also Elizabeth Bloch-Smith, *Judahite Burial Practices and Beliefs about the Dead* (JSOTSup 123; Sheffield: JSOT Press, 1992) 95–96, on goddess figurines in Judah through the seventh century.

38. Otto Eissfeldt (*The Old Testament: An Introduction* [New York: Harper & Row, 1965]) provides comments on the editorial process for each individual biblical book

data appearing in the Torah that might have derived from the kingdom of Judah must be understood to have a Jerusalem cult bias. The postexilic editing ensured that the idea of a single deity for the entire cosmos had a central position. The books outside of the Torah all passed through the hands of the same Jerusalem religious community, resulting in a consistent editorial vision of non-Judean religions throughout the Hebrew Bible.

Biblical references to the deities of people who were considered by the authors to have wrong notions presupposed that those deities, in most cases, did not exist. In spite of this the biblical texts do at times contain passages that confirm the existence of deities other than the one god of Judah. Often these passages now appear in a form that does not directly refer to the gods but implies that the deities did exist. It is uncommon for the names of "other" deities to appear in any text that presents them as active, real entities in the universe, though there are exceptions. Any passage in the Bible that deals with gods must be scrutinized, not only to see what the gods are supposed to be doing, but also to see how the author of the extant passage intended it to appear. Furthermore, the origin of the passage's idea of the gods needs to be given some consideration.

The most frequently cited passage regarding divine hierarchy in the Bible is Deut 32:8–9. Since the study of this passage by Otto Eissfeldt in 1958 and Albright's reconstruction of a supposed original version in 1959, this portion of biblical poetry has been used to show that the nations of the earth were, in some ancient and primordial time, allotted to proper patron deities by a supreme god.[39] But actually, this poetic fragment does not demonstrate a divine hierarchy. Eissfeldt's theory depends on the supposition that Elyon and Yahweh were considered two distinct deities by the poet, yet in the Bible both names are used to refer to Yahweh. Since one cannot simply assume an early date for the poem, neither should the two names be

---

and for the Old Testament as a whole; for the complications encountered in attempting to deal with "primary" data found in biblical texts as edited source, see, for example, the discussion of Jeremiah in Robert P. Carroll, *From Chaos to Covenant: Prophecy in the Book of Jeremiah* (New York: Crossroad, 1981) 5–30.

39. Otto Eissfeldt, *Das Lied Moses Deuteronomium 32 1–43 und das Lehrgedicht Asaphs Psalm 78 samt einer Analyses der Umgebung des Mose-Liedes* (Berichte über die Verhandlungen der sächsischen Akademie der Wissenschaften zu Leipzig 104.5; Berlin: Akademie, 1958); and William Foxwell Albright, "Some Remarks on the Song of Moses in Deuteronomy XXXII," *VT* 9 (1959) 342–43. Note how for Richard J. Clifford (*The Cosmic Mountain in Canaan and the Old Testament* [HSM 4; Cambridge: Harvard University Press, 1972] 46–47) and E. Theodore Mullen, Jr. (*The Divine Council in Canaanite and Early Hebrew Literature* [HSM 24; Chico, Cal.: Scholars Press, 1980] 119, 202–4), among others, the emended text has become the real text.

expanded to refer to two deities. Albright's thesis depends on a conflation of the Hebrew text of the Masoretic canon, selected Greek translations, and a fragment of a Dead Sea Scroll. None of these manuscript traditions, by itself, actually supports such a reading of the text, however, though the Greek renditions of the passage *may* be interpreted as showing a hierarchy. Keeping in mind that this has been the most accepted proof text for divine hierarchy in the biblical corpus, one can see that the Bible provides at best elusive evidence about the gods.

Dating any material from the Bible is a major problem. It is often assumed that the narratives now occurring in the biblical books were based on earlier traditions, written or not. This appears to be a reasonable hypothesis in general, but to what extent the traditional content has been retained in its retelling is quite impossible to determine. Moreover, it is impossible for scholars even to agree on dates for the composition of the extant narratives in their current form, let alone to agree on dates for the composition of sources for the texts. One belief held by several scholars regarding the antiquity of biblical narratives is that poetic sections should be seen as the oldest material embedded in narrative compositions.[40] Proponents of this theory contend that certain poetic characteristics present in some biblical poems show that the poetry belongs to the earliest period of Judean literary traditions. The central basis of this theory is the observation that narratives of early "Israelite" traditions contain poetic sections and a premise that there is a discernible form for all "early" poetry.[41] Any poem that appears to have a similar form is then considered premonarchical in origin. However, none of the arguments for a set progression in poetic style are credible without precise dating, which is impossible for periods prior to the Exile. Furthermore, as poetry critics surely know, a text in poetic form need not predate a prose form with the same content, nor does it need to relate the same

40. See, for example, John Bright, *A History of Israel* (Philadelphia: Westminster, 1959) 66, or Siegfried Herrmann, *A History of Israel in Old Testament Times* (Philadelphia: Fortress, 1975) 63. On the convoluted problems of suggesting a primacy of poetry over prose in such texts; see, on the two renditions of Deborah's section of Judges, Baruch Halpern, *The First Historians: The Hebrew Bible and History* (San Francisco: Harper & Row, 1988) 76–97.

41. The foundational work for this theory was laid by William Foxwell Albright ("The Earliest Forms of Hebrew Verse," *JPOS* 2 [1922] 69–86), though it is best known from the joint project of Frank Moore Cross, Jr. and David Noel Freedman (*Studies in Ancient Yahwistic Poetry* [SBLDS 21; Missoula, Mont.: Scholars Press, 1975], originally produced as a joint dissertation in 1948 and 1950). However, it has long been known that prose may be retained orally for as long a period and as completely as poetry (Eduard Nielsen, *Oral Tradition: A Modern Problem in Old Testament Introduction* [SBT 11; London: SCM, 1954] 32).

material in the same manner as a prose account—neither now nor in the past.

With very few exceptions, no material now contained in the Bible may be unequivocally dated to a time earlier than the Babylonian Exile. The historical narratives clearly were given their final form after the destruction of Jerusalem and its temple in 587.[42] The poetry that comprises the book of Psalms must have been compiled after the return from the Exile, no matter when the songs themselves may have been written.[43] All prophetic materials underwent lengthy, partisan editing well after the building of the second temple, in the Persian Period, with a theological bias that may not have been recognizable even to the original prophets.[44] None of the canonical books as it now appears could have been written, let alone reached sacred status, prior to the Persian Period. This must be considered seriously, not only when one asks questions about the theology of the texts themselves, but also when one attempts to reconstruct the religious beliefs of Judah or Israel in preexilic times.

The deities mentioned in the narrative sections are most often "the foreign gods" that Judah and Israel were not to worship—Baal, Asherah, Shemesh, and a host of others. Even the clear statements prohibiting the worship of gods must be viewed with suspicion. Since the historical narratives derive from Judean circles (groups whose loyalty to Jerusalem and its national cult clearly set them at odds with what in their eyes was the "renegade" northern Israelite

42. For a short survey of the dates for the historical books (Joshua, Judges, Samuel, Kings, Chronicles, Ezra, Nehemiah), see Jacob M. Myers, *I Chronicles* (AB 12; Garden City, N.Y.: Doubleday, 1965) 19–30. A strong scholarly tradition continues to argue that the major portion of the historical literature (the so-called "deuteronomistic history") was composed before the Exile: Cross, *Canaanite Myth*, 274–89; and Halpern, *First Historians*, 181–235. Yet, the existence of a continuous history from Deuteronomy through Kings was originally proposed and dated to the exilic period by Martin Noth (*Überlieferungsgeschichtliche Studien I: Die sammelnden und bearbeitenden Geschichtswerke im Alten Testament* [Halle: Niemeyer, 1943] 133), and his exilic date for the completed history is acknowledged even by those who see it as a "second edition": Cross, *Canaanite Myth*, 287–89; Richard Elliott Friedman, "From Egypt to Egypt: Dtr[1] and Dtr[2]," in *Traditions in Transformation: Turning Points in Biblical Faith* (ed. Baruch Halpern and Jon D. Levenson; Winona Lake, Ind.: Eisenbrauns, 1981) 191–92, which is a work expanding on Cross, *Canaanite Myth*, 167–68. Halpern (*First Historians*, 181–82, 234) sees an exilic historian using and preserving earlier historical narrative, so that the material of the preexilic narrative provides the understanding for a later author.

43. The inclusion of a poem such as Psalm 137, which is certainly from the Babylonian Exile, proves that the collection itself can be no earlier; Artur Weiser, *The Psalms: A Commentary* (OTL; Philadelphia: Westminster, 1962) 100.

44. Eissfeldt, *Old Testament*, 345–46, 350–65, 372–74, and 383–84; Rolland Emerson Wolfe, "The Editing of the Book of the Twelve," *ZAW* 53 (1935) 128; Carroll, *Chaos to Covenant*, 18, 25–26.

religion), any picture of northern Israel's religious traditions may have been slanted toward the negative. In the same manner, the religious activities of Judean rulers who were perceived by the authors, for whatever reasons, to be evil monarchs were shown in the worst possible terms, while Judean kings who were considered to be good appeared in what may have been unrealistically pious renditions related to the beliefs of the authors rather than to the beliefs of the monarchs themselves.[45] The extent to which any of the deities were worshiped in the two nations may not in fact be discernible in the narratives purporting to provide such information. Therefore, any attempt to reconstruct the religious beliefs in either Judah or Israel prior to the Exile solely from biblical data is dubious.[46]

The relationship between the divine and human realms, on the other hand, is much more extensively portrayed in the Bible than is the heavenly world. The question of a monarch's right to rule the land belonging to God (or a god) is dealt with both in narrative and poetic form. What the deity was expected to do for a loyal ruler and a righteous populace is a theme commonly touched on in both its positive and negative ramifications. Biblical texts concerned with the way the king was supposed to function within the cosmic realm are a rich source of information about divine rule. This is also true concerning the way divinity communicated with humanity. Usually, of course, the biblical material deals only with the relationship between Yahweh and the nations of Judah and Israel; however, occasionally other gods and their lands make an appearance in the texts. In these cases it is necessary to remember that the writers who recorded the information were outsiders explaining foreign religious matters in terms

---

45. An example of each may suffice: Hezekiah is painted in broad strokes as a veritable paradigm of the good and pious ruler, though it is reasonable to suggest that he himself merely survived an Assyrian invasion in what appeared to contemporaries to be a miraculous fashion. Such divine intervention in their eyes would have required a just and pious ruler, so Hezekiah may well have become "wonderful" only in retrospect. On the dubious nature of the cult reform ascribed to this ruler, see Lowell K. Handy, "Hezekiah's Unlikely Reform," *ZAW* 100 (1988) 111–15. Manasseh, on the other hand, may simply have been replacing the destroyed cult of Judah, which contained elements later authors felt to be heretical and therefore portrayed him as the very embodiment of evil (p. 115); Ahlström, *Royal Administration*, 75–81.

46. Note the effort by Mark S. Smith (*The Early History of God: Yahweh and the Other Deities in Ancient Israel* [San Francisco: Harper & Row, 1990] 145–52) to create a history of Yahwistic religion prior to the Exile. While Smith is capable of making over a hundred pages' worth of comments on parallels to Yahweh and other deities, he is able produce a mere seven pages on the religion of the nations Judah and Israel; and even this reconstruction suffers from an incapacity to distinguish between biblical narrative and the reality that lies behind it. On the archaeological data, which appears to confirm a religion of several deities during the time of the monarchies, see Helga Weippert, *Palästina in vorhellenistischer Zeit* (Handbuch der Archäologie: Vorderasien 2/1; Munich: Beck, 1988) 620–31.

of their own religious understanding. Whether the understanding expressed in such passages was common to the various nations to which the texts ascribe it or whether it was solely a Judean vision of the way the cosmos was supposed to function may not be discernible from the biblical texts alone. Whether one deals with God's relations with Judeans and Israelites or the gods' dealings with their nations, one must bear in mind the possibility that the Judean postexilic belief that regarded Yahweh as the only existing deity may have colored the presentation of the deities' dealings with mortals.

One other general observation can be made about certain biblical texts concerned with the divine realm. There are passages in both prose narrative and poetic compositions that quite clearly presuppose a knowledge, on the part of the audience, of a divine realm populated by a monarchical hierarchy of divine beings.[47] In some of these texts the beings on the heavenly plane are quite simply called "gods" (אלהים; בני־אלים; בני־האלהים). In these passages, especially compositions that must be considered literary or liturgical, it is probably safe to assume that the authors took it for granted that people who heard the productions knew there was a heavenly world populated by the gods. The question that arises is whether the heavenly realm of gods was understood to be a reality functioning on a divine level in the contemporary religious thought or whether the references were a literary allusion to some "classical," but later incredible, beliefs.[48] To some extent the answer to this question rests on a decision about the purposes of the biblical authors for their individual compositions. If, for example, the references to the gods appear in the psalms, it makes a difference whether the songs were intended for laity outside the cult ritual, in which case the references were probably less serious than if the composers wrote the passages to be sung in the temple cult, because then it would be necessary to assume that the cult included a belief in the gods referred to.

It is clear that the texts of the Bible may be taken as primary source material for the religious world of Syria–Palestine, but the texts contain data of a unique type. They are the books of a particular religious heritage. This religion had reduced its vision of the pantheon to a single deity before any of the texts included had received their final form. It is neither clear when most of the biblical literature

---

47. 1 Kgs 22:19–23; Job 1:6–12, 2:1–7; Psalm 82. See H. Wheeler Robinson, "The Council of Yahweh," *JTS* 45 (1944) 151–57; Mullen, *Divine Council*, 111–244; and Handy, "Dissenting Deities or Obedient Angels: Divine Hierarchies in Ugarit and the Bible," *BR* 35 (1990) 26–28.

48. The use of mythological motifs in literary work by those who no longer hold to the reality of those gods, even people with religious and/or political intentions, is a common enough aspect of more modern authors: Dante, Milton, and Mao have all used deities in which they do not believe for their serious poetry.

was first composed, nor certain when the final form was completed. The intent of both the authors and the redactors can only be guessed from the modern vantage point. Any reconstruction of religious beliefs backward from the "Yahweh-as-only-god" position of the final canonical editors to a previous view that there were several deities must be understood to be at best provisional and always open to question. The few passages remaining in the Bible referring to divine populations ruled by Yahweh must be investigated, each according to its own purpose, origin, reliability, and usefulness.

THE HISTORY OF THE PHOENICIANS BY PHILO OF BYBLOS

After the Ugaritic tablets of the late second millennium B.C.E., the next extended narratives that purport to be myths from Syria–Palestine are contained in the *History of the Phoenicians*, written around the end of the first century C.E. by Philo of Byblos.[49] The selections that have survived from this history do not come from any manuscript or copy of the history itself. The majority of surviving passages are found in Eusebius of Caesarea's *Preparation for the Gospel*; the other few fragments or references that remain have been collected, along with Eusebius's quotations, by Felix Jacoby.[50] The relevant material in Greek and in English translation is now available in two books: Albert Baumgarten's commentary is extensive in its coverage of the passages, while Harold Attridge and Robert Oden's monograph is less thorough, but immensely more readable.[51]

The stories that relate the myths of Syria–Palestine alluded to in Philo's history were passed down by a series of writers who lived after he did. The fourth-century Christian author Eusebius, who provided almost all the surviving passages, may have been dependent for his sources on the third-century philosopher Porphyry. It appears that Eusebius can be considered a trustworthy conveyor of the written tradition,[52] yet, if it was Porphyry whom Eusebius was copying and not Philo himself, then it is necessary to question how well Por-

---

49. The majority of fragments surviving from this work appear in Eusebius of Caesarea, *Preparation for the Gospel*, available with French translation in Jean Sirinelli and Édouard des Places (eds. and trans.), *Eusèbe de Césarée: La Préparation évangélique, Livre I: Introduction, texte grec, traduction et commentaire* (Paris: Cerf, 1974).

50. Felix Jacoby (ed.), *Die Fragmente der griechischen Historiker* (Leiden: Brill, 1958) 3.C:802–24.

51. Albert I. Baumgarten, *The "Phoenician History" of Philo of Byblos: A Commentary* (Études préliminaires aux religions orientales dans l'Empire Romain 89; Leiden: Brill, 1981); Harold W. Attridge and Robert A. Oden, Jr., *Philo of Byblos, the Phoenician History: Introduction, Critical Text, Translation, Notes* (CBQMS 9; Washington, DC: Catholic Biblical Association, 1981).

52. Attridge and Oden, *Philo of Byblos*, 2 n. 5, and references cited there.

phyry handled the material. It is clear from the evidence that Porphyry changed his sources to suit himself. Thus the texts that survive from Philo of Byblos had at least one questionable redactor before reaching a fairly safe witness. Since it is not clear whether Eusebius of Caesarea had an independent source apart from Porphyry (it is clear that he used Porphyry), it is not certain that Philo's original text has survived. The material in Eusebius is at least material considered to be genuine in Eusebius's time, which was two centuries after Philo wrote.

On the other hand, Philo wrote that the narratives that he presented as the earliest history of Phoenicia came to him from other trustworthy sources. Nearest to his time was the figure Sanchuniathon, who, if he really existed at all, probably had the Semitic name Sakkunyaton (or something like it).[53] The information that Philo insisted came from the very earliest times had already been collected by the Phoenician Sakkunyaton, from various earlier sources. These reports were then translated, very carefully, to create the "factual" rendition of Phoenician early history, as Philo reports. This Sakkunyaton was supposed to have been a Phoenician chronicler, whose information came from numerous cult centers that had retained ancient documents with facts on Phoenician culture. All of this work was supposed to have been carried out around the time of the Trojan War, Moses, and Semiramis, which is to say, sometime in hoary antiquity.[54] It is not certain that Philo believed that Sakkunyaton lived in that ancient age, but he did state that he believed the material derived from Sakkunyaton originated well before the time of Greek culture.[55] Philo believed that behind the collected data arranged by Sakkunyaton was the original form of the texts written by the "renowned" scribe Taautos. That the great scribe Taautos had lived in most ancient antiquity was not doubted by Philo, since the creation of writing was attributed to Taautos. Taautos, it is said, was later considered to have been a god and was worshiped in Egypt as the divinity Thoth.[56]

In this alleged chain of transmission, the earliest date that can in any sense be considered reliable is that of Philo of Byblos himself. It is fairly certain that Taautos may be deleted as a historical entity from this series of chroniclers; the attribution of ancient material to a god is not uncommon in religious traditions, but it is not acceptable to use them in recreating the history of the tradition.[57] The figure of

53. James Barr, "Philo of Byblos of his 'Phoenician History'," *BJRL* 57 (1974) 36.
54. F. Løkkegaard, "Some Comments on the Sanchuniaton Tradition," *ST* 7 (1954) 75.
55. Philo of Byblos I.9.24 (numbers are from Eusebius's *Preparation for the Gospel*).
56. Attridge and Oden, *Philo of Byblos*, 72 n. 6.
57. Barr, "Philo of Byblos," 37.

Sakkunyaton is more of a problem. Dates seriously proposed for his lifetime range from early in the second millennium B.C.E. to the first century C.E., the latter being the time of Philo of Byblos.[58] Since the stories contained in Philo's history have some parallels in the narratives from Ugarit, dates around the time of the fall of Ugarit have often been suggested, which would be an incredible coincidence.[59] More likely than having been a contemporary of Ilimilku, Sakkunyaton may well have been a literary creation of Philo of Byblos himself.[60] This leaves the modern scholar with the necessity of treating the material in the history as no earlier than Philo of Byblos and, at the same time, of remembering that the selections may not even have survived as Philo originally wrote them.

The text of the *History of the Phoenicians* reflects the hellenistic interest in ethnic historiography.[61] Moreover, the manner in which the deities of Syria–Palestine are presented, as human actors from the earliest history of Phoenicia, conforms to the euhemeristic interpretation of myths common in hellenistic Greek works.[62] For James Barr the euhemerism in the history is the work of Philo of Byblos himself, even though the sources he used are seen to have come from a period of extensive Greek influence on Phoenician writing.[63] The history of Philo of Byblos deals with human beings, though occasionally the text reports that those being told about were in fact gods. It is clear from these references that the material used to recreate the earliest history of Phoenicia came from the mythology of the area. Not enough of that material has survived to make a coherent series of

58. Patrick D. Miller, Jr. (*The Divine Warrior in Early Israel* [HSM 5; Cambridge: Harvard University Press, 1973] 10) dates the material to an earlier stage of Canaanite culture than the texts from Ugarit. Attridge and Oden (*Philo of Byblos,* 8–9) suggest a date no earlier than the Hellenistic Era and perhaps during the Roman Period.

59. O. Eissfeldt (*Ras Schamra und Sanchunjaton* [Beiträge zur Religionsgeschichte des Altertums 4; Halle: Niemeyer, 1939] 70–71) posits a date in the thirteenth century B.C.E. for both Sakkunyaton and the Ugaritic tablets. Others have found the material in Philo of Byblos to agree fully with that found at Ugarit; Pope, *El in the Ugaritic Texts,* 4–5; Mitchell J. Dahood, "Ancient Semitic Deities in Syria and Palestine," in *Le Antiche divinità semitiche* (ed. Sabatino Moscati; SS 1; Rome: Centro di studi semitici, 1958) 70.

60. Baumgarten, *Phoenician History,* 265–66; however, M. J. Edwards, "Philo or Sanchuniathon? A Phoenician Cosmology," *Classical Quarterly* 41 (1991) 216–17, sees a Semitic author behind Philo's work, though Porphyry and Philo are assumed to have created much of the "historical background" for the author and at least some of the book's content themselves.

61. Robert A. Oden, "Philo of Byblos and Hellenistic Historiography," *PEQ* 110 (1978) 115–26; John Van Seters, *In Search of History: Historiography in the Ancient World and the Origins of Biblical History* (New Haven, Connecticut: Yale University Press, 1983) 206–7.

62. Oden, "Philo and Historiography," 118–19.

63. Barr, "Philo of Byblos," 35, 49, and 55.

narratives out of the fragments appearing in Philo's history. Nor can it be assumed that Philo recorded a complete record of myths or legends from any period of Phoenician religious history. It would have been fortunate if the section of Philo's history dealing with the transition from primordial times to the clearly historical human age had been preserved so that historians could compare the way Philo wrote history taken from myths with the way he wrote history taken from historical data, but that material has not survived.

Because Philo of Byblos accumulated mythological material for his history, it is likely that the myths underlying his work were part of the religious life of the Phoenician cult at the time of Philo, and thus, quite late. If this is true, the *History of the Phoenicians* provides modern scholars with information on Syro-Phoenician religious thought from the first century C.E. Undoubtedly the religious traditions revealed in the texts stretched backward into the first millennium B.C.E. While mythological material from Egypt and Greece can easily be found in the Phoenician history, it is not appropriate to assume that they were therefore foreign elements added to the original Phoenician material by either Philo or his sources. They may reflect indigenous mythological thought reported in a Grecian manner, better known in similar narratives from Greek or Egyptian religion. Or they may indeed have been taken from foreign sources and became a part of the religious culture of Phoenicia. If the latter were true, culling the foreign elements from the source would falsely slant the vision of reality as seen in the religious world in that area at that time.

The history, as it is now preserved, is constructed to form a consistent narrative. If the sources for these stories originally came from a number of different temple archives, as Philo insists, numerous local traditions must have been conflated to produce the uniform history that now appears. Any other theory would suggest that the tradition of the myths was constant throughout the area and the only reason for collecting materials from various sites was to compile a dispersed, not a varied, tradition. It is possible that the various localities from which the tales were collected had their own traditions and their own widely differing dates of origin. It is not possible at this juncture to separate the strands wrapped together to create this history. Whatever the original myths, the history was constructed by means of a progression centered around three major themes: cosmology, technogony, and theogony, giving the current narrative a unified structure.[64] The original myths may or may not have had a unifying narrative into which they all could be fit.

64. Ibid., 22.

Determining exactly which Syro-Palestinian deities are referred to in Philo's history is a confusing task. Some gods are clearly defined. El is called Kronos, and this equation is flatly stated in the text of the history itself (Ἦλον, τὸν καὶ Κρόνον).[65] In the case of Athena (Ἀθηνᾶ), often the reference is clearly to the Greek goddess (as when Attica is presented to the deity as her personal allotment), yet sometimes it appears that the goddess Anat is intended (as when she is engaged in warfare). It is generally agreed that Baal appears in the history, but as a minor figure and with no little confusion because of the Greco-Semitic names being used for him. Where the Greek divine names are used without any explanation, one must guess which, if any, known deity of Syria–Palestine is intended. It is possible that some gods appear more than once with different names. The use of Egyptian deities in the stories does not aid in identifying the Semitic divinities.

How representative of mythological narration these tales were is impossible to determine. Written in Greek, in a Grecian historiographical manner, apparently for a Greek audience, the selections may well have been chosen with an eye to what the Greek audience would have found interesting or novel. One does well to ask whether the current form of the work was something the Phoenician religious populace would have understood as coming from their own culture or whether the history was a Greek form into which Phoenician material was shaped. Clearly Greek thought influenced the narratives, but enough Syro-Palestinian data appear in the history to demonstrate that there was a genuine local tradition in Philo of Byblos's work. Any use of these mythological tales retold must take into account the impossibility of knowing the number of layers of interpretation within and without the Phoenician tradition purported to be the basis of this work. The extent of the alterations from any original Phoenician material is unknown.

DE DEA SYRIA

The final major source for this study is a work ascribed to Lucian of Samosata and entitled *The Syrian Goddess*.[66] The author is, in fact, unknown. The work has been attributed to Lucian by arguing that either the author was attempting to mimic the writing style of He-

---

65. Philo of Byblos I.10.16.

66. The text, with modern translation, is available in English by Harold W. Attridge and Robert A. Oden, *The Syrian Goddess (De Dea Syria) Attributed to Lucian* (SBLTT 9; Missoula, Montana: Scholars Press, 1976); and in French by Mario Meunier, *Lucian de Samosate: La Déesse syrienne: Traduction nouvelle avec prolégomènes et notes* (Paris: Éditions Janick, 1947).

rodotus by writing in an overly literary Ionic Greek, or he was intending a satirical and ironic parody of a travel tour guide.[67] Neither of these suggestions seems very satisfactory. Ionic Greek is at best rare, if attested, in the acknowledged genuine writings of Lucian of Samosata, and when irony and satire appear in other works of his, there has been no doubt whether he intended them as such. *The Syrian Goddess* simply does not fit in with the corpus of genuine compositions by Lucian of Samosata. But since the author is unknown, I shall follow tradition and call the author Lucian, in spite of the fact that the real author's name will probably never be known.[68]

The work itself consists of a series of descriptive accounts of religious sites along the coast of the Levant. Whether the presentation was intended to be serious or to be a parody of the religious beliefs of the local population remains a debated topic, though nothing in the text mandates that the work be regarded as a lampoon. The descriptions of the temples conform to what is known of Syro-Palestinian sanctuaries, and the brief selections from temple-foundation narratives do not conflict with what would have been possible in Phoenician cult belief. The person who wrote the work seems to have had reliable information concerning the cult in Syria–Palestine in the second century C.E., whether from first- or second-hand experience. The manner in which the report is written is that of popular Greek travel reflections. The visitor describes the appearance of temples in Phoenicia, their statues, pantheon, and patron deities, the rituals performed in them, anecdotes about the cult personnel, and occasionally short summaries of foundation myths and legends from various sacred sites. The center of the author's attention is the temple dedicated to the goddess at the city of Hierapolis, but the goddess is always referred to by the Ionic Greek name "Ἥρη (Hera).

A number of problems relate to the use of this work as a source for mythological information. First is the basic problem of the stories that appear. When a tale is told about the founding of a temple, it tends to be a very short rendition, obviously retold by the author from longer explanations provided by the cult itself. The author, however, acknowledges no original source for the tales. Several quite different narratives are proffered as foundation stories for a single site, leading one to wonder whether one of the given stories was the

---

67. See A. M. Harmon (ed. and trans.), *Lucian* (LCL; Cambridge: Harvard University Press) 4.337; Franz Cumont, *Oriental Religions in Roman Paganism* (n.p.: Routledge, 1911; reprint, New York: Dover, 1956) 14. For a summary of the debate see Robert A. Oden, *Studies in Lucian's "De Syria Dea"* (HSM 15; Missoula, Mont.: Scholars Press, 1977) 11–13.

68. So Monika Hörig, *Dea Syria: Studien zur religiösen Tradition der Fruchtbarkeitsgöttin in Vorderasien* (AOAT 208; Kevelaer: Butzon & Bercker/Neukirchen-Vluyn: Neukirchener Verlag, 1979) 3 n. 2.

official rendition or whether the author collected the narratives from others visiting the shrines who had their own ideas about how the temples were founded. Some of the tales are presented in a decidedly Greek form, complete with Greek names and plots known from other Greek sources. Again, questions arise in one's mind. Do these stories reflect Greek travelers' renditions of the foundation stories, the author's rendition of a Syro-Palestinian legend in Greek dress, or a story common to Phoenician and Greek civilizations? Perhaps each temple did have a battery of foundation narratives; perhaps there were multiple explanations for the existence of a single temple. All options are possible.

The second problem is the uncertainty of identifying the Syro-Palestinian deities being referred to in the texts. The author consistently gives the gods Greek names. Hera, Aphrodite, Zeus, and Apollo may all be interpreted as being gods of some kind, but when the author mentions their statues, the information he gives the reader is whether the likenesses fit or do not fit their Greek manifestations. This does not help in determining which local deities were intended, and it certainly provides no information about the attributes of the local pantheon. While there is some material that aids the process of equating a Greek name with a known Semitic name, the process is less certain than it sometimes appears. Though some scholars identify Apollo (Ἀπόλλων) with the god El, their arguments are neither convincing nor indisputable.[69] None of the gods identified only with Greek names in the work may with any certainty be identified with any particular Semitic deity.

Third, the audience for whom the book was intended may have had a major influence on the content. If this was a travel booklet intended to entertain Greek readers with stories of far-away places, the author no doubt wrote in a manner that would attract the Greek populace. Not only would he have selected stories based on the interests of the potential readers, but also he would have chosen sites based on their interests. If the Greeks enjoyed stories about Semiramis, complicated love novels, sexual adventures, bizarre cultic practices, and temple oracles that actually worked (and there is ample evidence that these themes were popular at the time), then the author of the work would have sought for tales that had these themes.[70] For the same reason, stories familiar to the Greek audience

69. René Dussaud, "Peut-on identifier l'Apollon barbu de Hiérapolis de Syrie?" *RHR* 126 (1943) 147–48. This identification is accepted by Attridge and Oden, *The Syrian Goddess*, 4.

70. Thomas Hägg, *The Novel in Antiquity* (Berkeley: University of California Press, 1983), deals with popular literary topics in classical narratives. On Semiramis, see

that he found in foreign cultures would have been most likely to be chosen. If this type of selection process was utilized, it is safe to assume that the stories now appearing in the work are not even a representative sample of the contemporary Syro-Palestinian myths of sanctuary foundations.

Finally, stories provided in "Lucian's" work were selected because they were related to the particular *sanctuaries* mentioned. This is a highly select type of tale, since the mythology of a sanctuary would ordinarily have included the stories of the *deity* of that temple. The tales told by this author are narratives concerned with the founding of the temples themselves, making the center of attention the temple and not the deity. This was, of course, a legitimate and reasonable topic for the author, but it did not develop into a well-rounded mythology. In fact, it was not intended to provide a comprehensive mythology, nor was it intended to explain the divine realm as seen by the residents of the areas visited. Therefore, the information that survives in this work is severely limited both by the fact that only a few cults were considered and by the restricted purposes of the author. General statements about which gods were of major or minor importance in the culture should not be deduced from this text.

While the information that may be gleaned from *The Syrian Goddess* is not voluminous, it does help us to understand how people viewed divine activities in the early first millennium C.E. As with the inscriptions described above, these tales deal mostly with the intersection of the divine and human realms. In this case the major concern is for the human world's response to and proper respect for (if not dread of) the divine realm, as displayed in the cult described for each patron deity. The work can be used for observations regarding the form and function of the cult in the Syro-Palestinian world, but we must remember that the amount of information is very small in relation to the amount of cultic activity in the civilization. The uncertainty about identifying the deities involved in the tales requires us to draw only general, conditional conclusions from them.

MINOR SOURCES

There are other sources of information that deal with the deities of Syria–Palestine. For this study they are of less importance than the six already mentioned above. However, material from the minor

---

Diodorus Siculus, *Library of History* 2.3.4–20.5 (LCL; Cambridge: Harvard University Press); and on cultic notations from the "foreign" nations, consider Herodotus, *The Histories* (also LCL).

sources may be useful as supplemental or tangential evidence to the major narrative texts.

Art

There is no lack of artistic representation of the gods of Syria–Palestine from the Bronze Age through the Roman Era. In metal and pottery, numerous figurines in human and animal form have been discovered that are understood to be artistic representations of various deities.[71] The most familiar figures are, no doubt, the statues and reliefs of female figures in human form, usually nude with hands often holding one or both breasts; these have usually been interpreted as "Astarte plaques."[72] It may be true that these figures were intended to represent the fertility goddess of the region, but the statues themselves do not tell the observer which goddess was intended by the artist. There is still some debate about whether any or all of the figurines actually depict deities.[73] In some cases, however, the depictions of the stance, hair, or objects held by the women do conform to artistic figures of goddesses from neighboring cultures that have identification imprinted on them.[74] Assuming that at

71. Ora Negbi (*Canaanite Gods in Metal: An Archaeological Study of Ancient Syro-Palestinian Figurines* [Tel Aviv: Tel Aviv University Press, 1976]) has collected photos of a majority of published metal images of deities. Caquot and Sznycer (*Ugaritic Religion,* plates) have presented a fine sample of Ugaritic representations. J. B. Pritchard (*ANEP,* 160–70, 352–53) presents a few examples, though many of them are depictions of Syro-Palestinian deities as seen from outside of Syria–Palestine. On clay figurines, see T. A. Holland, "A Study of Iron Age Baked Clay Figurines with Special Reference to Jerusalem: Cave 1," *Levant* 9 (1977) 124–54; figs. appear on pp. 138 and 146. See now the extensive study of deity symbols and figures by Othmal Keel and Christoph Uehlinger, *Göttinnen, Götter, und Gottessymbole: Neue Erkenntnisse zur Religionsgeschichte Kanaans und Israels Auf Grund bis Lang Unerschlossener Ikonographischer Quellen* (Quaestiones Disptutatae 134; Freiburg im Breisgau: Herder, 1992).

72. A decidedly out-of-date, but accessible, list of these figurines may be found in James B. Pritchard, *Palestinian Figurines in Relation to Certain Goddesses Known through Literature* (AOS 24; New Haven, Conn.: American Oriental Society, 1943); a small sample of these figurines appears in his *ANEP,* plate 469.

73. For a short summary of the current positions and a statement that these are not figurines of deities, see Jeffrey H. Tigay, *You Shall Have No Other Gods: Israelite Religion in the Light of Hebrew Inscriptions* (HSS 31; Atlanta: Scholars Press, 1986) 91; but see Weippert, *Palästina,* 620–21. Joan B. Townsend, "The Goddess: Fact, Fallacy and Revitalization Movement," in *Goddesses in Religions and Modern Debate* (ed. Larry W. Hurtado; University of Manitoba Studies in Religion 1; Atlanta: Scholars Press, 1990) 191–93, presents a variety of interpretations possible for the female figurines (this article was brought to my attention by Erica Treesh).

74. Compare, for example, the figurines in *ANEP,* plate 469 (upper left two examples), with plates 471, 473, and 474, which have very similar representations of female

least some of these Syro-Palestinian figurines probably do represent goddesses, one can only conjecture whether they were intended for the purpose of creating fertility in humans or crops.[75] The fact that nude goddess statues were made does not necessitate their having been made for the purpose of producing fertility. In fact it is not certain how these goddesses related to humans. Were the statues intended to be kept by women or men or both?[76] Because this particular type of art constitutes the representation of a single deity, there is little information to be derived from the artwork itself that helps to describe relationships among gods or between the divine and mortal worlds.

A large number of statues have been catalogued that do not fit into the "Astarte plaque" category. Of these, two types may be distinguished as being possible representations of divinities. One type is the animal figurine, with some indication that the beast should be interpreted as representing a deity. This type includes any number of horse figurines found bearing a disk on the head, apparently designating the sun god/goddess.[77] In the same way, snake and dove figurines are often considered to be representations of particular deities, while bovine (bull, heifer, and calf) figures seem to signify divinity in a more general manner in Syria–Palestine.[78]

---

forms and stance plus the name of a goddess, though the latter stelae come from Egypt.

75. Raphael Patai (*The Hebrew Goddess* [New York: Avon, 1978] 22–23, 48, 50), though not quite certain which goddess is portrayed by which figurine, is certain that the goddesses are related to fertility.

76. The theory that the goddesses were intended for fertility suggests that they were intended for use by women; it is within the realm of possibility that the adornment of living establishments with portrayals of half or wholly naked women (goddesses or not) is not necessarily a product of modern photographic print media and that men might have used such icons for decor in antiquity. On the impossibility of telling what these figurines were used for (or which deity was represented) from archaeological data, see Joachim Bretschneider, "Götter in Schreinen: Eine Untersuchung zu den Syrischen und Levantinischen Tempelmodellen, ihrer Bauplastik und ihren Gotterbildern," *UF* 21 (1991) 20–25.

77. John W. McKay, *Religion in Judah under the Assyrians 732–609 BC* (SBT 2d series 26; Naperville, Ill.: Allenson, 1973) 33–34.

78. See, for example, *ANEP*, plate 585, for birds and snakes; plates 828 and 832 for bulls. The snake has often been connected with healing deities (John Gray, "The Canaanite God Horon," *JNES* 8 [1949] 27–34); and with fertility cults (Karen Randolph Joines, *Serpent Symbolism in the Old Testament: A Linguistic, Archaeological, and Literary Study* [Haddonfield, N.J.: Haddonfield House, 1974] 74). The dove has long been associated with Syrian goddess worship (W. R. Smith, *The Religion of the Semites: The Fundamental Institutions* [New York: Schocken, 1972] 294 [first published in 1891]). For bull imagery used in Judah, see E. W. Heaton, *Solomon's New Men: The Emergence of Ancient Israel as a National State* (New York: Pica, 1974) 85, 91–92.

The second type is anthropomorphic. While these statues show the divinities as being human in form, they may include crowns, horns, or even wings to indicate the superiority of the entity being portrayed.[79] Common among these portrayals are the striding deities, often holding a weapon that may have been intended to signify that the deity was a god/goddess of war or to portray the idea that the deity was acting in a protective manner, unrelated to the usual representation of that particular deity. Several examples of seated deities have also been recovered; these appear to be representations of enthroned divinities, but since the context for these representations is lacking, more mundane situations may have been intended by the artists.

Similar portrayals of the gods are found carved on stelae, stone reliefs, and other objects.[80] One advantage provided by some of these carvings is that occasionally the name of the deity represented has been inscribed on the sculpture. Stelae were produced throughout the area during the entire period of Syro-Palestinian religious culture, though again, they often only portray a single deity, which does not help very much in understanding the relationships among different deities. A few carvings depict more than one image of the god itself. A seated, bearded god shown on a stela from Ugarit displays the worship of a human or divinity before an enthroned god.[81] Another stela from Ugarit displays a goddess suckling what appear to be two human lads, and from references in the Ugaritic texts, it is reasonable to assume that this is a picture of either Asherah or Anat suckling royal princes.[82] Among the small pictures found at Palmyra is one

79. Examples of each of these types may be found in Negbi, *Canaanite Gods in Metal*, figs. 51 and 54–56, plates 22, 27, and 31, all of which include crowns and horns; fig. 122 has both crown and horns and also wings.

80. For Ugarit, see Caquot and Sznycer, *Ugaritic Religion*, plates 7, 10, 11, 12, 26, 28a, and 29b. At the other temporal extreme, see for Palmyra, Teixidor (*Palmyra*, plates III.2, VII.2, VIII, XIII, XVIII, and XXI.2), who has also included plates of contemporary reliefs derived from other Syrian cities; Drijvers (*Religion of Palmyra*, plates) provides a wide assortment of deity representations.

81. Caquot and Sznycer, *Ugaritic Religion*, plate 7; Cassuto, *Anath*, plate 8; *ANEP*, plate 493. Recently a sculpture in the round has been discovered that appears to present the same seated figure, assumed to be El: Marguerite Yon and Jacqueline Gachet, "Une statuette du dieu El à Ougarit" (*Syria* 66 [1989] 349): "Il a en effet l'aspect à la fois vénérable et bienveillant du «père des dieux» et «père des ans»."

82. Caquot and Sznycer, *Ugaritic Religion*, plate 29b; *ANEP*, plate 829. Claude F. A. Schaeffer, "Les Fouilles de Ras Shamra–Ugarit quinzième, seizième et dix-septième campagnes (1951, 1952 et 1953): Rapport sommaire," *Syria* 31 (1954) 54–55, plate VIII. Paolo Matthiae (*Ars Syra: Contributi alla storia dell'arte figurativa siriana nella etè del medio e tardo bronzo* [SARC 4; Rome: Centro di studi semitici, 1962] 87–89) takes the two suckling figures to be a double image of the young king. See *KTU* 1.14.VI.25–27; and William A. Ward, "La Déesse nourricière d'Ugarit," *Syria* 46 (1969) 225–39.

with a scene that has been interpreted as a depiction of the Adonis myth, though this interpretation is open to serious doubt. The understanding of the enigmatic little scene is significant, since the whole Adonis mythology, while ascribed to Phoenicia, is attested only in Greek sources.[83] But the number of carvings depicting recognizable scenes is extremely small. For this reason the artwork of Syria–Palestine does not add a great deal of information to what may be gleaned from the major narrative sources.

Syro-Palestinian Gods Abroad

The Hellenistic Age was neither the first, nor the only, time period when deities from Syria–Palestine were adopted into other cultures. In the second millennium B.C.E. several West-Semitic deities were taken into the Egyptian cult. These deities were at times simply equated with indigenous Egyptian gods,[84] but sometimes they retained their own identities.[85] These deities were incorporated into Egyptian literature and mythology as well as portrayed in works of art.[86] In certain cases the Egyptian data provide most of what is known about a particular Syro-Palestinian deity. This is true, for example, of the god Reshep, though the reliability of the Egyptian material for defining the Syro-Palestinian god in his homeland is suspect due to the thorough incorporation of the deity into Egyptian religious culture.[87] In most cases, however, it is the study of the god as he appeared in Egypt that benefits from what is known about him from Syro-Palestinian sources. Such is the case with the popular

---

83. Otto Eissfeldt, *Adonis und Adonaj* (Leipzig: Akademie, 1970) 9–10. The "ticket" clearly refers to Tammuz, so there would have to be agreement on an equation of the two deities for this scene to reflect Adonis, which is a dubious assertion at best. See below on the Greek Adonis myth.

84. Consider Baal "who is almost completely absorbed by Seth" (Morenz, *Egyptian Religion*, 238); H. Te Velde, *Seth, God of Confusion: A Study of His Role in Egyptian Mythology and Religion* (Probleme der Ägyptologie 6; Leiden: Brill, 1967) 122–29.

85. This appears to have been the case with the goddesses Anat and Astarte; see Morenz, *Egyptian Religion*, 238–39.

86. See Rainer Stadelmann, *Syrisch-palästinensische Gottheiten in Ägypten* (Probleme der Ägyptologie 5; Leiden: Brill, 1967).

87. Ibid., 47–76; William Kelly Simpson, "Reshep in Egypt," *Or* n.s. 29 (1960) 63–74; William J. Fulco, *The Canaanite God Rešep* (AOS Essay 8; New Haven, Conn.: American Oriental Society, 1976). On the arrival and incorporation of the deity into Egyptian culture, see Bernhard Grdseloff, *Les Débuts du culte de Rechef en Égypte* (Cairo: Institut Français d'archéologie orientale, 1942).

goddesses Anat and Astarte, though the descriptions of Astarte are insufficient in the sources available at present.[88]

For the most part the gods of Syria–Palestine who appear in Egyptian sources do not have narratives devoted to their activities but are shown in incidental roles scattered in various texts. The names of gods from Syria–Palestine appear in royal statements regarding a ruler's patron deities. There are two exceptions. One is a work, variously titled, which contains Astarte and the "Insatiable Sea."[89] The badly fragmented narrative lacks a clear plot line, and in order to create a readable reconstruction of the work as a narrative whole, a great deal of inventive repair work has been done on the text. It has been argued that this is an Egyptian translation of a Syro-Palestinian myth.[90] Yet, because there are so many deities that are clearly Egyptian in the story, even within the tattered fragment that remains, and because of the possibility of parallel narratives based on the same plot motif in earlier Egyptian writings, other Egyptologists have concluded that it is an Egyptian story into which Astarte has been inserted.[91] It has also been suggested that the "Sea" appearing in the tale is a god imported from Syria–Palestine, the god Yam.[92] This identification is harder to substantiate. It may be true that the goddess Astarte (and perhaps also the god Yam) was used by an Egyptian author because she fit the needs of the tale. If this is true, like the gods of the Hittite Elkunirsha myth, she may be displaying the same characteristics that she displayed in Syria–Palestine, but she may also have been redesigned for an Egyptian audience. It is also possible that "The Sea" does not even refer to Yam, but even if it does, the possibility of poetic license again

88. On Anat in Egypt, see Stadelmann, *Syrisch-palästinensische Gottheiten*, 91–96; and Charles Howard Bowman III, "The Goddess ʿAnatu in the Ancient Near East" (Ph.D. diss., Graduate Theological Union, 1978) 228–34. On Astarte and Asherah, see Robert du Mesnil du Buisson, *Études sur les dieux phéniciens hérités par l'Empire Romain* (Études préliminaires aux religions orientales dans l'Empire Romain 14; Leiden: Brill, 1970) 73–76, 79–84.

89. Edward F. Wente, Jr., "Astarte and the Insatiable Sea," in *The Literature of Ancient Egypt: An Anthology of Stories, Instructions, and Poetry* (new ed., ed. William Kelly Simpson; New Haven, Conn.: Yale University Press, 1973) 133–36; and John A. Wilson, "Egyptian Myths, Tales, and Mortuary Texts," in *ANET*, 17–18.

90. Wilson, "Egyptian Myths," 17; Stadelmann, *Syrisch-palästinensische* Gottheiten, 127; and J. van Dijk, "ʿAnat, Seth and the Seed of Prēʿ," in *Scripta Signa Vocis: Studies about Scripts, Scriptures, Scribes and Languages in the Near East Presented to J. H. Hospers by His Pupils, Colleagues and Friends* (ed. H. L. J. Vanstiphout et al.; Groningen: Forsten, 1986) 32.

91. Georges Posener, "La Légende égyptienne de la mer insatiable," *AIPHOS* 13 (1953) 461–478; followed by Adolf Erman, *The Ancient Egyptians: A Sourcebook of Their Writings* (New York: Harper & Row, 1966) xxxiii; and Wente, "Astarte," 133.

92. Van Dijk, "ʿAnat, Seth," 32; Erik Hornung, *Conceptions of God in Ancient Egypt: The One and the Many* (Ithaca, N.Y.: Cornell University Press, 1982) 79.

arises. Since this mythological shred of a story contains clear references to Egyptian religious traditions (the Ennead, Ptah, and Nut), the narrative is less likely to have had a Syro-Palestinian origin than the Elkunirsha fragment.

The other Egyptian story that deals with Syro-Palestinian deities is about Anat and Seth.[93] It is argued that the god called Seth is actually Baal and that the work may reflect the myths of Syria–Palestine; however, it appears more likely that the tale is totally Egyptian in origin.[94] Nothing in the narrative suggests a source outside of Egypt and nothing in the contents specifically defines individual gods. Thus neither of the Egyptian narratives with Northwest-Semitic goddess names appears to be a reasonable source for Syro-Palestinian myths.

A certain amount of information may be discovered in correspondence preserved in Egyptian soil. From Amarna several tablets in Akkadian from the fourteenth century B.C.E. have been recovered, letters from minor kings in Syria–Palestine (and elsewhere) to the king of Egypt.[95] The gods who are formally acknowledged in these letters are the pantheon of Egypt, especially the sun-god king of the land, but occasionally a reference is made to one of the gods of Syria–Palestine. A relatively small collection of fifth-century B.C.E. papyrus letters from a colony of Syro-Palestinians who had settled in Yeb has been recovered.[96] This colony had brought their gods with them to their new homes and even had built temples for the deities in Egypt.[97] Among the deities who have been identified in these letters are Yahweh, Anat, and Beth-El.[98] In addition to these collections of letters, at times a single letter has survived that mentions Syro-Palestinian deities, as is the case with an Aramaic papyrus from

93. Van Dijk, "ᶜAnat, Seth," 31–51.

94. Ibid., 45.

95. J. A. Knudtzon, *Die El-Amarna-Tafeln* (2 vols.; VAB 2; Leipzig: Hinrichs, 1907–1915); and William Foxwell Albright, "Akkadian Letters," in *ANET*, 483–90.

96. The texts are collected in two books: A. Cowley, *Aramaic Papyri of the Fifth Century B.C.* (Oxford: Clarendon, 1923); and Emil G. Kraeling, *The Brooklyn Museum Aramaic Papyri: New Documents of the Fifth Century B.C. from the Jewish Colony at Elephantine* (New Haven, Conn.: Yale University Press, 1953).

97. While the letters refer to the temples, excavations failed to find a trace of these buildings. See W. Honroth, O. Rubensohn, and F. Zucker, "Bericht über die Ausgrabungen auf Elephantine in den Jahren 1906–1908," *ZÄSA* 46 (1909–1910) 14–61; and Werner Kaiser et al., "Stadt und Tempel von Elephantine: Siebter Grabungsbericht," *Mitteilungen des Deutschen archäologischen Instituts, Abteilung Kairo* 33 (1977) 63–100.

98. Albert Vincent, *La Religion des Judéo-Araméens d'Éléphantine* (Paris: Geuthner, 1937) 25–60, 86–87, 567–69; and Bezalel Porten, *Archives from Elephantine: The Life of an Ancient Jewish Military Colony* (Berkeley: University of California Press, 1968) 165.

King Adon to the Egyptian Pharaoh in the seventh century B.C.E.[99] Usually these letters mention the gods only in passing (in salutations, for example) and thus supply only a name and the fact that a deity was acknowledged at the time.

More closely related to the homeland of these deities are the colonies established by the Phoenicians throughout the Mediterranean. It is clear that the Phoenician settlers took their religious beliefs with them.[100] Inscriptions and art confirm the continuity between the colonies and the homeland; however, as with the inscriptions of Syria–Palestine, problems arise in attempting to use materials from the colonial centers. The inscriptions for the most part merely name deities and do not explain how the gods related to each other. Moreover, the same problem that was encountered in Syria–Palestine, that of identifying the various divinities named in the inscriptions, is also encountered in the documents from the colonies. An additional difficulty is the identification of the gods mentioned in colonial inscriptions with deities known from the homeland, Phoenicia. So far, narratives of legendary or mythological nature have not been uncovered at the sites of Phoenician colonies, though it is probably safe to assume that the Phoenician people living in these commercial ports maintained their traditional religious heritage and literature.

Even less is known about Syro-Palestinian deities who passed into other religious communities. Mesopotamia, from early times, was aware of the gods of the region to the west, but the narratives discovered so far show no clear sign of influence by "western" thought.[101] The Roman Empire also accepted the spread of Syro-Palestinian deities throughout the empire and into the many cults in Rome itself.[102] The problem is that the records are likely to present

---

99. See discussion and references in Bezalel Porten, "The Identity of King Adon," *BA* 44 (1981) 36–52.

100. This may be seen from the numerous inscriptions (see *KAI* 61–171). Note the dependency on colonial inscriptions for the reconstruction of Phoenician religion in Brian Peckham's "Phoenicia and the Religion of Israel: The Epigraphic Evidence," in *AIR*, 79–99; and Sergio Ribichini, "Beliefs and Religious Life," in *The Phoenicians* (ed. Sabatino Moscati; Milan: Bompiani, 1988) 104–25.

101. Deities with names Il, Dagan, Adad, Rashap, Shamash, etc., occur in even the earliest documents from Mesopotamia (J. J. M. Roberts, *The Earliest Semitic Pantheon: A Study of the Semitic Deities Attested in Mesopotamia before Ur III* [Baltimore: Johns Hopkins University Press, 1972] 13–14, 18–19, 31–34, 48, 51–52), none of which demonstrates that the gods had necessarily come from Syria–Palestine or were thought to be related to Palestinian deities in antiquity, despite Roberts' conclusions (p. 60).

102. Robert M. Grant (*Gods and the One God* [LEC 1; Philadelphia: Westminster, 1986] 30–32) follows the course of Baal of Serepta on the journey toward Rome. For the adoration of the Syrian goddess during the period of the Roman Empire, or at least her possible influences, see the study by Hörig, *Dea Syria*, 247–61.

these deities as local manifestations of Greek or Roman gods better known to the classical readers.[103] By and large, then, there is not much material that is useful for describing the interrelationships of the deities from the references to them in documents from neighboring states or in the narratives of conquering empires.

The Greek Adonis Myth

One exception to the observation that neighboring or conquering peoples left no solid information about the divine world of Syria–Palestine may be the Greek cult devoted to "Adonis." Even in ancient Greece it was acknowledged that this cult originated in the Semitic world. The name by which the god was known, *Adonis*, is clearly a Semitic title; but since it is a title, we cannot know for certain which Semitic god might have been intended originally. It is common to identify Adonis with the otherwise little-known deity Eshmun of Sidon.[104] The fact remains, however, that this entire cult is known only from Greek sources. It is mentioned in the poems of Sappho for the first time anywhere and then is found in references to the Greek cult scattered among the various classical texts, but nowhere is the entire mythological cycle set forth in one consistent narrative.[105]

Much of what is assumed to have been the cult of Adonis in Syria–Palestine derives from the knowledge of cultic mythologies

103. The problem of trying to determine the deity "hiding" behind each divine name is noted by Ramsay MacMullen, *Paganism in the Roman Empire* (New Haven, Conn.: Yale University Press, 1981) 5–6; on the confusion of Semitic gods with classical divine names, see Teixidor, *Pagan God*, 19–60. The confused state of these deities is not helped much by the material from Syria in the Roman period since the Syrians did not hesitate to inquire for divine advice from "foreign" deities, as well as from their own and from their own under the name of Roman and Greek gods. Youssef Hajjar ("Divinités oraculaires et rites divinatoires en Syrie et en Phénicie à l'époque gréco-romaine," in *ANRW* II.18.4:2240–89) presents a thoroughly mixed group of deities recorded in the inscriptions of the time; note the predominance of Greek and Roman divine names, though Hajjar's attempt to correlate Greco-Roman names with known Syro-Palestinian deities may not reflect any understanding of the relationship among the deities that would have been recognizable to the Syrians and Phoenicians of the Roman period, even if the Romans or Greeks might have accepted such one-for-one correspondences.

104. The classical study proposing this identification remains Wolf Wilhelm Grafen Baudissin, *Adonis und Esmun: Eine Untersuchung zur Geschichte des Glaubens an Auferstehungsgötter und an Heilgötter* (Leipzig: Hinrichs, 1911).

105. For references, see Roland de Vaux, *The Bible and the Ancient Near East* (Garden City, N.Y.: Doubleday, 1971) 224–28; and Walter Burkert, *Greek Religion* (Cambridge: Harvard University Press, 1985) 176–77; 421 nn. 7–12. For the passage from Sappho, see John Pairman Brown, "Kothar, Kinyras, and Kythereia," *JSS* 10 (1965) 218.

in Mesopotamia (Dumuzi/Tammuz and Inanna/Ishtar) and Egypt (Horus and Isis).[106] The major Greek literary source for the Semitic origin of this cycle is *The Syrian Goddess*.[107] The story seems to tell of the beautiful young god who was killed in a hunting accident by a boar, causing all the devotees to weep and wail. It is not even clear whether or not the deity was thought to have been revivified.[108] The evidence for this cult in Syria–Palestine is minimal and may even be

106. Walter Burkert, *Structure and History in Greek Mythology and Ritual* (Sather Classical Lectures 47; Berkeley: University of California Press, 1979) 99–102, 105–11; Sergio Ribichini, *Adonis: Aspetti "orientali" di un mito greco* (SS 55; Rome: Consiglio nazionale delle ricerche, 1981) 171–97. For Mesopotamia, see the studies by Thorkild Jacobsen, *Toward the Image of Tammuz and Other Essays on Mesopotamian History and Culture* ([HSS 21; Cambridge: Harvard University Press, 1970] 73–101) and *The Treasures of Darkness: A History of Mesopotamian Religion* ([New Haven, Conn.: Yale University Press, 1976] 25–73), which provide ample evidence for the precariousness of interpretations concerning this mythological cycle. For Egypt, see Erik Hornung (*Conceptions of God*, 151–53), who accentuates how piecemeal the mythological fragments are in the Egyptian sources from which this myth would have to be reconstructed. The full cycle is derived, in fact, only from Greek sources: Plutarch, *On Isis and Osiris*; or Diodorus Siculus, *Library of History* 1.13.4–27.6. It has reasonably been suggested that the resurrection element of the cult derives only from Egyptian renditions of the tale, in which Osiris mythology was the actual source of the story; de Vaux, *Bible and the ANE*, 227 and 236.

107. *De Dea Syria* 6–8 (paragraph numbers for this work are taken from Attridge and Oden, *Syrian Goddess*).

108. The "dying and rising god" has been popular in modern scholarly circles since the studies of James George Frazer (*Adonis, Attis, Osiris: Studies in the History of Oriental Religion*, 3d rev. ed., vol. 6: *The Golden Bough* [New York: Macmillan, 1935]; 1st ed., 1906), so much so that if a myth recounts the death of deity but no evidence for the return of the dead deity to life exists, a search for such an event is made. Samuel Noah Kramer ("'Inanna's Descent to the Nether World' Continued and Revised," *JCS* 5 [1951] 1–17) made an ending available from Sumerian sources for the Inanna and Dumuzi story; but in this account there is no evidence for the return of Dumuzi from the dead. Adam Falkenstein (review of *Ur Excavations Texts VI: Literary and Religious Texts*, by C. J. Gadd and Samuel Noah Kramer, *BO* 22 [1965] 281) suggested that a broken text at the end of a tablet, preceded by a section of missing lines, provided the evidence required for showing that Dumuzi did in fact return for half a year. This evidence consists of the line: *za-e mu-bar-àm niĝ-zu mu-bar-[à]m* 'Your half year; your sister half year'. Kramer ("Dumuzi's Annual Resurrection: An Important Correction to 'Inanna's Descent,'" *BASOR* 183 [1966] 31) accepted this correction and revised his view of the myth to include the return of Dumuzi. He went on to posit this Dumuzi myth as the basis for all similar cultic myths, including Adonis and the Christian Christ story (*The Sacred Marriage Rite: Aspects of Faith, Myth, and Ritual in Ancient Sumer* [Bloomington: Indiana University Press, 1969] 133 and 160 n. 48), though he acknowledges that the resurrection of Dumuzi rests on speculation (pp. 154–55 n. 4). On the other hand, it has long been known that Osiris in the Egyptian material was believed to have taken up the rule of the underworld rather than return to the realm of the living (Morenz, *Egyptian Religion*, 189–93). On the problems with the Greek rendition of Adonis and its relationship to the ancient Near Eastern myths, see Burkert, *Structure*, 101.

nonexistent.[109] What relationship the Greek cult may have had to an otherwise unknown Semitic cult is not very clear, and it is possible that the Greek cult arose in Greece based on ideas of what such a foreign cult ought to have looked like.

The goddess of the Greek story is Aphrodite, goddess of love. There is no substantial reason to assume that a goddess of love had to be imported to Greece from the Semitic world, as though the Greeks had no sense of love or sex before easterners informed them of these matters.[110] The goddess is nowhere referred to by a Semitic name in the sources, and the god appears only with a title, not a Semitic divine name. For these reasons, one could speculate that the story was indeed concocted by the Greeks, even though they may have used aspects of Syro-Palestinian religious traditions to color the tale. Of course, it is still possible that the Adonis mythology derived from a major cult in the Phoenician religious world, evidence for which simply has not yet been uncovered. However, until some further evidence comes to light, the Adonis myth and its attendant cult should be considered a Greek cult with certain but ambiguous Syro-Palestinian roots rather than an example of religion as practiced in Syria–Palestine.

Excavations at Ebla

Since the discovery of extensive archival tablets at Tell Mardikh in 1974, extravagant claims have been made about the significant religious content of the literature. At first, attention was focused on possible biblical references, hopes for which have proved more sensational than realistic.[111] The material found at Ebla is, of course, earlier than the time limit set for this study, but a certain amount of data derived from the site is relevant to Syro-Palestinian theology. To begin with, Ebla was a third-millennium Syrian city-state, so its religion was Syro-Palestinian, even though most of the deities referred

109. Burkert, *Greek Religion* (177), and Ribichini (*Adonis*, 199), who sees the cult's origin in Ebla; but see Peckham ("Phoenicia," 96 n. 70), who assumes that *ʾdn* is a name and not a title.

110. Burkert (*Greek Religion*, 152–53) argues unconvincingly that the Greek goddess Aphrodite must derive from the eastern civilizations, where goddesses of sex and love were common.

111. For an overview of this stage, see Chaim Bermant and Michael Weitzman, *Ebla: A Revelation in Archaeology* (New York: Times Books, 1979) 178–99. W. G. Lambert ("Notes on a Work of the Most Ancient Semitic Literature," *JCS* 41 [1989] 1) observes that the majority of early claims for the Ebla texts were simply false.

to in the texts are clearly southern Mesopotamian in origin. Moreover, the gates and quarters of the city, which would reflect the religious beliefs of the governing populace when the areas were named, were designated in honor of four deities known from other sources in Syria–Palestine: Dagan, Baal, Reshep, and the "sun-god" (^{d}UTU, which may have been from Sumer as easily as from West-Semitic Shapshu or Shemesh).[112]

Perhaps as many as 500 deities are mentioned in the tablets from Ebla, but no information is given about the structure of the pantheon, or more to the point, about the way the deities dealt with each other.[113] So far, scholars have been unable to say much more about the West-Semitic divinities appearing at Ebla than that their names exist.[114] There are ritual texts that provide both offering instructions with the names of gods and feast days for particular deities. These lists show an official pantheon composed of Mesopotamian, West-Semitic, and Hurrian elements.[115] What is helpful for the purposes of this book is the fact that many of the deities of the pantheon appearing in Syria–Palestine in the second millennium B.C.E. can be shown to have a history in the area reaching back into the third millennium.

The actual texts from Ebla are being published at a fairly steady pace in the ARET series. Unfortunately, any literary compositions from the civilization of Ebla itself have so far eluded the compilers of the tablets. There is one extended mythological piece that does deal with the activities of the pantheon, but it is the pantheon of southern Mesopotamia, praising Shamash, and the piece itself is clearly Old Akkadian mythology, probably composed in Sippar and copied for use at Ebla.[116] It is possible, but not certain, that more literary texts deriving from Syro-Palestinian scribes may yet appear. Such findings would help to define the relationships among the deities, but at

112. Giovanni Pettinato, *The Archives of Ebla: An Empire Inscribed in Clay* (Garden City, N.Y.: Doubleday, 1981) 44; the patron deity of the city appears to have been Dagan (p. 246).

113. Ibid., 245.

114. Mitchell Dahood, "Ebla, Ugarit and Phoenician Religion," in *La religione fenicia: Matrici orientali e sviluppi occidentali atta del colloquio in Roma, 6 marzo 1979* (SS 53; Rome: Consiglio nazionale delle ricerche, 1981) 55–56; Giovanni Pettinato, *Ebla: Nuovi orizzonti della storia* (2d ed., Milan: Rusconi, 1986) 331; Cyrus H. Gordon, "Ebla, Ugarit and the Old Testament," *Orient* 25 (1989) 136. However, not all the deities alleged to be present at Ebla actually have been attested there in texts published thus far.

115. Pettinato, *Archives*, 252–58; and Pettinato, *Ebla*, 331.

116. The piece is published in Dietz Otto Edzard, *Hymnen, Beschwörungen und Verwandtes aus dem Archiv L.2769* (ARET 5; Rome: Missione archeologica italiana in Siria, 1984) #6. An English text appears in Lambert, "Notes," 33; on the origins of the piece, see pp. 3 and 25.

this time it is a hope, not a reality. The publications of Ebla material should be consulted as they continue to appear, but at present Ebla is far from being a helpful source of information.

Polemic

Finally, a short note should be made about another type of literature that mentions the deities of Syria–Palestine, the religious polemic. There are two primary types of polemical material, from three religious traditions. At times, the author of such material has attempted merely to describe the worship practices of and deities worshiped by members of another faith as a comparison to the religion of the author. But more often, the material is provided as examples of false, if not malevolent, behavior. Jewish writers included a few references to the worship of Asherah in the Talmud, stating that such worship should be condemned.[117] Christian authors in the first half of the first millennium C.E. wrote about the fallacy of pagan peoples' worship and the falsity of their gods. In the eastern sections of the Christian world, these tracts could also refer to the false worship of Syro-Palestinian deities.[118] A favorite argument of the early Christian writers was that the gods had originally been humans, the argument set forth by the Greek scholar Euhemerus.[119] Numerous observations made by Christians concerning the devotees of Syro-Palestinian deities found their way into the works of Muslim scholars as well, especially the encyclopedic work on books by al-Nadim in the tenth century.[120] Under Islamic rule, the faith appears to have died out as a public institution in Syria–Palestine, and therefore contemporary accounts of the religion ceased in that period.

117. See *ʿAboda Zara* for references to "foreign" cults; Asherah is dealt with in sections 48–50.

118. For a survey of such texts, see Teixidor, *Pagan God*, 152–56.

119. Ibid., 152. On Euhemerus, see Frederick C. Grant, *Hellenistic Religions: The Age of Syncretism* (New York: Liberal Arts, 1953) 74.

120. Bayard Dodge (ed. and trans.), *The Fihrist of al-Nadim: A Tenth-Century Survey of Muslim Culture* (Records of Civilization: Sources and Studies 83; New York: Columbia University Press, 1970) 2.745–73; see his extensive bibliography for works by other Muslim authors on the Sabians of Harran; though al-Nadim records a great deal about the "Sabians of Harran," found in both Muslim and Christian authors, there is frustratingly little actually concerned with the pantheon. An attempt to correlate al-Nadim's material with what is known of earler Syro-Palestinian deities has recently been published by Basile Aggoula, "Divinités phéniciennes dans un passage du *Fihrist* d'Ibn al-Nadim," *Journal Asiatique* 278 (1990) 5–10.

Chapter 3

Authoritative Deities

Hierarchy is seldom seen as open-ended at the upper level. Whether the topic is theology, bureaucracy, or family, at some point in any authority structure there is a point of last appeal. It is this position over and above all other levels in the organization that is here referred to as *authoritative deities*. Neither in the modern nor in the ancient world need the theoretical or practical authority for a given bureaucracy rest in one person, though usually it is assumed that there is a single final court of appeal. This is the ideal, but few organizations function as perfectly in reality as they do in theory. In the religion of Syria–Palestine, highest authority was thought to extend beyond transitory mortal existence. Necessarily, this authority needed to be even higher than the fractious divine pantheon. Because it was necessary at times to consult the authoritative deities in order to maintain cosmic order, highest authority could not be perceived to exist among conflicting and chaotic human rulers, and it certainly could not be sought among the chaotic and conflicting deities. Highest authority had to be established on a higher level of the universe than that occupied by either of these two groups. Ultimate power over the cosmos was seen in theological terms and was described in mythological narrative using monarchical hierarchy as a model for the description of the office.

THE OFFICE

The position of highest authority in any hierarchy entails a certain number of responsibilities. Basic among the duties of one holding the highest position are the establishment of a working order within the organization, the maintenance of functional positions for those within the organization, knowledge about what transpires and ought to transpire within the organization, and dealing with problems that overwhelm those occupying lower levels in the hierarchy.[1] These duties break down into two types, one active and one inactive. The active duties of the highest authority figure consist of two spheres. First, the person holding the position must organize people and structures so that the organization as a whole will function properly. This aspect of highest authority is the initial step, that is, setting up the structure of the organization and giving it direction at the beginning of the enterprise. It is an activity that is done once and then, ideally, need not be done again. Second, the person holding the office of highest authority fulfills the function of the Chief Executive. That is, the maintenance of the organization is controlled by this office. When positions in the organization need to be filled, the Chief Executive sees that they are filled; when decisions affecting the entire organization need to be made, the Chief Executive makes them; when disputes within the higher levels of the hierarchy break out, the Chief Executive arbitrates them. Thus, after the structure of the organization is founded and the personnel to maintain it have been appointed, the activity of the holder of the office of highest authority is restrained and occasional.

The inactive duties are also twofold. One duty is related to the active duties insofar as the Chief Executive who has properly fulfilled the task of setting up the organization succeeds in properly carrying out the office of highest authority by not doing the work of the organization, since doing the work of the organization is the task of those on lower levels of authority. "Executive work is not that *of* the organization, but the specialized work of maintaining the organization in operation."[2] Proper work for the highest authority, then, appears in the guise of inactivity. The other obligation is knowledge. This is an activity of sorts, but it does not manifest itself in active behavior. Knowledge includes both the capacity to understand how the organization functions and the wisdom to handle the personalities serving under the highest authority.

The characteristics of a Chief Executive must conform to the needs of the office. Barnard has reduced the necessary characteristics

1. On the position of executives in hierarchical organizations, see Chester I. Barnard, *The Functions of the Executive* (Cambridge: Harvard University Press, 1951). Other works that deal with executive management as a functioning and flawed office within corporations or political structures, useful for understanding how the highest level of hierarchy operates, include: Peter M. Blau, *The Dynamics of Bureaucracy: A Study of Interpersonal Relations in Two Government Agencies* (Chicago: University of Chicago Press, 1955); Edward Franz Leopold Brech, *Organisation: The Framework of Management* (London: Longmans, Green, 1957); and Rosabeth Moss Kanter, *Men and Women of the Corporation* (New York: Basic Book, 1977).

2. Barnard, *Functions*, 215; Barnard's emphasis.

required of the executive to two.

> One is local, individual, particular, ephemeral. It is the aspect of indi-
> vidual superiority—in physique, in skill, in technology, in percep-
> tion, in knowledge, in memory, in imagination. This is the immediate
> aspect, highly variable through time and in place; subject to specific
> development by conditioning, training, education; significant chiefly
> in conjunction with specific conditions; relative; rather easily deter-
> minable; comparatively objective; essential to *positive* action; com-
> manding admiration, emulation.[3]

That is, the executive must possess a wisdom acknowledged and
sought after by those within the organization. This knowledge must
be used to encourage the proper functioning of the whole organization. Whoever holds the position of highest authority in any given
organization also is expected to have all the knowledge required to
form and maintain the proper function of the organization.

> The second aspect of leadership—the more general; the more con-
> stant; the least subject to specific development; the more absolute; the
> subjective; that which reflects the attitudes and ideals of individual
> superiority in determination, persistence, endurance, courage; that
> which determines *quality* of action; which often is most inferred from
> what is *not* done, from abstention; which commands respect, rever-
> ence. It is the aspect of leadership we commonly imply in the word
> "responsibility," the quality which gives dependability and determi-
> nation to human conduct, and foresight and ideality to purpose.[4]

That is, the executive provides character for the entire organization.
This is leadership that commands respect so that the rest of the organization will act. The actions themselves are not taken by the executive but by others in the organization.

If the executive functions perfectly as highest authority, decisions
are made impartially, almost mechanically. However, this office, like
any office, must be held by an individual. Individuals bring to an
office their own characteristics, which will always diverge from the
perfect ideal.[5] Even so, certain characteristic variations from the
ideal tend to be found in those who attain positions of Chief Executive. These aberrant characteristics usually express themselves in
various forms of preferential treatment toward certain personnel on

3. Ibid., 260; Barnard's emphasis.

4. Ibid.; Barnard's emphases.

5. Ibid., 12, 15, 18–19, 40, 77, 280. Barnard, whose book first appeared in 1938, is
credited, in the study of bureaucratic structures, with first stressing the individual
who holds an office over the office itself. Blau (*Dynamics*, 141) clearly points out the
fact that it is the individuals who function together for good or ill, not the offices
themselves.

the lower levels of the organization.[6] They may also display themselves in arbitrary actions or decisions that are not in the best interests of the organization as a whole.[7] Thus, a depiction of highest
authority as a functioning individual holding a position of highest
authority must distinguish between the realistic, occasional "malfunctioning" of the individual and the ideal office.[8]

When the deities of Syria–Palestine are considered in an organizational context, a few differences between the theology of ancient
mythological narrative and the hierarchy of modern corporate or
governmental organizations must be acknowledged. Most important
among these differences is the scale of the organization. However
large and powerful modern hierarchies become, they are limited in
size and effective power; there is always another world beyond the
bureaucracy of the organization itself. This is not true when a bu-
reauracy fills the universe; beyond the realm ruled by the gods there
was either chaos or nothing. Second, the bureaucracy characteristic of
the Syro-Palestinian pantheon was related to the notion of monarchy,
just as government on earth at that time was a monarchy. While monarchies function in many respects like corporate bureaucracies, there
are significant differences. Foremost among these is the fact that the
higher offices of a monarchical bureaucracy are generally filled by
members of the royal family. In a modern bureaucracy "nepotism" is
considered to be a malfunction of executive authority, but in the
royal courts of Syria–Palestine it was considered a requirement of
any good ruler. The same good behavior would have been expected
of a competent ruler in heaven. Therefore, the notion of *family* is important in understanding hierarchy in Syro-Palestinian religious
thought.[9] The interactions among the gods relied not only on the position the deities held within the universe but also on the positions
they held within the divine family. Finally, in this study the subject is
the divine realm. While it is certainly true that ancient Near Eastern

6. Brech, *Organisation*, 63–69; Kanter, *Men and Women*, 38–39.

7. Ibid., 39. These inappropriate actions may be called "malfunctions" and are
often perceived as a natural characteristic of bureaucratic and hierarchical organizations: Andreski, *Max Weber*, 100; Gerald M. Britan and Ronald Cohen, "Toward an
Anthropology of Formal Organizations," in *Hierarchy and Society: Anthropological Perspectives on Bureaucracy* (ed. Britan and Cohen; Philadelphia: Institute for the Study of
Human Issues, 1980) 16–17.

8. Blau, *Dynamics*, 49–50.

9. A. van Selms (*Marriage and Family Life in Ugaritic Literature* [POS 1; London:
Luzac, 1954] 10) assumes that the family life portrayed in the divine myths from
Ugarit is exactly the same as that of family life among the citizens of the city Ugarit.
This "one-for-one" correlation is unlikely to have been absolutely true. See Oden,
"Theoretical Assumptions," 51–52, 55; and Marjo C. A. Korpel, *A Rift in the Clouds:
Ugaritic and Hebrew Descriptions of the Divine* (UBL 8; Munster: Ugarit, 1990) 217.

writers used human behavior as a basis for describing and explaining the lives and actions of divine populations, there were certain differences between human beings and the deities that were understood to be major, not the least of which was the possibility of immortality.[10] These distinctions must also be taken into consideration.

THE GODS

The highest authority in Syro-Palestinian mythology was held by two deities, the couple El and Asherah. Not only were they the ultimate divine pair, but they filled the offices of King and Queen Mother on the highest cosmic level. Their status as the most important deities in Syria–Palestine is not always, or even generally, acknowledged.[11] That El, at least at some point in the history of Syro-Palestinian religious traditions, was the acknowledged leader of the pantheon has been widely recognized, but the status of Asherah has usually been presented as minor and undistinguished. In the narratives from Ugarit, however, the two deities together functioned as the highest authority in the Syro-Palestinian hierarchy of the universe.

El

As early as 1951, Otto Eissfeldt argued that El was the single deity of highest authority and power in the Ugaritic pantheon, but he went on to insist that all the other deities who appeared in the city-state were merely hypostases of the one true god, El.[12] His reconstruction

10. For one study on the relationship between human and divine characteristics in ancient Near Eastern literature, see Thorkild Jacobsen, *Toward the Image of Tammuz and Other Essays on Mesopotamian History and Culture* (HSS 21; Cambridge, Mass.: Harvard University Press, 1970) 16–38, which, while it may in some aspects be inaccurate, well displays the sense of the divine realm being something beyond the grasp of humans.

11. Two recent volumes present El as impotent and of little importance in the Ugaritic myths: Johannes C. de Moor, *The Rise of Yahwism: The Roots of Israelite Monotheism* (BETL 91; Louvain: Louvain University Press, 1990) 105–7; and Oswald Loretz, *Ugarit und die Bibel: Kanaanäische Götter und Religion im Alten Testament* (Darmstadt: Wissenschaftliche Buchgesellschaft, 1990) 68. Both authors base their views on the earlier work of Marvin Pope, who has recently questioned his own notion that El was clearly not the ruler of the divine realm ("The Status of El at Ugarit," *UF* 19 [1987] 224). Asherah has tended to be relegated to a marginal status as some common form of *Fruchtbarkeitsgöttin* (Loretz, *Ugarit und Bibel*, 84); this is true even in the otherwise excellent observations on divine status made by Mark Smith, "Divine Travel as a Token of Divine Rank," *UF* 16 (1984) 359, and Susan Ackerman, *Under Every Green Tree: Popular Religion in Sixth-Century Judah* (HSM 46; Atlanta: Scholars Press, 1992) 191.

12. Otto Eissfeldt, *El im ugaritischen Pantheon* (Berichte über die Verhandlungen der sächsischen Akademie der Wissenschaften zu Leipzig 98/4; Berlin: Akademie, 1951).

of the Ugaritic myths reflects earlier attempts to find a basic "monotheism" in ancient Near Eastern religions.[13] The effect of accepting such a theory is to remove the pantheon altogether, leaving El not the highest god, but the only god. However, there is no evidence from the Ugaritic texts or any other Syro-Palestinian source to substantiate a thesis that somehow all the gods were taken to be aspects of one god.

Rather than considering all deities to be manifestations of a single god, El, most scholars have taken the narrative texts at face value and have found the god El to be (or at least to have been at one time) the leader of a pantheon of independent deities. One group of scholars cites the narratives from Ugarit, the Hittite Elkunirsha fragment, and the biblical texts in forming a theory that the god El was at one time the supreme deity in Syria–Palestine, but that the younger, more virile Baal came into the region from elsewhere, replacing the older, sedentary El.[14] Another group of scholars has taken the position that the pantheon remained relatively constant, with El always the highest authority.[15]

The position that El had once been, but no longer was, the supreme deity in the pantheons of Syria–Palestine was first elaborated by Kapelrud and then expanded in the works of Pope and Oldenburg.[16] This theory rested on three main observations. The first was that Baal must have been a foreign deity who entered Syria–Palestine in the early second millennium B.C.E. along with the Amorite migrations.[17] It is now clear, however, that there was no discernible mass migration of Amorites in the second millennium

13. In the nineteenth century, scholars studying ancient Near Eastern civilizations were able to find "monotheism" in any major culture. For such an interpretation of Egyptian religion, see Jacques Joseph Champollion-Figeac, *Égypte ancienne* (UHDP; Paris: Didot, 1839) 245. The classic work presenting this view of Mesopotamian culture in English is Friedrich Delitzsch, *Babel and Bible: Two Lectures* (New York: Putnam's Sons/London: Williams & Norgate, 1903) 69, 72.

14. Ditlef Nielsen, *Ras Šamra Mythologie und biblische Theologie* (Abhandlungen für die Kunde des Morgenlands 21/4; Leipzig: Deutsche morgenländische Gesellschaft, 1936) 108; most recently, de Moor, *Rise of Yahwism*, 105–6.

15. Mitchell J. Dahood, "Ancient Semitic Deities in Syria and Palestine," in *Le antiche divinità semitiche* (ed. Sabatino Moscati; SS 1; Rome: Centro di studi semitici, 1958) 70.

16. Arvid S. Kapelrud, *Baal in the Ras Shamra Texts* (Copenhagen: Gad, 1952); see also *The Ras Shamra Discoveries and the Old Testament* (Norman, Okla.: University of Oklahoma Press, 1963); Marvin Pope, *El in the Ugaritic Texts*; and Ulf Oldenburg, *The Conflict between El and Baʿal in Canaanite Religion* (Supplementa ad Numen, altera series 3; Leiden: Brill, 1969).

17. This is the thesis worked out by Oldenburg, ibid.; but see E. Theodore Mullen, *The Divine Council in Canaanite and Early Hebrew Literature* (HSM 24; Chico, Cal.: Scholars Press, 1980) 62–68.

B.C.E.[18] Moreover, neither El nor Baal can be demonstrated to have been the earlier of the two deities in Syria–Palestine.[19] The second observation was that El was impotent, while Baal was virile.[20] Two texts (the Elkunirsha fragment and the Ugaritic narrative of the Birth of the Gracious Gods) were presented as evidence that El was no longer capable of engaging in sexual activity and therefore was powerless.[21] However, neither text actually portrays El as impotent, and certainly neither displays El as powerless, so the argument is specious at best.[22] Moreover, it has become more evident as the texts are studied that the two gods represented two different aspects of the divine realm.[23] Third, it has been argued that El ceased to be of any importance to the pantheons known from Syria–Palestine after the second millennium B.C.E., with the exception of Israel and Judah, where a different trajectory in development took place.[24] Yet, it was not only the biblical texts that recognized the importance of El; inscriptions and the tales contained in Philo of Byblos's history singled out El as an important deity even into the first millennium C.E.[25] In short, nothing suggests that El was removed from a position of authority by Baal.

The more convincing position is that El remained the head of the pantheon throughout the period of Syro-Palestinian religious culture. This position was first articulated by Albright, who, though he agreed with Pope that El was in decline, argued that El was an otiose deity (far removed and inactive) but in some sense still the head of the pantheon.[26] Cross has been the foremost proponent of the theory

18. C. H. J. de Geus, *The Tribes of Israel: An Investigation into Some of the Presuppositions of Martin Noth's Amphictyony Hypothesis* (SSN 18; Amsterdam: van Gorcum, 1976) 211; Thomas L. Thompson, *The Historicity of the Patriarchal Narratives: The Quest for the Historical Abraham* (BZAW 133; Berlin: de Gruyter, 1974) 87.

19. De Moor in J. C. de Moor and M. J. Mulder, "Baᶜal," in *Theological Dictionary of the Old Testament* (Grand Rapids, Mich.: Eerdmans, 1975) 2.183. It is possible, though the evidence is at best questionable, that both deities were worshiped in the third millennium B.C.E. at Ebla: Giovanni Pettinato, *The Archives of Ebla: An Empire Inscribed in Clay* (Garden City, N.Y.: Doubleday, 1981) 44, 248.

20. See especially Marvin H. Pope, "Ups and Downs in El's Amours," *UF* 11 (1979) 706; and Loretz, *Ugarit und Bibel*, 68.

21. Oldenburg, *Conflict between El and Baᶜal*, 109–14.

22. Cross, *Canaanite Myth*, 22–24; Paolo Xella, *Il mito di ŠḤR e ŠLM: Saggio sulla mitologia ugaritica* (SS 44; Rome: Istituto di Studi del Vicino Oriente, 1973) 122–37.

23. Caquot and Sznycer, *Ugaritic Religion*, 12.

24. Ulf Oldenburg, "Above the Stars of El: El in Ancient South Arabic Religion," *ZAW* 82 (1970) 187–208.

25. See the Hadad inscription of Zenjirli, *KAI* 214:2–3 (= *TSSI* 2.64), in addition to the material collected by Philo of Byblos.

26. Albright, *Yahweh and the Gods*, 119–21; and idem, *From the Stone Age to Christianity: Monotheism and the Historical Process* (2d ed.; Garden City, N.Y.: Doubleday, 1957)

that El was consistently the highest authority in the Syro-Palestinian pantheon and not a marginal character.[27] El was the king (*mlk*) of the gods and Baal served a function subservient to him. They formed the minimal base of a divine hierarchy. The structure of this pantheon as hierarchy has been noted, if not worked out, by L'Heureux.[28] A series of set levels within the pantheon has been proposed by Mark Smith, who finds a four-stage hierarchy in the Ugaritic myths.[29] These four levels are based on the behavior of the various deities toward one another in the narratives; they conform to the levels examined in this study. The one major difference between Smith's divisions and mine is the status of Asherah. Smith places her on his second level. I argue that she was on the same level as El, the top level.

Asherah

The status of the goddess Asherah has been and still is less clearly defined than El's. Prior to the discovery of the tablets at Ras Shamra, in fact, there was a fairly widely-held position that *asherah* referred only to some kind of religious object and not to a goddess at all.[30] The appearance of this object in the Bible was taken as proof of tree worship in Judah and Israel.[31] Other scholars held out for the interpretation of the term as a deity of the "mother-goddess" type, a generalized abstraction of the nineteenth century, paired with the generic "sky-god."[32] With the discovery of the narratives from Ugarit, the reality of a specific goddess had to be acknowledged.

---

231. In this theory, the stories concerning El found in Philo of Byblos's history derived from a much earlier age than the myths of Ugarit: Patrick D. Miller, "El the Warrior," *HTR* 60 (1967) 414.

27. Cross, *Canaanite Myth*, 13–75.

28. Conrad E. L'Heureux, *Rank among the Canaanite Gods: El, Baᶜal, and the Rephaʾim* (HSM 21; Missoula, Mont.: Scholars Press, 1979) 106–7; see also Paolo Xella, *Gli antenati di Dio: Divinità e mita della tradizione di Canaan* (Verona: Essedue, 1981) 39–40; and Gibson, "Theology," 202, 207–9.

29. M. S. Smith, "Divine Travel," 359.

30. W. R. Smith, *The Religion of the Semites: The Fundamental Institutions* (New York: Schocken, 1972) 187–88; Elford Higgens, *Hebrew Idolatry and Superstition: Its Place in Folklore* (Port Washington, N.Y.: Kennikat, 1971; first published in 1893) 14; W. Carleton Wood, *The Religion of Canaan from the Earliest Times to the Hebrew Conquest* (Ontario: Newmarket, 1916) 23; and Charles F. Pfeiffer, *Ras Shamra and the Bible* (Baker Studies in Biblical Archaeology 1; Grand Rapids, Mich.: Baker, 1962) 30.

31. Wood, *Religion of Canaan*, 23; W. R. Smith, *Religion of the Semites*, 23.

32. Raphael Patai, *The Hebrew Goddess* (New York: Avon, 1978) 13, 142; William G. Dever, *Recent Archaeological Discoveries and Biblical Research* (Seattle: University of Washington, 1990) 145; and discussion in Joan B. Townsend, "The Goddess: Fact, Fallacy and Revitalization Movement," in *Goddesses in Religious and Modern Debate* (ed.

Several general designations for the goddess Asherah were, and continue to be, used. "Fertility-goddess" is still a favorite designation for the deity.[33] The use of general titles for this divine character suggests only that scholars do not know what to make of the individual goddess Asherah as she appears in the narratives. Curiously, this way of dealing with the goddesses of Syria–Palestine, treating them only in generic terms, has passed beyond the use of clichés for defining all female deities into the proposition that not only can modern scholars not tell the difference among the various goddesses, but even ancient Syro-Palestinians could not tell their own goddesses apart.[34] This is absurd. There may not be sufficient surviving material to describe Asherah thoroughly, but the information that remains appears to portray a distinct deity whose major sphere of activity was more than (if not entirely other than) fertility.

William Reed was the first to consider Asherah seriously as a distinct deity. In 1949 his monograph on the goddess demonstrated that there was a deity with the name Asherah and that the paraphernalia bearing her name had to have been related to her worship.[35] Reed observed that she was a deity common throughout Syria–Palestine, who was worshiped in Israel (Judah) in the same way that she was revered in the surrounding culture. He surmised that Asherah was

---

Larry W. Hurtado; University of Manitoba Studies in Religion 1; Atlanta: Scholars Press, 1990) 182.

33. Johannes Hehn (*Die biblische und die babylonische Gottesidee* [Leipzig: Hinrichs, 1913] 106) presented Asherah as a Canaanite Ishtar and a vegetation goddess, with phallic associations; U. Cassuto, *The Goddess Anath: Canaanite Epics of the Patriarchal Age* (Jerusalem: Magnes) 58. Helmer Ringgren (*Israelite Religion* [Philadelphia: Fortress, 1966] 157) calls her "the mother-goddess of fertility"; Gray, *Legacy*, 1976. William G. Dever ("Asherah, Consort of Yahweh? New Evidence from Kuntillet ʿAjrûd," *BASOR* 255 [1984] 22) uses the term "great goddess"; see now Dever, *Recent Archaeological Discoveries*, 157; Loretz, *Ugarit und Bibel*, 84. JoAnn Hackett ("Can a Sexist Model Liberate Us? Ancient Near Eastern 'Fertility' Goddesses," *JFSR* 5 [1989] 71–73) surveys a selection of twentieth-century scholars who have adopted the fertility and mothering definitions of all ancient goddesses, but points out (p. 75) that this derives from modern Western culture and that in fact there were a variety of distinctive goddess types. (This succinct statement of what ought to be obvious was published after the first draft of my manuscript, but clearly states what has been described here about the need for recognizing distinct goddesses' roles.) See now the cautious approach of Steve A. Wiggens, "The Myth of Asherah: Lion Lady and Serpent Goddess," *UF* 23 (1991) 392.

34. R. A. Oden, *Studies in Lucian's "De Syria Dea"* (HSM 15; Missoula, Mont.: Scholars Press, 1977) 72–98; Patai, *Hebrew Goddess*, 12–15; Oden, "The Persistence of Canaanite Religion," *BA* 39 (1976) 34–36; Dever, "Asherah, Consort of Yahweh?" 28–29; David Noel Freedman, "Yahweh of Samaria and His Asherah," *BA* 50 (1987) 246, picture caption.

35. William L. Reed, *The Asherah in the Old Testament* (Fort Worth: Texas Christian University Press, 1949).

the consort of Yahweh in Israel, as she was of El in Ugarit; however, he also noted that she appeared to be the consort of Baal as well, since the terms בעלים and אשרים often occur together in the biblical text. While it seems that El/Yahweh was Asherah's consort, evidence for Baal as Asherah's male counterpart has not yet appeared anywhere in Syria–Palestine.[36] Reed's study placed the goddess Asherah above the level of generic female deity by viewing her as an individual personality of great importance, a consort of the ruling god, with characteristics of her own.

Gösta Ahlström sought to prove that Asherah was related to a national *hieros gamos* rite performed in Jerusalem, and, as a result, he considered the goddess as the divine counterpart to the *gebîrāh* (Queen Mother) of the human ruling hierarchy.[37] While the proposed relationship between the goddess Asherah and a ritual of *hieros gamos* in Jerusalem is conjectural, the fact that Asherah should be seen as the divine Queen Mother has been firmly established.[38] Asherah's position in the cosmos as Queen Mother, corresponding to the human position of *gebîrāh*, made her the second most important and powerful deity after El.[39] Ahlström also insisted that the goddess was an integral part of the preexilic Judean cult.

Recent studies concerned with the goddess Asherah have concentrated on the status of the goddess in the Judean and Israelite cults.[40]

---

36. Saul Mitchell Olyan, "Problems in the History of the Cult and Priesthood in Ancient Israel" (Ph.D. diss., Harvard University, 1985) 84–105; and his *Asherah and the Cult of Yahweh in Israel* (SBLMS 34; Atlanta: Scholars Press, 1988) 61.

37. Ahlström, *Aspects of Syncretism in Israelite Religion* (Horae Soederblominae 5; Lund: C. W. K. Gleerup, 1963) 69–87.

38. Niels-Erik A. Andreasen, "The Role of the Queen Mother in Israelite Society," *CBQ* 45 (1983) 182.

39. Georg Molin, "Die Stellung der Gᵉbira im Staate Juda," *TZ* 10 (1954) 161. Holders of the position of Queen Mother in the ancient Near East attained their influence on their own initiative, by knowing how to manage the power spheres of the ancient hierarchy; Zafrira Ben-Barak, "The Queen Consort and the Struggle for Succession to the Throne," in *La Femme dans le proche-orient antique* (ed. Jean-Marie Durand; RAI 33; Paris: Éditions recherche sur les civilisations, 1987) 40; see now her "The Status and Right of the Gebîrâ," *JBL* 110 (1991) 33–34. In Mesopotamia, at least, it was not an office which *had* to be filled; W. G. Lambert, "Goddesses in the Pantheon: A Reflection of Women in Society?" in *La Femme dans le proche-orient antique*, 125–26; Susan Ackerman, "The Queen Mother and the Cult in Ancient Israel," *JBL* 112 (1993) 400–401.

40. Olyan, "Problems in History of Cult" and *Asherah and the Cult*; Richard J. Pettey, "Asherah: Goddess of Israel?" (Ph.D. diss., Marquette University, 1985); J. A. Emerton, "New Light on Israelite Religion: The Implications of the Inscriptions from Kuntillet ᶜAjrud," *ZAW* 94 (1982) 2–20; Zeᵓev Meshel, "Did Yahweh Have a Consort? The New Religious Inscriptions from the Sinai," *BAR* (March-April 1979) 24–35; Ziony Zevit, "The Khirbet el-Qôm Inscription Mentioning a Goddess," *BASOR* 255 (1984) 39–47; et al.; see the survey in John Day, "Asherah in the Hebrew Bible and Northwest Semitic

While it is generally accepted that the goddess was a revered member of the pantheon in both Judah and Israel, there are those who continue to argue that the אשרה mentioned in the Bible is only a cultic object.[41] The recognition that Asherah was a widely worshiped goddess, with a well-established cult throughout Syria–Palestine, has nonetheless been almost universally accepted. It is also less common to find scholars simply lumping Asherah together with Anat and Astarte, as though all goddesses were indistinguishable.

EL AND ASHERAH:
THE TITLES OF HIGHEST AUTHORITY

The titles that were attributed to El and Asherah are often given a great amount of importance for understanding what the deities represented. This is not an unreasonable thesis, but some caution must be used when dealing with divine epithets. It clearly meant something different for the Ugaritic tablet authors to call the gods *mlk* (translated 'king') than it meant in western Europe, for example, to call Henry the Eighth by the title "king." There were at least three levels of personnel designated at Ugarit by the title *mlk*: El, Baal, and the human ruler of the city-state.[42] This multiple attestation of a title, which in common English usage is generally restricted to a single individual within one governmental organization, clearly demonstrates that the word *mlk* had its own peculiarities of meaning at Ugarit, not shared by the English word *king*. If *king* was not a title peculiar to El, it is unlikely that it was intended to signify a supremely high position or to describe the unique character of the god

---

Literature," *JBL* 105 (1986) 385–408. Baruch Margalit, "The Meaning and Significance of Asherah," *VT* 40 (1990) 284–85, recently concluded that the name derived from a "forgotten" common noun for a female consort and that it surely referred to a goddess when used in cultic references, even in Israel. See also Manfried Dietrich and Oswald Loretz, *"Jahwe und seine Aschera": Anthropomorphes Kultbilt in Mesopotamien, Ugarit und Israel—Das biblische Bilderverbot* (UBL 9; Münster: Ugarit Verlag, 1992) 92–93, 120–22.

41. For a survey of this thesis, see Day, "Asherah in the Hebrew Bible," 397–404. See also Tigay, *You Shall Have No Other Gods: Israelite Religion in Light of Hebrew Inscriptions* (HSS 31; Atlanta: Scholars Press, 1986) 26–30; Robert North, "Yahweh's Asherah," in *To Touch the Text: Biblical and Related Studies in Honour of Joseph A. Fitzmyer* (ed. Maurya P. Hogan and Paul J. Kobelski; New York: Crossroad, 1989) 137; and M. S. Smith, *Early History*, 92–93; note now that inscriptions to the goddess Asherah (by herself) have been found at the site of Philistine Ekron, as reported by Trude Dothan and Seymour Gitin—noted in "Arti-Facts: News, Notes, and Reports from the Institutes," *BA* 53 (1990) 232.

42. Lowell K. Handy, "A Solution for Many *MLKM*," *UF* 20 (1988) 57–59; see *UT* and *WUS*, *s.v. mlk*.

El. There were two designations, however, that do appear to have belonged to El and Asherah alone and that were used to designate the pair as the pinnacle of the Ugaritic pantheon.

The "Owners"

In the texts at Ugarit, El and Asherah are referred to as the "owners." Asherah is clearly called *qnyt ilm*.[43] For a long time this title was treated as a form of 'creator', and Asherah was called the "creatrix of the gods," with the implication that the title was related to her as the "fertility-goddess" who had given birth to the deities.[44] The root *qny* is cognate to the Hebrew root קנה, as has generally been suggested. The meaning of the root, however, has been determined to be 'acquire/own' and not 'create'.[45] Therefore, Asherah's title must mean something like 'owner of the Gods'. The Ugaritic narratives also refer to El as "owner," but the phrase in which this word appears does not make clear what El is supposed to be owning: *il dyqny ddm* ('El who is owner of the grotto').[46] In the Ugaritic narratives it appears that "owner" was a designation for both of these deities, even if it is not clear what was meant by the title. It is not too speculative to suggest that the title has to do with control and authority.

If the title for El is uncertain in the texts from Ugarit, it is not so ambiguous in other Syro-Palestinian sources.[47] The name of the central deity in the Hittite fragment is ᵈel-ku-ni-ir-ša, which corresponds to the name El with the title 'owner of the earth'.[48] An inscription from Karetepe contains a similar name, *ᵓl qn ᵓrṣ*. Also related to this series of divine titles for El are two biblical attestations, אל עליון קנה שמים וארץ (El Elyon, 'owner of heaven and earth') and the name of Samuel's father, אלקנה (El, 'owner').[49] The multiple attestations of this title for El in several different sources of various times confirms the thesis that it was a significant and lasting characterization of the god.

Since El and Asherah were owners of the earth and heaven, they clearly had the greatest concern for the condition of the universe. All

---

43. *KTU* 1.4.I.22.

44. *UT*, s.v. *qny*; *WUS*, s.v. *qnṯ*; Gray, *Legacy*, 265.

45. Peter Katz, "The Meaning of the Root קנה," *JJS* 5 (1954) 126–31; and Bruce Vawter, "Yahweh: Lord of the Heavens and the Earth," *CBQ* 48 (1986) 466–67.

46. *KTU* 1.19.IV.57–58. The proper translation of *dd* remains unknown; for 'grotto', see Gregorio del Olmo Lete, "Notes on Ugaritic Semantics IV," *UF* 10 (1978) 43–44.

47. Vawter, "Yahweh," 465.

48. Heinrich Otten, "Ein kanaanaischer Mythus aus Boğazköy," *MIO* 1 (1953) 127.

49. *KAI* 26.A.3.18 (= *TSSI* 3.52); Gen 14:19; 1 Sam 1:1.

other divinities, let alone humans, were responsible to this pair for their activities in a universe that belonged to the couple. El and Asherah were the final arbitrators of any matter relating to their possession. This included the appointment of personnel, human or divine, to control the various portions of their cosmos.

Parents

As with the royal title *mlk*, the appellative "parent" was borne by other deities than El and Asherah.[50] However, both gods are referred to as the parents of the gods. Asherah is mentioned with the gods as a general group in the phrase "Asherah and her children" (*aṯrt w bnh*).[51] This suggests that she was seen as the mother of the pantheon, even though she did not necessarily bear all of the deities. In fact, it is clear that some of the deities derived from female divinities other than Asherah.[52] This is even true of the gods considered to have been sired by El, who mated with several female divinities.[53] There is no extant narrative clearly showing Asherah giving birth to any deity, yet she stood as the legal mother to them all. Moreover, it was as Queen Mother that Asherah determined which deity filled each role in the governing of the universe. It must be pointed out that any goddess apparently could have children or engage in sex with a god; this was an aspect of anthropomorphism in the mythology. This does not mean that just because a goddess had sex or bore children, she was assumed to be "in charge" of sexuality or fertility. Asherah, however, held the title of mother to all the gods, regardless of their parentage.

El is also presented as a father to the gods. It is possible that the generic phrase for gods, *bn ilm*, was intended to be read 'sons of El' rather than 'sons of the gods'.[54] In whatever manner the phrase is

---

50. The argument has been made by del Olmo Lete ("Estructura del panteón ugarítico," in *Salvación en la palabra: Targum-Derash-Berith: En memoria del professor Alejandro Diez Macho* [ed. Doming León; Madrid: Ediciones Cristiandad, 1986] 270–71, n. 10), who makes note of the exception of Baal's offspring. See also Baal as *bn dgn* (*KTU* 1.6.I.6, 52; Philo of Byblos I.10.19), though del Olmo Lete argues that El and Dagon are the same deity (p. 274), which is unlikely. However, Asherah and El, along with the rest of the gods, are "conceived as one big family, the sons (and daughters) of El and his spouse"; Carola Kloos, *Yhwh's Combat with the Sea: A Canaanite Tradition in the Religion of Ancient Israel* (Amsterdam: van Oorschot; Leiden: Brill, 1986) 17.

51. *KTU* 1.6.I.40.

52. *KTU* 1.23.

53. *KTU* 1.23.33–36, 49–51; Philo of Byblos I.10.22–24, 26, 44.

54. Del Olmo Lete, *Mitos y leyendas de Canaan segun la tradicion de Ugarit: Textos, versión y estudio* (FCB 1; Madrid: Ediciones Cristiandad, 1981) 528, *s.v.* "*bn* III."

taken, El is called the father of individual deities, including Baal, Mot, and Athena: *bᶜl abk il, bn ilm mt,* and Ἀθηνᾷ τῇ ἑαυτοῦ Θυγατρὶ.[55] The progeny of El are numerous in the narratives contained in Philo of Byblos's history and several goddesses give birth to them.[56] El also had children by more than one woman in the Ugaritic tablets, though it is not clear whether he mated with goddesses or mortals, or whether the two females were otherwise known, since no names are provided in the text.[57]

It is clear that El sired these deities in a manner consistent with normal human copulation.

> In kissing and conception,
> In embracing, pregnancy,
> They crouched and gave birth
> To Shahar and Shalim (*KTU* 1.23.51–52).

This was not magical creation of gods, though El could create divine beings without sexual procreation as well.[58]

> I will craft and I will establish;
> I will establish one who casts out pain,
> One who chases away lingering illness (*KTU* 1.16.V.25–28).

Even though El was not the father of all the gods by sexual procreation, he appears to have been considered the father of all the gods in terms of status among the deities, in the same way that Asherah was the mother of all the gods. Thus, the divine couple El and Asherah were the *de facto* parents of the entire Syro-Palestinian pantheon.

The fatherhood of El was not restricted to the divine realm. El was also called 'father of humanity' (*ab adm*).[59] In the Kirta Epic the protagonist, even though he is a mortal, is addressed as though he were the son of El.

---

55. *KTU* 1.14.II.24–25; 1.6.II.13; Philo of Byblos I.10.33.

56. Philo of Byblos I.10.18, 21–24, 26, 34, 44 (from Eusebius *Prep. Gospel*); though one may ask whether the numerous children in this Greek source were El's or simply ascribed to him by the author because El was the father of all the gods.

57. *KTU* 1.23; see del Olmo Lete, *Mitos y leyendas*, 434 n. 18; and Xella, *ŠḤR e ŠLM*, 119–22.

58. Pope (*El in the Ugaritic Texts*, 37) believes that this is a magical conception; but see Cross, *Canaanite Myth*, 22–24.

59. *KTU* 1.14.I.37. El's fatherhood of gods and humans has been noted by Korpel (*Rift*, 235–37).

Sacrifice to the Bull, your father El!
Cause Baal to descend by your sacrifice,
The Son of Dagon with your (game?) (*KTU* 1.14.II.25–26).[60]

Indeed, human rulers appear to have been treated as children of the god El in much the same way that the gods of the pantheon were considered his children. A monarch became a child of El when it was clear that he was the person who had been chosen to rule. In Ps 2:7 and 89:26 the new ruler is described as being accepted as a son by Yahweh; at the same time, heirs apparent in Syria–Palestine were presumed to be nurtured by suckling at goddesses' breasts.[61] One of these goddesses who is specifically mentioned as breast-feeding the prince is, as might be expected, Asherah.[62]

The cosmic ramifications of the parentage of El and Asherah appear to be clear. These two gods were the familial heads of both the divine and human populations. Familial authority, as well as universal power, lay with them. As owners of the earth and heaven, they controlled the physical entity that made up the cosmos; as parents to all who inhabited the cosmos, they were to be accorded all respect due to the heads of families. Moreover, as the rulers of the universe, they also were the heads of the monarchical hierarchy of *world* government. To be *the* parents in the cosmic scheme was to be the highest authority.

EL AND ASHERAH:
ACTING AS HIGHEST AUTHORITY

There were two major responsibilities for those in the position of highest authority: wisdom and order. The main purpose of El and Asherah was to have knowledge in order to operate the world properly, and then to have the capacity to create and maintain order within the cosmos.

Wisdom

The Ugaritic texts clearly designate El as the wise god above all other gods, as is stated by goddesses to the deity:

---

60. See also *KTU* 1.16.I.10.
61. *KTU* 1.15.II.25–28; Caquot and Sznycer, *Ugaritic Religion*, plate 29b.
62. *KTU* 1.15.II.26; W. A. Ward, "La Déesse nourriciére d'Ugarit," *Syria* 46 (1969) 225–39.

> Your word, El, is wise;
> Your wisdom throughout eternity;
> Your word is fortunate life (*KTU* 1.3.V.30–31).

This text has long been recognized as a statement about the qualitative wisdom of El over all other divine wisdom.[63] Yet, the passage does not explain what is meant by *ḥkm* (wisdom). The narratives in which this line is reproduced in the mouths of the goddesses Anat and Asherah both deal with the procurement of permission for construction of Baal's house. The context shows only that El's consent was mandatory for the construction of the temple; it does not clearly explain what was meant by the attribution of wisdom to the god. On the surface the passage appears to suggest that whatever El declared was, in fact, wisdom. This would mean that El was the source of secure knowledge. The reliability of this source of knowledge is stressed by reference to eternity (*ᶜlm*). Moreover, the good life seems to be tied to the declaration of El: if El decreed a "fortunate life," it was so. Therefore, it appears that the deities in effect came to seek a fortunate life for Baal. Underlying the passage is the belief that El was the source of wisdom itself, which would imply that he had the knowledge with which to run the universe. It was El, then, who must be consulted by other gods when major decisions were to be made.

While the data are sparse, incomplete, and largely inferential, some conclusions may be drawn concerning the wisdom of El. The description of this wisdom must be illustrated from the narratives. In attempting to define El's wisdom, however, it must be remembered that the conclusions drawn are closer to wild guesses than the results of systematic research, simply because, with the present amount of information available, this is the best that can be accomplished.

First, El's wisdom was in knowing how the cosmos ought to function and how to facilitate this end. This is suggested by El's appointment of gods and kings to their offices. Mot, Yam, Baal, and human rulers owed their positions to El.[64] In the inconclusive battle between Baal and Mot, it was El who decided the outcome of the fray. It was

---

63. Pope, *El in the Ugaritic Texts*, 42–43; Gray, *Legacy*, 159; Hartmut Gese, "Die Religionen altsyriens," in *Die Religionen altsyriens, altarabiens, und der Mandäer* (ed. Hartmut Gese, Maria Höfner, and Kurt Rudolph; Die Religionen der Menschheit 10/2; Stuttgart: Kohlhammer, 1970) 98. The biblical texts also portray Yahweh (often called אל) as the source of all wisdom, or the only being to truly possess wisdom; see Prov 2:6; 8:22–31; Job 28:23. For El and Yahweh as "the wise one" in Ugarit and Israel, see Glendon E. Bryce, *A Legacy of Wisdom: The Egyptian Contribution to the Wisdom of Israel* (Lewisburg: Bucknell University, 1979) 199.

64. See, for example, *KTU* 1.6.VI.26–29; 1.2.III.17–18; 1.4.IV.48; *KAI* 214.2–3 (= *TSSI* 2.64).

also El who noticed that Asherah's choice of a replacement for Baal would not be able to manage the position.[65] These instances suggest that it was El's wisdom that kept the cosmos functioning properly. This form of wisdom is related to the type of wisdom tradition that deals with proper procedure and bureaucratic knowhow.

Second, as an extension of his wisdom in maintaining order in the universe, El also ordered the state of governing offices and personnel in the universe. This was not creation of these institutions, but the power and knowledge to be able to assign territory to specific deities so that they might rule under the discretion of El himself.[66] In both the Ugaritic narratives and the Philo of Byblos tales, the deities that ruled under El remained subject to him and could be dismissed at his will. This type of wisdom is related to creating order from chaos, a capacity for order.

Third, in the texts there is an acknowledged recognition of El's wisdom in carrying on the business of the gods and human rulers. The assembly of the gods (from the little that is known about its make-up, organization, and function) is presented as having been under the formal rule of El.[67] The gathering of the gods under El's guidance even extended to the drinking-feast, where El appeared as host and father to the gods.[68] Human rulers sought the aid of El by

65. *KTU* 1.6.I.47–55.

66. Despite several attempts to find a "creation" story at Ugarit, no creation narrative appears in the extant Ugaritic texts. Those who have "found" a creation myth include: Loren R. Fisher, "Creation at Ugarit and in the Old Testament," *VT* 15 (1965) 316; Johannes C. de Moor, "El the Creator," in *The Bible World: Essays in Honor of Cyrus H. Gordon* (ed. Gary Rendsburg et al.; New York: KTAV, 1980) 171–87; Gese, "Religionen altsyriens," 114; Gray, *Legacy*, 33; and Richard J. Clifford, "Cosmogonies in the Ugaritic Texts and in the Bible," *Or* 53 (1984) 184, 201. However, see the studies by Arvid S. Kapelrud, "Baꜥal, Schöpfung und Chaos," *UF* 11 (1979) 408; and Baruch Margalit, "The Ugaritic Creation Myth: Fact or Fiction?" *UF* 13 (1981) 141. The creation story recorded in Philo of Byblos is acknowledged to be devoid of deities (Eusebius *Prep. Gospel* I.9.30–10.2), but all biblical creation stories agree that El (יהוה = אלהים = אל) was the creator (Gen 1:1, 2:5; Ps 33:6–7, 148:1–6; Job 38:4; Prov 3:19–20; etc.). In the Philo of Byblos history, however, it is clear that El assigns the individual realms of rule to the gods (I.10.31–32, 34, 38).

67. El appears to be understood as the head of the divine assembly at Ugarit (*KTU* 1.1–2, Baal and Yam; 1.16.V, Kirta), in Judah and Israel (1 Kgs 22:19–23, Micaiah; Psalm 82, death of the gods; Job 1:1–2:12, God and Satan), and in Transjordan (Deir ꜥAllā, Combination I.2, 5–6). On Ugarit and Israel, see Mullen, *Divine Council*, 111–284. The highly fragmented Deir ꜥAllā passage is currently being interpreted as "a typical Divine Council scene" (Hackett, *Balaam Text*, 75, based on P. Kyle McCarter, "Balaam Texts from Deir ꜥAllā: The First Combination," *BASOR* 239 [1980] 57), though this may turn out to be an example of a very tight circular argument.

68. *KTU* 1.114. The feast represents a gracious banquet presented by El. It is not a representation of the deity's ineptness, but, as at all good drinking bouts, the guests do get rather rambunctious. See Baruch Margalit, "The Ugaritic Feast of the Drunken

petitioning lesser deities.[69] This is acknowledged wisdom of a governing leadership.

Fourth, El's wisdom seems to have taken on a humorous vein in the Elkunirsha fragment. If the narrative has been properly interpreted, the god El was wily, knowing how to entrap and embarrass the goddess. The storm-god sought this knowledge from El. It was El who knew how to manipulate the other deities and who was clever enough to out-maneuver them. This is a type of wisdom akin to craftiness, possessed by the character referred to in folklore studies as the trickster.

Finally, El appears to be the one god who knew when and what should be done. This was not only true of major events (such as temple-building), but of minor events. He was credited with founding cults in the tales of Philo of Byblos.[70] It is possible that even mundane everyday activities were understood to have been determined by El, though the evidence for this is suspect.[71] This is a wisdom for knowing the proper time for events and proper ritual and places El at the peak of the religious world within the cult.

While El was seen as the supreme source of wisdom, Asherah was not without her own wisdom as well. Two major forms of wisdom are attributed to her. First, Asherah is credited with choosing the individual deities to be established by El in positions of power in the pantheon.[72] This presupposes that Asherah knew the gods and the various offices that needed to be filled. This also is a type of wisdom related to control, but it is made clear in the narrative of Athtar that El's wisdom in this regard was deeper than Asherah's.

Second, as consort to El, Asherah knew how to gain his consent for projects, After Anat failed to receive the required permission that she was seeking from El, even with threats, she had to turn to Asherah for aid in obtaining her desire. Asherah, apparently without effort, succeeded where Anat failed. Whether this entailed El's desire for Asherah or not (a point from a narrative section that is not entirely clear), the goddess clearly enjoyed favor with El that the

---

Gods: Another Look at RS 24.258 (KTU 1.114)," *MAARAV* 2 (1979–80) 107. The need for El to be carried out by two gods (his sons) in a state of inebriation marks the respect of the gods for their father. See Samuel E. Loewenstamm, "Eine lehrhafte ugaritische Trinkburleske," *UF* 1 (1969) 76.

69. Note how Baal approaches El on behalf of Kings Kirt and Danil (*KTU* 1.15.II.12–26; 1.17.I.16–23).

70. Philo of Byblos I.10.20, 29, 34.

71. *De Dea Syria* 36, though this is based on the dubious identification of Ἀπόλλων with El, as made by René Dussaud, "Peut-on identifier l'Apollon barbu de Hiérapolis de Syrie?" *RHR* 126 (1943) 147–48.

72. Xella, *Gli Antenati di Dio*, 56; *KTU* 1.6.I.47–55.

other deities did not have. Being able to bring topics before and manipulate the desired response from El was, in fact, a very useful form of wisdom, especially within the realm of a bureaucratic structure.

Order

By far the most fully illustrated aspect of rule in the surviving sources is that of maintaining order in the cosmos. Maintaining order involves two types of actions. One action is the creation of order in the first place and the other is the maintenance of order once it is established. In the available source material, maintenance is far more evident than creation, though certain narratives about establishing order are available. There is only one extant extrabiblical narrative of the creation of the universe from Syria–Palestine, and it does not credit creation of the universe to any particular deity.[73] However, while creation is not well represented (and establishment narratives are scarce), a great deal of information about the establishment of order may nonetheless be derived from the sources.

The division of the world into regions of authority is ascribed to El in the narratives related by Philo of Byblos. These regions were distributed to various deities to govern under the care of and with the consent of El.[74] Both material and immaterial regions were allocated by El. Even the realm of the dead was assigned to Mot by El.

> And after a little while, another of his sons by Rhea, named
> Mouth, having died, he hallowed (him) and the Phoenicians
> named this one Death and Pluto (Philo of Byblos I.10.34).

And, since El established Mot in his realm, El could remove him from his realm.

> How will Bull El, your father, not hear you,
> Will not pull up the support of your seat,
> Will not overthrow the throne of your reign,
> Will not shatter the sceptre of your rule? (*KTU* 1.6.VI.26–29).[75]

This represents the power El had to determine the gods who ruled each area, as well as the continuing authority he had over them. In

73. Philo of Byblos I.10.1–2.

74. As has been noted above (nn. 64 and 66), the religious and political divisions of the universe have their origins in the decisions of El.

75. Though the tablets from Ugarit do not describe the establishment of Mot as ruler of his kingdom, this passage clearly assumes that El is in charge of the personnel for this realm.

the Ugaritic texts, not only Mot, but also Baal and Yam are mentioned as owing their positions to the decisions of El. One way that
El controlled these gods was to remind them that their right to office
was dependent on his continuing favor.[76]

The process by which a deity was established in his or her position of rule in the universe is described in the narrative about the attempt to place Athtar on the throne of Baal after Baal died at the
hands of Mot. When the situation was made known to El, he turned
to Asherah and said:

> Hear, oh Lady Asherah of the Sea!
> Give one among your sons; I will make him king!
> And Lady Asherah of the Sea answered:
> "Yea, let us make king one knowing, he will have
>   understanding!"
> And kind El, who is good, answered:
> "One of feeble strength will not run,
> With Baal he will not release the spear
> With the Son of Dagon (?)!"
> But Lady Asherah of the Sea answers:
> "Yes, but we will make Athtar, the Tyrant, king!
> Athtar, the Tyrant, will be king!" (*KTU* 1.6.I.47–55).

It is clear that Asherah's decision to make the god Athtar a king in
Baal's stead was sufficient sanction for the god to become the legitimate heir to the position. El's objections did not change the right of
Athtar to attempt to claim the throne of Baal. Here Asherah was
clearly fulfilling the role of the *gebîrāh*. As Queen Mother she was
able to nominate the child who was to be next to rule.[77] The office of
Queen Mother was sufficiently powerful that Asherah's decision was
final. Athtar was heir to Baal's throne on the basis of her word alone.

While Asherah nominated, El established. El's original request
made this dual role quite clear; the duty of Asherah was to present a
candidate from among the gods, who were her children, and then El
would make a king (*amlk*) of the selected candidate. Here *to make a
king* (*mlk*) is the term used for the establishment of the deity in his
office; elsewhere it is stated that El had installed (*km*) Baal in his position.[78] It was the official act by El that established the deities in

---

76. *KTU* 1.2.III.17–18; 1.6.VI.26–29.

77. Molin, "Stellung der Gᵉbira," 163. On the influence of the Queen Mother on the
choice of heir to the throne in the ancient Near East, see Hayim Tadmor, "Autobiographical Apology in the Royal Assyrian Literature," in *History, Historiography and
Interpretation: Studies in Biblical and Cuneiform Literatures* (ed. H. Tadmor and M. Weinfeld; Jerusalem: Magnes, 1983) 38–39, 55, 57.

78. *KTU* 1.3.V.36; 1.4.IV.48.

their rightful realms. In the case of Athtar, it is not certain that El actually ever established him on Baal's throne; however, the passage cited above clearly demonstrates that, if Athtar were to hold that position in the pantheon, El would have had to "make him king." In this particular instance it appears to be Athtar himself who realized he could not fulfill the office vacated by Baal:

> Then Athtar, the Tyrant,
> Goes up to the peaks (?) of Saphon,
> He sits on the throne of Victorious Baal,
> His feet do not come to the footstool,
> His head does not come to its top.
> And Athtar, the Tyrant, responded:
> "I will not rule in the peaks of Saphon!"
> Athtar, the Tyrant, comes down,
> He comes down from the throne of Victorious Baal
>   (*KTU* 1.6.I.56–64).

Due to the large lacuna that follows this section, it is impossible to tell what happened next.

This narrative about the nomination of Athtar demonstrates that the process of placing a deity in his or her proper position in the cosmos was the joint work of Asherah and El. They both functioned in the placement of the gods in their respective offices. Asherah, as mother of the gods, Queen Mother in the universal organization, and owner of the gods, selected the candidates for the respective positions of authority. El, as father of the gods, King of the cosmic organization, and owner of heaven and earth, then officially placed the candidate in the office. It is fairly certain that this was the process by which Mot, Yam, Baal, and Athtar (and probably all the children of Asherah and El) were understood to have achieved their divine positions in the Ugaritic world view. It is also clear that the ruling deities in Philo of Byblos's history owed their realms to the decisions of El.

In addition, the establishment of religious cult was ascribed to El. In the texts from Ugarit it is shown that construction of temples had to be cleared through El. Repeated requests on behalf of Baal to El for consent to enlarge his house only make sense if it was well known that all changes in religious matters were the concern of El. The desire to expand Baal's house was not an attempt to found a new temple cult, though this often has been argued.[79] Baal's cult, as well

---

79. Julian Obermann, *Ugaritic Mythology: A Study of Its Leading Motifs* (New Haven, Conn.: Yale University Press, 1948) 5–6; Norman C. Habel, *Yahweh versus Baal: A Conflict of Religious Cultures* (New York: Bookman, 1964) 78; Cassuto, *Anath*, 68; Gray, *Legacy*, 168; and Cyrus H. Gordon, "Canaanite Mythology," in *Mythologies of the Ancient World* (ed. Samuel Noah Kramer; Garden City, N.Y.: Doubleday, 1961) 203.

as a temple, already existed and is presupposed in the narrative; this was a request to remodel and expand the temple to conform with the temples belonging to the rest of the gods.[80] This modification in the religious sphere could not be begun without the consent of El. It is no doubt true that the improvement in the house of Baal also signaled a change in the status of Baal among the deities, in some way, and consequently El's consent to the building project would also have been seen as an approval of the rise in status of Baal. What is clear in this story is that such a change in the religious world could not legitimately be made by any deity other than El. This, in turn, implies that El was seen as the ultimate authority on religious matters.[81]

There may be evidence that El was seen as the founder of religious cults generally. In Philo of Byblos's history there is a passage that suggests that El was considered the first builder of a temple complex in Phoenician tradition:

> After these things Kronos [= El], building a wall surrounding his own house, also founded the first city in Phoenicia, Byblos (Philos of Byblos I.10.19).

There is ample reason to assume that this story was originally a myth of the foundation of the first temple complex. The standard architectural plan for temple complexes in Syria–Palestine consisted of the house of the deity surrounded by a wall.[82] These formations frequently stood at the center of the city, which, along with the palace of the ruler, created the area of rule for the city-state.[83] Moreover, temples were generally seen to have been instigated by the gods, so this tale in Philo of Byblos could be taken as the story of El building a wall around his own temple to form such a complex.[84]

---

80. *KTU* 1.4.V.1–2: *in.bt.bᶜl.km.ilm.wḫẓr.kbn.aṯrt*. The construction of the house is to begin by hauling the building materials "into Baal's house" (1.4.V.36); see Ahlström, *Aspects*, 70; and Matitiahu Tsevat, "A Window for Baal's House: The Maturing of a God," in *Studies in Bible and the Ancient Near East Presented to Samuel E. Loewenstamm on his Seventieth Birthday* (ed. Yitschak Avishur and Joshua Blau; Jerusalem: Rubinstein, 1978) 152–54. The need for a "proper" house for the god necessitates the expansion (del Olmo Lete, *Mitos y leyendas*, 118).

81. If Ἀπόλλων in *De Dea Syria* should happen to be El, this material would also confirm the status of El as the highest determiner of proper times for cultic and even daily activities, but the identification is too tenuous to be assumed.

82. Magnus Ottosson, *Temples and Cult Places in Palestine* (Boreas 12; Uppsala: University of Uppsala Press, 1980) 10, 115.

83. Ahlström, *Royal Administration*, 4–5.

84. Arvid S. Kapelrud (*God and His Friends in the Old Testament* [Oslo: Universitetsforlaget, 1979] 184–90) describes the general ideology of temple building; see also the various foundation narratives in *De Dea Syria* 4, 6–8, 12–27.

These passages appear to confirm the theory that, in mythological ideology, El founded the major bases of West Semitic religion. The divisions of the world, both on the divine and the human levels, were credited to El. Both divine and human beings who served as rulers were established in their offices by the two deities. The religious sphere, with its cult and ritual centered in temple worship, was felt to have its ultimate authority in the god El. Therefore, both political and religious institutions owed their existence to Asherah and El.

The maintenance of these realms was also the province of El and Asherah. The case of Athtar, already mentioned, was an instance in which El and Asherah tried to find a proper replacement to fill a post vacated by the deceased Baal. They clearly were obligated to fill such positions on the divine plane. In a similar manner, it was El's responsibility to keep order among the deities, even to the extent of removing a god from his or her position in the pantheon if the behavior was chaotic enough that the cosmos might cease to function properly. This is most evident in the narrative of the battle between Baal and Mot.[85] In order to end this dispute, El sent word through Anat to Shapshu for Mot to cease the battle. Mot was the equal of Baal in the fight in which they were engaged and had bested Baal in a prior confrontation. Therefore, he had no reason to concede the contest. At the word of El, however, Mot stopped the battle, and Baal regained his throne, permitting the earth to thrive again through his storms. It was not the gods as a group who kept order in the cosmos. Even Anat did not directly confront the combatants but sought the intervention of El. Keeping proper order among the deities appears to have been a major task for El.[86] In this duty El was the organizer of the cosmos; it was his job to see that the universe functioned properly and that all of the deities properly filled their positions in the divine scheme. El did not do the work of running the universe but made certain that those who were supposed to do the work, both human and divine, functioned correctly.

85. *KTU* 1.6.III–VI.

86. This aspect of the deity is presented in the tablets from Ugarit, the narratives in the Bible, and the fragment of the Elkunirsha myth from the Hittite Empire, so keeping order is a constant throughout the sources. It should be noted that the Muslim sources for the tenth century A.D. Sabians report a theological question among them as to whether they ought to sacrifice to the greatest of the gods or to those whom the highest divine authority allocated spheres of administration in the universe under his control; Bayard Dodge, ed. and trans., *The Fihrist of al-Nadim: A Tenth-Century Survey of Muslim Culture* (RCSS 83; New York: Columbia University, 1970) 2.747–48 and n. 15. This clearly implies that the hierarchy of deities under one of supreme authority was understood as central to the faith and lasted until its demise.

When a situation arose in which there was no deity to perform a necessary task, El did not step in and do the work, but he did provide a deity to accomplish the task. This was true in the story about Kirtu's illness. It was a situation that required the immediate attention of a deity who could cure the disease. Unfortunately, there was no such deity. El asked, and the gods replied by not replying:

> Who among the gods is one who casts out pain,
> One who chases away lingering illness?
> No one among the gods answers him (*KTU* 1.16.V.10–13).

It was after interrogating these deities several times that El finally responded:

> Sit, my children, in your seats,
> On your princely thrones.
> I will craft and I will establish;
> I will establish one who casts out pain,
> One who chases away lingering illness (*KTU* 1.16.V.24–28).

The problem led El to create a goddess (*š^ctqt*) precisely for the situation. Again, it was not merely enough to fashion the divinity; the deity had to be officially and formally established in the office to which she belonged. In this situation, El moved to provide continuous order in the world by filling a gap in the divine structure, creating a new goddess as soon as the need became known.

El also was a source of information regarding the running of the cosmos. While deities could approach El, it was more common to find that the lines of communication were kept open by means of messengers who served the various deities. The gods sent messengers in order to receive the words of El.[87] Human kings entreated El through lesser deities.[88] The attention of the god could be obtained either directly or through Asherah.[89] In the other direction, El could communicate with the other gods directly, by speaking to them,[90] or he might deal with them through "normal channels," the assembly and messengers.[91] When El needed to communicate with kings, he

---

87. So Yam sends messengers to El; *KTU* 1.2.I.11.

88. *KTU* 1.15.II.12–16; 1.17.I.16–23.

89. Anat seeks to sway El's decision by means of Asherah on behalf of Baal (*KTU* 1.3–4); the storm-god goes directly to El in the Elkunirsha tale.

90. In the tablets from Ugarit El speaks directly with Anat, Asherah, and the assembled gods. In the Elkunirsha fragment he speaks to the storm-god and to the goddess assumed to be Asherah. In Ps 82:2–7 אלהים speaks directly to the gods as a group; Lowell K. Handy, "Sounds, Words and Meanings in Psalm 82," *JSOT* 47 (1990) 62.

91. El not only sits at the head of the assembled deities, but also sends messages to the gods by way of other deities (as with Shapshu to Mot).

did so by means of dreams or more indirectly through the divine assembly and messengers.[92] Thus, the wisdom of the highest authority was available to the rulers of the cosmos, from deity to king.

Not only was El called upon to settle disputes, he was also expected to be the final arbiter of justice. A common theme of biblical psalms, this aspect of El's responsibilities is less clearly drawn in the sources from the rest of Syria–Palestine. The divine disputes between Baal and his two adversaries, Yam and Mot, came before El, who made decisions in both instances. The proclamation of El was regarded as important, even though self-interest might move a deity to disregard the decision made by El.[93] In the same fashion, when Anat felt herself abused because she wanted the bow of Aqhat, she turned to El for permission to take the weapon and the life of Aqhat.[94] Whether or not the position taken by El was just, it was his consent she sought and received.

The actions of both divine and human personalities were subject to the justice of El. In Psalm 82 all members of the divine pantheon are condemned to death for abusing their offices as rulers of the universe.

God stands up
In the assembly of El;
In the midst of the gods he judges:
"How long will you rule unjustly?
And honor the wicked?
Judge the lowly and the fatherless!
Do justice for the needy and the poor!
Rescue the lowly and oppressed!
From the hand of the wicked, rescue!
They do not know,
And they do not understand.
In darkness they wander around;
All the foundations of the earth totter!
I, I say:
'You are gods,
And sons of the Highest are all of you.'
Nevertheless, you will die like a man,
And like one of the leaders you will fall!"

92. *KTU* 1.17.I.1–15 (vision of El to Danil); Deir ꜥAllā, Combination I.2, 5–6 (Divine Assembly contacting Balaam); 1 Kgs 22:19–23 (Divine Assembly with Micaiah in attendance); Ezek 1:1–3, etc. (God speaking directly to a prophet, who is in turn to speak to others in the name of God).

93. Baal refuses to submit to Yam, even though that is the decision of El (*KTU* 1.2).

94. *KTU* 1.18.I.

Arise God!
Rule the earth!
For you possess
All the nations! (Psalm 82).[95]

This poem supports the Ugaritic narratives by showing that El could remove deities from their positions if they misbehaved. This prerogative was understood to extend to human rulers as well. Though there is not a great deal of source material from Syro-Palestinian texts regarding the susceptibility of kings to divine removal, the threat of reprisal against kings for disturbing another ruler's sarcophagus is recorded.[96] For better or worse, it appears that the highest authority for justice in the universe was thought to be El. Gods and humans alike could petition him for redress in moral issues.

The importance of El for the maintenance of order in the cosmos is also displayed in the description of his abode. El was pictured in the Ugaritic texts as dwelling at the center of the universe, where waters merged, authority resided, and order was preserved.[97] The nebulous location and the description of El's house, characteristic of descriptions of the cosmic center, symbolically set it apart as the center of order around which the earth's existence was dependent.[98] The house of El was located on a mountain, with its connotations of "world mountain," and the other gods at Ugarit were thought to live on mountains as well.[99] El, however, also lived at the source of the waters:

Then she surely set her face
Toward El, the source of the rivers,
The midst of the springs of the oceans (*KTU* 1.4.IV.20–22).

The term *thm* suggests a site where the chaotic waters, from which creation took place, arose and were retained by El's house.[100] The

---

95. Psalm 82, as translated in Handy, "Sounds," 51–52. Note that the word translated both 'God' and 'gods' is אלהים.

96. *KAI* 26.A.III.12–IV.1; and 1.2; see 1 Sam 15:11 as well.

97. Richard J. Clifford, *The Cosmic Mountain in Canaan and the Old Testament* (HSM 4; Cambridge, Mass.: Harvard University Press, 1972) 51; Cross, *Canaanite Myth*, 37–38. These are in contrast to Edward Lipiński, "El's Abode: Mythological Traditions Related to Mount Hermon and to the Mountains of Armenia," *OLP* 2 (1971) 13–69.

98. It is rather misguided to attempt to find a geographical location for El's house; ibid., 42; Cross, *Canaanite Myth*, 38; Albright, *Yahweh and the Gods*, 120.

99. See the survey in Clifford, *Cosmic Mountain*, 34–97.

100. *Thm* is perhaps to be compared with Tiamat, whose body (sea water) became the material of creation in the *Enuma Elish* (though it should not be seen as deriving from the Mesopotamian myth); it is certainly the same as the unformed waters (תהום) that appear in Gen 1:2 at the beginning of creation. All three words suggest chaos

waters of the rivers (*nhrm*) flowed from El's abode and gave life at the same time that the waters of the chaotic cosmic oceans (*thmtm*) were kept in check. Thus El was continually staving off a return to chaos while simultaneously being the source of life.[101] The combination of mountain and waters' source is a standard description of the world's center in mythology.[102]

Besides being the location of living and chaotic waters, the dwelling of El was the place of final authority in the entire universe and therefore the preserve where order was maintained. El was consulted before major projects were undertaken: placing gods in positions of authority, building temples, or acquiring heirs for kings. To the house of El were brought questions of life and death, both of which the god appears to have controlled. At least some of the time the divine council met at El's mountain.[103] The preservation of cosmic order was maintained by the commands of El, issuing from his house. His word itself was sufficient to end strife among the deities (as with Baal and Mot, for example). El was the highest authority, and to him all questions came for final arbitration.

It is important to note that Asherah did not dwell in the same house as El. When she desired to see El, she came to him from her own temple. While on the one hand this mythological vision of their living arrangements removed her from the center of cosmic power, on the other hand it demonstrated that she was not simply an adjunct of El, but a primary deity in her own right. Clearly she was not seen as a hypostatic form of El (or Yahweh, or any other god) but was known as an independent goddess of great importance.[104]

---

waters and the order of creation. See Herbert G. May, "Some Cosmic Connotations of *Mayim Rabbîm*, 'Many Waters,'" *JBL* 74 (1955) 9–21. For a discussion on chaos waters in relation to the temple in Jerusalem, both in biblical and Jewish legendary sources, see Raphael Patai, *Man and Temple in Ancient Jewish Myth and Ritual* (London: Thomas Nelson, 1947) 24–165.

101. Both types of waters are to be found at the cosmic mountain; Mircea Eliade, *Patterns in Comparative Religion* (New York: New American Library, 1958) 377; and Othmar Keel, *The Symbolism of the Biblical World: Ancient Near Eastern Iconography and the Book of Psalms* (New York: Seabury, 1978) 113–14, 116–18, fig. 153a. Notice the combination of mountains and streams, also found in the ideology of the temple in Jerusalem (Ezek 47:1).

102. Eliade, *Patterns*, 375–76.

103. Mullen (*Divine Council*, 166–68) concludes that the divine assembly met at the abode of El; while this is certainly true some of the time, the council seems to be able to meet at many places, Baal's house and Danil's dinner party among them.

104. The argument that Asherah must have been some aspect of a central male deity comes from reflection on the "Israelite" cult, where Asherah appears both in biblical and epigraphic texts. The resort to this interpretation appears to be linked to a theological necessity to retain a single deity at the center of "Israelite" religion; see

Asherah's house not only provided access to her, but through her one could obtain the "ear" of El. Her house was the second most important place for a devotee to petition.

The ideal of highest authority in Syria–Palestine lay in the deities El and Asherah, the divine royal couple, the parents of all ruling personnel, mortal or immortal. In El was the repository of all wisdom and practical knowledge for the general functioning of the universe. He sat as final judge in all matters of justice and dispute, a position through which all other deities could be controlled. The work of the universe was performed in this mythology by gods other than El, though the other deities were established, promoted, and overseen by El. Asherah held a position only slightly below that of El in divine power, and certainly she was thought to be on the same level of the divine hierarchy. It was she who chose the deities for their positions in the pantheon, in her role as Queen Mother. She was also a counselor to El and therefore the goddess through whom others could influence the decisions of El.[105] Thus, ideally, these two deities maintained the order of the cosmos by making ultimate decisions and providing the highest authority on political, religious, and judicial matters.

MALFUNCTIONING

When a hierarchical office functions smoothly, it is represented as functioning ideally. Smooth, ideal operation seldom occurs in real life, and it is not observed very often in the mythological narratives. Deviation from the ideal is known as "malfunctioning." Malfunctioning was particularly apparent in El and Asherah's preferential treatment of certain deities. However, other manifestations of their malfunctioning also are attested in the sources. Both deities were at times partial to other gods, and this partiality resulted in behavior detrimental to the cosmos in general. This type of malfunctioning has been analyzed in modern times by studying basic behavior pat-

---

P. Kyle McCarter, Jr., "Aspects of the Religion of the Israelite Monarchy: Biblical and Epigraphic Data," in *Ancient Israelite Religion* (ed. P. D. Miller, P. D. Hanson, and S. D. McBride; Philadelphia: Fortress, 1987) 143–49.

105. F. O. Hvidberg-Hansen, *La Déesse TNT: Une Étude sur la religion canaanéo-punique: I Texte* (trans. F. Arndt; Copenhagen: Gad's, 1979) 71; Andreason illustrates from human government ("Role of Queen Mother," 191): "chief function of the position of queen mother in Jerusalem was that of senior counsellor to King and people." On the Queen Mother as the second official to the king and almost as powerful, see Molin, "Stellung der Gᵉbira," 161; and Tadmor, "Autobiographical Apology," 38, on Naqiʾa-Zakutu (wife of Sennacherib who made her son Esarhaddon the heir apparent).

terns within a hierarchical organization.[106] One example of partiality in ancient mythological texts can be singled out for each of the two highest gods.

In spite of his incapacity to handle the office to which he was nominated, Athtar received Asherah's support. This support was given even after El noted the incapacity of the god to fill the position. The situation demonstrates either that Asherah had less insight into Athtar's capacities than El or that she had some inordinate preference for Athtar that took precedence over the need for a competent candidate. In either case, the situation displays a fallibility on the part of Asherah that was less than ideal for her position.

El's attitude toward Anat, especially concerning her visit with him in the tale of Aqhat, displays the same type of preferential treatment. In the legend of Aqhat, Anat's demand for the human's bow appears unjustified, yet El gave in to the spoiled goddess's request. This behavior on the part of El not only corresponds to typical malfunctioning by those in a position of highest authority, but also corresponds to a type of narrative that described spoiled children in ancient Near Eastern literature.[107] El's compliance with the malevolent behavior of Anat reflected the lenient attitude of her father toward her. The consequences of this leniency did not bode well for the order and justice of the universe.

In the Elkunirsha fragment from the Hittite Empire the narrative appears to have been developed primarily from the personal lives of these two gods rather than from their roles as ruling deities. The goddess, who may have been Asherah, is pictured as attempting to seduce the storm-god; this seems to have been an abuse of power. The author of the tale considered it unacceptable behavior and it was also considered unacceptable by both El and the storm-god, who together devised a way to ensnare and embarrass her. It is not quite clear from the small fragment whether El was displeased with her because she attempted to engage in illicit sex (the point may not have been the illicit sex, since the plot developed by El and Baal still entailed the liaison) or because she attempted to force herself on an unwilling subordinate. In either case the goddess was expected to pay the consequences. At the same time, the El who appeared in this story was not portrayed as a judge or ruler making a clear moral decision but as a crafty and underhanded dealer who exacted retribution in the role of husband. Clearly, neither El nor Asherah was an ideal authority figure.

106. Kanter, *Men and Women*, 39.
107. The motif of the spoiled divine/royal child is discussed in the following chapter with respect to the goddess Anat.

Favoritism on the part of the ruling deities was even taken one step further. Asherah was accused by Anat of taking great joy in the demise of Baal.

> Now Asherah and her children will rejoice!
> The Goddess and the gang of her relatives,
> For dead is Victorious Baal! (*KTU* 1.6.I.39–42).

Anat obviously considered Asherah capable of evil emotions. It must be kept in mind, however, that Anat is not portrayed in these myths as the most emotionally stable character, and her speeches appear to have been written with the purpose of revealing her inflammatory character. It is possible that Asherah was glad to hear of the death of Baal for some reason that the extant mythological sources do not record. Asherah's dislike for Baal may have led her to wish one of her children on his throne in his stead; perhaps Baal was one of the gods who was mothered by another goddess; or perhaps Asherah disliked having a deity as dumb as Baal in such a powerful position. That there was such animosity can only be conjectured, and there is, in fact, little evidence in the existing texts that Asherah was an opponent of Baal. Speeches by Anat, like the one above, were written to demonstrate Anat's belligerence and not necessarily to describe reality as perceived by the devotees.

In Philo of Byblos's history, El was also pictured as being happy about the death of certain gods, though in these instances it was El himself who killed them. In one such case it was El's father (called Οὐρανὸς in the Greek text) whom El killed in revenge for the abuse suffered by his mother.[108] Though this version has much in common with Hesiod's *Theogony*, it may reflect a Phoenician mythological belief at the time of Philo of Byblos or even earlier. In this story there was a motive for the deicide/patricide, which turned the tale into a pursuit of justice on the part of El. Another story told about El, however, related the murder of his son and daughter out of sheer paranoia.[109] It was recounted with the comment that El's actions were considered to be strange behavior. In this story El was depicted as defending his status and position by violent and unacceptable means.

In short, the gods of the highest level were pictured just as humans holding similar positions on the mortal plane. The King and Queen Mother had vast power and wielded it with more self-interest than ideally would benefit the entire earth. The universal

---

108. Philo of Byblos I.10.21. Note how this story parallels Hesiod's *Theogony*; see Baumgarten, *Phoenician History*, 235–42.

109. Philo of Byblos I.10.21.

temptation to treat favored underlings with special concern and to allow less-favored personnel to be abused was a temptation to these deities as well. Power and authority, paranoia and preference—all appeared on the highest level of cosmic hierarchy in Syria–Palestine.

Chapter 4

Active Deities

The highest authority in the pantheon was responsible for ordering and maintaining earth and cosmos but was not actively engaged in the actual work necessary to maintain the universe. The next lower level of deities performed this function. Serving under the authority of those who actually owned the universe, the active gods were expected to perform in a way that would enable the cosmos to operate smoothly. Each of the gods at this level of the pantheon had a specific sphere of authority over which to exert his or her control. Ideally, all the gods were to perform their duties in a way that would keep the universe functioning perfectly in the manner desired by the highest authority. Yet, the gods, like human beings, are portrayed as having weaknesses and rivalries that kept the cosmos from operating smoothly.

THE OFFICE

The active deities correspond in important respects with the level of authority in modern bureaucracies that may be called "management," in a general sense. "The role of management is to promote efficiency and economical operating."[1] Managers, therefore, are responsible for the smooth operation of their area of specialty. They make decisions but are in turn held accountable for carrying out these decisions by the highest authority in the organization.[2] Each individual at this level of bureaucracy holds an office, the right to which lies not with the individual, but with the superiors in the

1. E. F. L. Brech, *Organisation: The Framework of Management* (London: Longmans, Green, 1957) 11; see also p. 13.
2. The following characteristics conform to those already noted in Max Weber, *Theory of Social and Economic Organization Theory* (trans. Henderson and Parsons; New York: Free Press, 1947) 330–32.

structure. In order to maintain the office, the individual must adhere to the rules that govern both the bureaucracy as a whole and the office in particular, The authority of the office-holder derives from the status of the office, not the individual as an individual. In order for an individual to be considered for an office in the hierarchical structure, he or she must demonstrate competency for the position being considered. In holding such an office, the individual does not "own" the office or the administration of the office; however, competency obligates the individual to carry out the functions of the office properly. To do this the individual is invested by his or her superiors with sufficient authority and adequate means for success in the bureaucracy. Should he or she fail to perform adequately, various consequences may follow, up to and including removal from the office.

Within a hierarchy the managerial level is at the upper end of the bureaucracy. Most of the functioning levels of the organization are lower and are subject to the managers. The responsibilities of the managerial officeholder are twofold: (1) the installation and maintenance of proper procedures to ensure adherence to plans; and (b) the guidance, integration, and supervision of the personnel comprising the enterprise and carrying out its operations.[3] The manager has both considerable authority and also an active role to play in the functioning of the organization.

In a sense, management is an extension of ownership in the organization.[4] In theory, managers work under strict rules that maintain the proper behavior of each member of the level, resulting in a smoothly functioning organization. In reality, this level provides most of the blatant examples of "malfunctioning" to be found in bureaucratic organizations. It is at this level that conflict, self-interest, competition, and the clash of opposing aims become most apparent in functioning hierarchies.[5] Such malfunctioning often involves personnel attempting to "get ahead" in the organization by means not always advantageous to the organization as a whole. The problem of incompatible personalities forced to deal with each other on this level can lead to considerable friction. This type of behavior disrupts any efficient flow of authority within the organization but does not necessarily reflect any general antipathy to the organization itself.[6]

There is one other form of malfunctioning common at this level, though it is a problem that begins outside the level itself. Managerial

3. Brech, *Organisation*, 10.

4. Ibid., 11–13.

5. Ibid., 63–69.

6. R. M. Kanter, *Men and Women of the Corporation* (New York: Basic Books, 1977) 99–101.

personnel of the higher levels are often "coddled" by the chief executive.[7] The rules that are supposed to maintain order within the organization may be bent, broken, or overruled to mollify people who are deemed essential to the organization. People who find themselves being treated in this manner tend to behave in a way that would be unacceptable to the organization if practiced by other people not considered necessary by the highest authority. This treatment extends, it seems, only to the managerial level; lower-level personnel in the organizational structure are perceived as being replaceable, and therefore similar behavior on their part is not tolerated.[8]

THE GODS

The more famous deities of Syria–Palestine fit into the category of active gods. This is the level of the divine hierarchy in which the powerful and active deities function. The extended myths that survive from Ugarit deal for the most part with the gods Baal and Anat, making them the most well-known of the active deities. However, there is reason to believe that other major deities would belong to this same group if more information were known about them. Deities such as Shemesh (Shapshu), Yareah, Reshep, Astarte, Yam, and Mot (among others) share characteristics of this level of the divine populace. For purposes of describing the level, the two best-known deities from the myths are used here to exemplify the behavior of gods belonging to this level, with other deities brought in as supporting data.

Baal

Early in the twentieth century it was generally believed that *baʿal* was only a title and not a name given to a particular deity. It was thought that the word *baʿal* was used for all local deities; each locality was supposed to have its own specialized god who was known as the "lord" (*baʿal*) of that locale.[9] It was thought that the *baal* of any

7. Ibid., 37. Kanter calls the personnel of this level the "exempts," because of their special treatment, which also extends to their families, 38–39.

8. Ibid., 39. Kanter calls those who cannot expect preferential treatment the "non-exempt" ones.

9. W. A. Hauser, *The Fabulous Gods Denounced in the Bible: Translated from Seldon's "Syrian Deities"* (Philadelphia: Lippincott, 1880) 72, 77 (John Seldon's work originally appeared in 1613); Julius Wellhausen, *Prolegomena to the History of Ancient Israel* (Cleveland: World Publishing, 1957) 234 (originally published in 1883). W. R. Smith, *The Religion of the Semites: The Fundamental Institutions*, 93–94; Elford Higgens, *Hebrew Idolatry*

given area was responsible for the fertility of that location; therefore, the *ba^{c}alim* were often referred to simply as fertility gods.[10] The local deities were taken to be either nature gods or tribal totems but of no particular importance beyond their local cults.[11] W. Carleton Wood went so far as to state that "Ba^{c}al never became a proper name for a deity as ^{c}Ashtart or Zeus."[12]

From Egyptian sources it was known that *baal* was used as a divine title for the god Seth. The equation of Baal with the native Egyptian Seth was so complete that the individual personality of Baal was lost behind the Egyptian god.[13] *Baal* does appear in literary references in texts from Egypt as a symbol of divine terror in warfare.[14] Still, it was not certain that a specific deity, not just a divine title, was intended when the Egyptians used the name of Baal.

It was only after the discovery of the Ugaritic narratives that the existence of a deity with the name Baal became undisputed. This deity went by several names and titles in the mythological tablets, including Baal and Hadad. For a period of time after the discovery of the tablets, the various names and titles led scholars to assert that several distinct deities were intended.[15] In 1933 Hans Bauer demonstrated that the name Aliyan did not refer to a separate deity but was a title for the god Baal.[16] Once it was established that a major deity was present in the narratives under several names, the storyline of the mythological tales could be cleared up considerably.

---

and Superstition: Its Place in Folklore (Port Washington, N.Y.: Kennikat, 1971) 53 (first published in 1893); and J. Hehn, *Die biblische und die babylonische Gottesidee* (Leipzig: Hinrichs, 1913) 115–16.

10. W. R. Smith, *Religion of the Semites*, 104–8; Theodore H. Robinson in W. O. E. Oesterley and Theodore H. Robinson, *A History of Israel* (Oxford: Clarendon, 1932) 1:167; and W. C. Wood, *Religion of Canaan: From the Earliest Times to the Hebrew Conquest* (Ontario: Newmarket, 1916) 235.

11. W. R. Smith, *Religion of the Semites*, 93–110; Lewis Bayles Paton, "Baal, Beel, Bel," in *Encyclopedia of Religion and Ethics* (ed. J. Hastings; 12 vols.; Edinburgh: T. & T. Clark, 1908–1922) 2.283–84; W. W. G. Baudissin, *Adonis und Esmun: Eine Untersuchung zur Geschichte des Glaubens an Auferstehungs-götter und an Heilgötter* (Leipzig: Hinrichs, 1911) 15–56.

12. Wood, *Religion of Canaan*, 23; see also Paton, "Baal, Beel, Bel," 285.

13. S. Morenz, *Egyptian Religion* (trans. Ann Keep; Ithaca, N.Y.: Cornell University Press, 1973) 238; and H. Te Velde, *Seth, God of Confusion: A Study of His Role in Egyptian Mythology and Religion* (Problème der Ägyptologie 6; Leiden: Brill, 1967) 122–29.

14. See examples in Miriam Lichtheim, *Ancient Egyptian Literature, Volume 2: The New Kingdom* (Berkeley: University of California Press, 1976) 64, 67, 69, 71.

15. On Aliyan-Baal and Baal, see Charles Virolleaud, "Le Déchiffrement des tablettes alphabétiques de Ras-Shamra," *Syria* 12 (1931) 22.

16. Hans Bauer, "Die Gottheiten von Ras Schamra," *ZAW* 51 (1933) 96–97.

Since Baal is referred to in the texts as the king (*mlk*) and ruler of the earth, it was assumed that Baal was the head of the pantheon.[17] The idea that there could only be one "king" in a given pantheon led one segment of scholarly tradition to the conclusion that Baal was the "new" king who had overthrown El, the "old" king of the Syro-Palestinian pantheon.[18] Once it was determined that Baal should be seen as the head of the divine realm, it was further determined that he must, as a matter of course, be equated with the stereotypical "sky-god," which would make him supreme in rule and fertility.[19] The role of Baal in fertility then became the major concern of scholarly research.[20]

An increasing number of scholars, however, recognized that El remained the active head of the Ugaritic pantheon.[21] This in turn led to the realization that the pantheon had a hierarchical structure in which Baal served in a position subordinate to El.[22] Baal's sphere of influence in the natural world was the thunderstorm, with its life-giving rains; to that extent Baal was still seen as a fertility-deity but not, perhaps, *the* fertility-god.[23] This view also placed more

---

17. W. F. Albright, *Yahweh and the Gods of Canaan: A Historical Analysis of Two Contrasting Faiths* (Garden City, N.Y.: Doubleday, 1968; repr. Winona Lake, Ind.: Eisenbrauns, 1978) 125; U. Cassuto, *The Goddess Anath: Canaanite Epics of the Patriarchal Age* (trans. I. Abrahams; Jerusalem: Magnes, 1971) 59.

18. Ibid.; Arvid S. Kapelrud, *Baal in the Ras Shamra Text* (Copenhagen: Gad, 1952) 133; Mircea Eliade, *History of Religious Ideas* (3 vols.; Chicago: University of Chicago Press, 1978–1985) 1.151.

19. M. Eliade, *Patterns in Comparative Religion* (New York: New American Library, 1958) 83, 88. Note that the relationship of the local Baal gods with the "Solar Deity" had already been suggested by Hehn (*Biblische und babylonische Gottesidee*, 105).

20. Cassuto, *Anath*, 60. Also see Peter J. van Zijl (*Baal: A Study of Texts in Connexion with Baal in the Ugaritic Epics* [AOAT 10; Kevelaer: Butzon & Bercker/Neukirchen-Vluyn: Neukirchener Verlag, 1972] 323–24), who sees all Baal narratives as fertility myths. J. C. de Moor bases his entire work on the premise that all Baal narratives are related to the fertility cycle in nature (*The Seasonal Pattern of the Ugaritic Myth of Ba^clu according to the Version of Ilimiku* [AOAT 16; Kevelaer: Butzon & Bercker/Neukirchen-Vluyn: Neukirchener Verlag] 1971). Eliade sees Baal primarily as *the* fertility deity (*History of Religious Ideas*, 152).

21. Albright, *Yahweh and the Gods*, 120; F. M. Cross, *Canaanite Myth and Hebrew Epic: Essays in the History of the Religion of Israel* (Cambridge, Mass.: Harvard University Press, 1973) 43; G. R. Driver, *Canaanite Myths and Legends* (OTSt 3; Edinburgh: T. & T. Clark, 1956) 21.

22. A. Caquot and M. Sznycer, *Ugaritic Religion*, (Iconography of Religions 15/8; Leiden: Brill, 1980) 12; P. Xella, *Gli antenati di Dio: Divinità e miti della tradizione di Canaan* (Verona: Essedue, 1981) 39–40; C. E. L'Heureux, *Rank among the Canaanite Gods: El, Ba^cal, and the Rephaim* (HSM 21; Missoula, Mont.: Scholars Press, 1979) 69–79.

23. Caquot and Sznycer, *Ugaritic Religion*, 12; John Gray, *The Legacy of Canaan: The Ras Shamra Texts and Their Relevance to the Old Testament* (2d rev. ed.; VTSup 5; Leiden: Brill, 1965) 165–66; and J. C. L. Gibson, "Theology of the Ugaritic Baal Cycle," *Or* 53 (1984) 206.

importance on the role of Baal as the patron deity of Ugarit, with
influence decidedly more political in nature than merely controlling
rain. Both roles were carried out by Baal under the authority of El.

Now that Baal does not have to be understood in terms of a
stereotyped ruler deity, it is possible to see him, in the mythological
narratives, as a deity highly dependent on other gods. While it is true
that he is presented in the myths as a mighty, virile deity, he also is
shown to possess a vast amount of what may only be called stupidity.
His victories over the gods Yam and Mot may well have been the reason he was given the title "victorious" (*aliyan*), but his victories came
only with the aid of other deities. As for Baal's lack of intelligence,
two examples will suffice. First, when Baal finally had a remodeled
house and had thrown a celebration for the other deities, he issued a
challenge to Mot.[24] For a deity who could prevail in a contest with
Mot this would be a reasonable, though boastful, action to take, but
Baal was incapable of withstanding the attack by Mot and the challenge was merely foolhardy. Baal ended up in the realm of the dead,
from which his sister Anat had to extract him. Second, Baal warned
his messengers in some detail that when they visit Mot they must be
very careful not to fall into Death's grasp; yet, Baal himself fell into
Mot's clutches by behaving in the manner he had warned his messengers to avoid.[25] Because these narratives were found near the Baal
temple, it must be assumed that the portrayal of Baal in the texts is
in accord with the cult's accepted character for him, namely, as a
somewhat virile lummox, hardly as an ideal of strength and wisdom.

Anat

The existence of a Semitic goddess in Syria–Palestine by the name of
Anat was uncertain prior to the translation of the Ugaritic tablets. Not
much was known about her other than that some place-names in
Syria–Palestine had been named after her.[26] In the Egyptian sources,
Anat appeared as a significant goddess during the eighteenth and
nineteenth dynasties in the role of a goddess of war.[27] Along with Astarte, Anat became a foreign god whom the Egyptians incorporated
into their own mythology.[28] In Egypt the Syro-Palestinian goddesses

24. *KTU* 1.4.VII.47–52.

25. *KTU* 1.4.VII.14–20; 1.6.II.22–23.

26. W. R. Smith, *Religion of the Semites*, 211; Wood, *Religion of Canaan*, 264.

27. Ibid., 263; Lewis Bayles Paton, "Canaanites," in *Encyclopedia of Religion and Ethics* (ed. J. Hasting; 12 vols.; Edinburgh: T. & T. Clark, 1908–1922) 3:182; Stephen Herbert Langdon, *Semitic* (Mythology of All Races 5; Boston: Jones, 1931) 30.

28. Hehn, *Biblische und babylonische Gottesidee*, 321; Morenz, *Egyptian Religion*, 259;
see also Lichtheim, *Ancient Egyptian Literature*, 2:215.

Kadesh, Astarte, and Anat were merged into an Egyptian multiple deity.[29] Anat was also worshiped in the Semitic colony that had settled at Yeb (Elephantine), where the goddess appeared as Anat-Bethel and Anat-YHW.[30] The title "queen of heaven" was accorded Anat in some Egyptian texts.[31] Outside of Egypt, in one Cypriot inscription of the fourth century B.C.E., the goddess Anat was equated with the Greek goddess Athena.[32] This identification of two goddesses from separate cultures was also attested in Philo of Byblos's texts, where Anat, the daughter of El, was conflated with the patron deity of Athens, Athena.[33]

The Ugaritic narratives provide the first literary texts that give a fairly clear description of this goddess. The first readers of these texts tended to view her as yet another example of the ubiquitous "fertility-goddess," this time as the spouse of Baal.[34] The narratives cited to demonstrate that Anat was a goddess of fertility are all, unfortunately, so broken as to be inconclusive about this role for her.[35]

29. Stanley A. Cook, *The Religion of Ancient Palestine in the Light of Archaeology* (Schweich Lectures 1925; London: Oxford University Press, 1930) 104–5; Morenz, *Egyptian Religion*, 143, 241.

30. Cook, *Religion of Ancient Palestine*, 104–5; A. Cowley, *Aramaic Papyri of the Fifth Century B.C.* (Oxford: Clarendon, 1923), no. 22; Albert Vincent, *La Religion des Judéo-Araméens d'Éléphantine* (Paris: Geuthner, 1937) 652.

31. Bezalel Porten, *Archives from Elephantine: The Life of an Ancient Jewish Military Colony* (Berkeley: University of California Press, 1968) 165.

32. *KAI* 42.1.

33. Philo of Byblos I.10.18, 32 (from Eusebius *Prep. Gospel*); see also Robert du Mesnil du Buisson, "Origine et évolution du panthéon de Tyr," *RHR* 164 (1963) 150; Barbara G. Walker, *The Woman's Encyclopedia of Myths and Secrets* (San Francisco: Harper & Row, 1983) 30. Aside from the sound of the names, it is uncertain that the goddesses Anat and Athena were related, except by classical authors searching for a corresponding deity in the Semitic world.

34. Albright, *Yahweh and the Gods*, 128, 135; Charles F. Pfeiffer, *Ras Shamra and the Bible* (Baker Studies in Biblical Archaeology 1; Grand Rapids, Mich.: Baker, 1962) 31; Eliade, *History of Religious Ideas*, 152; Cyrus Gordon, "Canaanite Mythology," in *Mythologies of the Ancient World* (ed. S. N. Kramer; Garden City, N.Y.: Doubleday, 1961) 185; Anton Jirku, *Der Mythus der Kanaanäer* (Bonn: Habelt, 1966) 53; Arvid S. Kapelrud, *The Violent Goddess: Anat in the Ras Shamra Texts* (Oslo: Universitetsforlaget, 1969) 92–93; Walker, *Women's Encyclopedia*, 30; de Moor, *An Anthology of Religious Texts from Ugarit* (Nisaba 16; Leiden: Brill, 1987) 7; and Loretz, *Ugarit und die Bibel: Kanaanäische Götter und Religion im Alten Testament* (Darmstadt: Wissenschaftliche Buchgesellschaft, 1990) 84.

35. Ringgren, *Religions of the Ancient Near East* (Philadelphia: Westminster, 1973) 142–43, 150–51; Kapelrud, *Violent Goddess*, 94–97; see the reconstructed texts in de Moor, *Anthology of Religious Texts*, pp. 109–16. Recently it has been acknowledged that there is no evidence for Anat as a fertility goddess; see Neal Hugh Walls, Jr., *The Goddess Anat in Ugaritic Myth* (Ph.D. diss., Johns Hopkins University, 1991) 142–96, 288; and Peggy Day, "Why Is Anat a Warrior and Hunter?" in *The Bible and the Politics of Exegesis: Essays in Honor of Norman K. Gottwald on His Sixty-Fifth Birthday* (ed. David

However, there is good reason to doubt the correlation between Anat's role and fertility. Though some of the Ugaritic texts describe the goddess and Baal copulating and perhaps even bearing offspring (bovine though they may be), this demonstrates only that the deities were presented in anthropomorphic fashion. Since sexual activity is a normal human pastime and could, one suspects, be engaged in by any divinity, it cannot be assumed just because a goddess was sexually active that she was therefore a fertility-goddess.[36] Moreover, the fact about Anat that is inescapable is that she was a war-goddess.[37] So dominant is the figure of Anat in the extant myths that it was thought for awhile that the narratives must have come from her cult.[38] Even though the tablets clearly note that the narratives are concerned with Baal, Anat appears in them as the most physically powerful, or at least the most active, of all the deities represented.[39]

More recent theories hold that if these texts had their origin in the cult of Baal, Anat must have been viewed as subject to and under the control of Baal. Petersen and Woodward, in their quasi-structuralist approach, argue that the missing sections of "the myth" certainly showed Baal appointing Anat to her rank in the pantheon, a position where she would be under his control.[40] Bowman concludes his study of the goddess Anat by stating that "ᶜAnatu's main function was to support Baᶜlu in his efforts to maintain his supremacy in the pantheon."[41] In Bowman's study Anat is reduced from being an independent deity to being a personified aspect of Baal ("his will"), a

---

Jobling, Peggy L. Day, and Gerald T. Sheppard; Cleveland: Pilgrim, 1991) 142, but the suggestion that Anat is "Mistress of the Animals" (p. 143) rests on even more shakey suppostions.

36. Marjo Korpel, *A Rift in the Clouds: Ugaritic and Hebrew Descriptions of the Divine* (UBL 8; Munster: Ugarit, 1990) 216–17, and Walls, "The Goddess Anat," 19–20.

37. Cassuto, *Anath*, 64; Kapelrud, *Violent Goddess*, 49; Gordon, "Canaanite Mythology," 197–98; Ringgren, *Religions of the Ancient Near East*, 143; del Olmo Lete, *Mitos y leyendas de Canaan segun la tradicion de Ugarit: Textos, versión y estudio* (FCB 1; Madrid: Ediciones Cristiandad, 1981) 72; Caquot and Sznycer, *Ugaritic Religion*, 14; and P. Day, "Why is Anat a Warrior?" 142.

38. Cassuto, *Anath*, 2; Driver, *Canaanite Myths*, 10–11; Gray, *Legacy*, 92. See René Dussaud (*Les Découvertes de Ras Shamra (Ugarit) et l'Ancien Testament* [2d ed.; Paris: Geuthner, 1941] 115–16), who also sees a relationship with human sacrifices in the goddess's activities.

39. Henri Cazelles, "Essai sur le pouvoir de la divinité à Ugarit et en Israël," *Ugaritica* 6 (1969) 28: "La divinité apparement la plus puissante, mais peut-être seulment la plus active, est Anat."

40. D. L. Petersen and M. Woodward, "Northwest Semitic Religion: A Study of Relational Structures," *UF* 9 (1977) 195.

41. Charles Bowman, "Goddess ᶜAnatu in the Ancient Near East" (Ph.D. diss., Graduate Theological Union, 1978) 195.

theory already suggested by Kapelrud.[42] In such a reconstruction the violence engaged in by the goddess is not thought to be the activity of a goddess so much as an extension of the activities of the god Baal.

There is no reason to view Anat as an aspect or hypostasis of Baal; nor is there any evidence that she was in any way subject to the will of Baal. While Anat acknowledged the authority of El, though not with a subservient demeanor, she never demonstrated any sense of being under Baal's control. She extricated Baal from disasters of his own making, but she took on these tasks as his sister, of her own volition, without having to be seen as Baal's lackey. Furthermore, it cannot be assumed that the pair Anat and Baal were considered to be a fertility god and goddess couple, since it was Baal's rain that brought life to the land, not the two deities' sex life. Anat was considered by the Syro-Palestinian religious world to be a goddess of war and mayhem. In the few narratives that survive, she is portrayed as a deity given to excesses of violence, greed, and vengeance, all of which would make good traits for a war-goddess.

Mot

It was long assumed that there was a god of the dead and of the underworld in the Syro-Palestinian pantheon. Certain biblical passages suggested to some that "Death" (מות) was a deity,[43] and some biblical passages were thought to imply such a deity without naming a particular god.[44] A name for this deity was already known through the story of Muth (Μούθ), who was made the deity of the dead by El in Philo of Byblos's history.[45] By the turn of the twentieth century he was sometimes recognized by scholars as a genuine Syro-Palestinian deity, even though there was no narrative known at that time in which Mot played a role.[46]

However, in the myths from Ugarit, Mot plays a major part in the plot, so major, in fact, that the entire religion of Ugarit has at times

42. Ibid., 260–63; Kapelrud, *Violent Goddess*, 54–55; note also Caquot and Sznycer, *Ugaritic Religion*, 14: "Anat is in some ways a caricature of Baal." Walls ("The Goddess Anat," 296) correctly declares that Anat was an independent, individual goddess.

43. Wood, *Religion of Canaan*, 268–69; biblical passages such as Isa 28:15 and Jer 9:20 seem to deal with a deity of death.

44. This had been noticed especially in the phrase "king of terrors" in Job 18:14, which was interpreted as a reference to a god of the netherworld; Samuel Rolles Driver and George Buchanan Gray, *A Critical and Exegetical Commentary on the Book of Job* (ICC 14; New York: Scribner's Sons, 1921) 1.160; Paul Dhorme, *Le Livre de Job* (Paris: Lecoffre, 1926) 241.

45. Philo of Byblos I.10.34.

46. Paton, "Canaanites," 184.

been interpreted as a fertility cult centered on an eternal cosmic struggle between Baal and Mot.[47] In this interpretation Mot is seen as embodying infertility, waste, and death.[48] As the god of death, Mot was pictured as having an insatiable appetite, a characteristic attested in both biblical and Ugaritic sources.[49] Moreover, the deity Mot held a special status with the highest authority; beloved of El (*ydd bn il*), he was assured of receiving all living things in the end.[50]

Recently some major questions have been raised concerning the status of Mot as a deity. Healey has suggested that Mot was not a god at all. His argument is that the deity did not receive food offerings in the ritual texts at Ugarit and that the name does not appear in standard god lists.[51] Astour had made the same observation concerning ritual texts earlier, but he noted that Mesopotamian offering texts also omitted the god Nergal, who is well attested as a god of the dead and is not dismissed as non-divine.[52] It has been suggested that, instead of being an independent deity, Mot was an aspect of either El or Yam, though neither possibility is at all convincing.[53] Even scholars who accept Mot as a deity debate the basic nature of his existence. While it is generally agreed by those who see him as a god that he was the ruler of the realm of the dead, Astour has raised the possibility that he was related to fertility and the source of good health.[54]

47. Gordon, "Canaanite Mythology," 184; Ringgren, *Religions of the Ancient Near East*, 134; T. C. Vriezen, *The Religion of Ancient Israel* (Philadelphia: Westminster, 1967) 41; see M. S. Smith, "Interpreting the Baal Cycle," *UF* 18 (1986) 321–22.

48. Cassuto, *Anath*, 61; Gray, *Legacy*, 53; Cross, *Canaanite Myth*, 116; Gordon Paul Brubacher, "The Canaanite God of Death in the Myth of Baal and Mot" (Ph.D. diss., Drew University, 1987) 20.

49. *KTU* 1.5.I.14–22; Hab 2:5; see Nahum M. Sarna, "The Mythological Background of Job 18," *JBL* 82 (1963) 316–17.

50. *KTU* 1.5.I.13; Job 30:23; Jesús-Luis Cunchillos Ylarri, "Le Dieu Mut, guerrier de El," *Syria* 62 (1985) 210. N. Wyatt notes that the Ugaritic belief presented in the epic and mythological narratives is that death is inescapable ("Cosmic Entropy in Ugaritic Religious Thought," *UF* 17 [1985] 386).

51. John F. Healey, "The Ugaritic Dead: Some Live Issues," *UF* 18 (1986) 29.

52. Michael C. Astour, "The Netherworld and Its Denizens at Ugarit," in *Death in Mesopotamia* (ed. Bendt Alster; Mesopotamia 8; Copenhagen: Akademisk, 1980) 231. There appears to be little relation among the deities listed in ritual, mythological, and proper name sources; see Dennis Pardee, "An Evaluation of the Proper Names from Ebla from a West Semitic Perspective: Pantheon Distribution According to Genre," in *Eblaite Personal Names and Semitic Name-Giving: Papers of a Symposium Held in Rome July 15–17, 1985* (ed. Alfonso Archi; Archivi Reali di Ebla Studi 1; Rome: Missione Archeologica Italiana in Siria, 1988) 141.

53. Respectively, Cunchillos Ylarri, "Le Dieu Mut," 218; and M. S. Smith, "Death in Jeremiah IX, 20," *UF* 19 (1987) 292–93. Since the mythological texts from Ugarit present Mot as taking orders from El, the former theory is untenable. There is nothing in the narratives to suggest that Yam (Sea) and Mot have anything in common aside from their mutual antipathy to Baal, so the latter theory is unlikely as well.

54. Astour, "Netherworld and Its Denizens at Ugarit," 231.

Along the same line of reasoning, Margalit argues that the realm of Mot was a pleasant place, much like the Elysian Fields of the Greeks.[55] Klaas Spronk is probably correct, however, in seeing no trace of a benign side to Mot in the extant sources.[56]

Shemesh / Shapshu

Solar deities have long held a fascination for scholars. That there had been worship of the sun in Syria–Palestine was known from references to such a deity and its cult in the Bible.[57] Prior to the discovery of the mythological narratives of Ugarit, the character of the deity worshiped as sun-god in Syria–Palestine was defined by the Mesopotamian Shamash.[58] Unlike some deities, the gender of the sun-deity in Syria–Palestine was uncertain, since Mesopotamia had a masculine solar-god, while South Arabia had a feminine solar-goddess.[59] The areas of responsibility for the deity, however, were presumed to be the same as those for Mesopotamian Shamash: law and justice, life and joy, divination and purification.[60] But scholars had to arrive at this description without benefit of any primary source material from Syria–Palestine.

The sun-goddess of the cult at Ugarit, Shapshu, appeared in two of the longer narratives as a spokesperson for the god El. She delivered El's word in an attempt to bring order to the pantheon. In this role she was portrayed as a representative of El and a preserver of order.[61] Because she aided Anat in the search for Baal (which finally resulted in Baal's return to life), Shapshu also has been described as a fertility-goddess. This is a strained argument at best.[62] Most recently the role of Shapshu as the ruler of the *rpᵓum* has kindled interest in her as traverser of the netherworld.[63]

55. Baruch Margalit, *A Matter of "Life" and "Death": A Study of the Baal-Mot Epic (CTA 4-5-6)* (AOAT 206; Kevelaer: Butzon & Bercker/Neukirchen-Vluyn: Neukirchener Verlag, 1980) 127.

56. Klaas Spronk, *Beatific Afterlife in Ancient Israel and in the Ancient Near East* (AOAT 219; Kevelaer: Butzon & Bercker/Neukirchen-Vluyn: Neukirchener Verlag, 1986) 203–4.

57. Hauser, *Seldon's Syrian Deities*, 139; Cook, *Religion of Ancient Palestine*, 32; Hehn, *Biblische und babylonische Gottesidee*, 364, 366; see 2 Kgs 23:5 and Ezek 8:16. See now Eduard Lipiński, "Le culte du soleil chez les Sémites Occidentaux du Iᵉʳ Millénaire a.v. J.-C.," *OLP* 22 (1991) 57–72.

58. Wood, *Religion of Canaan*, 72–74; Paton, "Canaanites," 180; Langdon, *Semitic*, 150.

59. Ibid., 4.

60. Ibid., 150; Wood, *Religion of Canaan*, 72–74; Paton, "Canaanite," 180.

61. Olmo Lete, *Mitos y leyendas*, 73; J. W. McKay, *Religion in Judah under the Assyrians 732–609 BC* (SBT 2d series 26; Naperville, Ill.: Allenson, 1973) 51.

62. Ibid., 103 n. 77.

63. A theory suggested as early as D. Nielsen (*Ras Šamra Mythologie und biblische Theologie* [AKM 21/4; Leipzig: Deutsche Morgenländische Gesellschaft, 1936] 27–37),

Little-Known Deities

A large number of deities are known to have been worshiped in Syria–Palestine, but so little about them is related in the surviving sources that positive statements about their relationships with other gods, or even their personal characteristics, are at best incomplete and at worst nonexistent. Many of these little-known deities must have fit into the category of active deities in the divine world. A sample of the more noteworthy is given here.

By far the most renowned deity of Syria–Palestine prior to the twentieth century was *Astarte*. She was seen as the perfect example of the fertility goddess.[64] From this association her name was connected with all the figurines of female form found throughout the region of Syria–Palestine.[65] Yet, the description of the goddess and the characteristics that have been ascribed to her came from references to Astarte in Egyptian literature and from the stories of Ishtar in Mesopotamia, who was assumed to be an earlier form of the goddess Astarte.[66] While the name Astarte appears in the Ugaritic texts, she is so little represented in the narratives that the traditional view of her as "Ishtar-west" remains, often with the added observation that she was confused with Anat and Asherah.[67] The fact remains that not nearly enough data have been recovered to describe her in any detail.

---

this aspect of the solar deity has consistently been mentioned. See also Gray, *Legacy*, 71, 187–88; Caquot and Sznycer, *Ugaritic Religion*, 14; and del Olmo Lete, *Mitos y leyendas*, 73, who connects travel through the netherworld with the notion of wisdom. The role of Shapshu as ruler of the *rpʾum* in the guise of a chthonic deity has been proposed: Margalit, *Matter of Life and Death*, 85; John F. Healey, "The Sun Deity and the Underworld: Mesopotamia and Ugarit," in *Death in Mesopotamia* (ed. Bendt Alster; Mesopotamia 8; Copenhagen: Akademisk, 1980) 239–40; and Spronk, *Beatific Afterlife*, 162–63. However, note that L'Heureux rejects both the netherworld aspect of Shapshu and her rule of the *rpʾum* (*Rank among the Canaanite Gods*, 190–91).

64. Hauser, *Sheldon's Syrian Deities*, 115; Wood, *Religion of Canaan*, 235; Lewis Bayles Paton, "Ashtart (Ashtoreth), Astarte," in *Encyclopedia of Religion and Ethics* (ed. James Hastings; Edinburgh: T. & T. Clark, 1908–1922) 2.116; Hehn, *Biblische und babylonische Gottesidee*, 109; Andrew Lang, *Myth, Ritual and Religion* (London, 1906; repr., New York: AMS, 1968) 2.271.

65. Ibid., 34.

66. Paton, "Ashtart (Ashtoreth), Astarte," 115–16; Langdon, *Semitic*, 8, 14; Cook, *Religion of Ancient Palestine*, 107–8; Hehn, *Biblische und babylonische Gottesidee*, 106.

67. Cassuto, *Anath*, 58; Gray, *Legacy*, 175; Eliade, *History of Religious Ideas*, 422; R. A. Oden, "Persistence of Canaanite Religion," *BA* 39 (1976) 34–36; D. N. Freedman, "Yahweh of Samaria and His Asherah," *BA* 50 (1987) 246, caption. See now Susan Ackerman, "'And the Women Knead Dough': The Worship of the Queen of Heaven in Sixth-Century Judah," in *Gender and Difference in Ancient Israel* (ed. Peggy L. Day; Minneapolis: Fortress, 1989) 110–14.

The god *Dagon* was long thought of as a fish-god (from the resemblance of the name to דג 'fish').[68] It was also believed that he had come from Mesopotamia.[69] In more recent studies, scholars have noted that the center of Dagon worship appears to have been at Terqa on the Middle Euphrates, and aspects of the cult may have spread both to Mesopotamia and to Syria–Palestine from Terqa. At this site Dagon was the patron deity of the region, with responsibility for prophecy and rule of the area, but little is known about his character aside from his position as patron.[70] In Syria–Palestine even less is known about him, aside from the fact that he was worshiped throughout the region from the middle of the second millennium B.C.E. His name appears at Ugarit in cultic texts, and in narratives he is mentioned only as the father of Baal, though he appears to have had a temple in the city. All biblical references refer to Dagon in the context of Philistine temples.[71] It appears that he was a god of grain, though fertility- and storm-deity titles have been proposed.[72] The references to Dagon in the history of Philo of Byblos do not clear up the ambiguity surrounding him.[73] It is clear that Dagon was an important deity, but currently little is known about him.

Reshep was long known as a demon or god of disease and pestilence.[74] From Egyptian inscriptions it has been determined that Reshep was worshiped there as a god of war.[75] The ritual texts from Ugarit show that Reshep was worshiped there, but the two references to him in the Kirta Legend do not give any information other than that he appeared with the other gods at a banquet and had something to do with a death.[76] Reshep has been associated with the

---

68. Hauser, *Sheldon's Syrian Deities*, 101; Lewis Bayles Paton, "Dagan, Dagon," in *Encyclopedia of Religion and Ethics* (ed. J. Hastings; Edinburgh: T. & T. Clark, 1908–1922) 4.387.

69. Langdon, *Semitic*, 77–78.

70. Jean-Robert Kupper, "Un Governement provincial dans le royaume de Mari," *RA* 41 (1947) 150–52.

71. Del Olmo Lete, *Mitos y leyendas*, 69–70; 1 Sam 5:1–7; Judg 16:23; 1 Chr 10:10; 1 Macc 10:83–84, 11:4.

72. See the survey in Knut Holter, "Was Philistine Dagon a Fish-God? Some New Questions and an Old Answer," *SJOT* 1 (1989) 142–47.

73. Philo of Byblos I.10.16–19; see Albright, *Yahweh and the Gods*, 124; H. W. Attridge and R. A. Oden, *Philo of Byblos, The Phoenician History: Introduction, Critical Text, Translation, Notes* (CBQMS 9; Washington, D.C.: Catholic Biblical Association, 1981) 87 n. 87.

74. Wood, *Religion of Canaan*, 238; Cook, *Religion of Ancient Palestine*, 113.

75. Hehn, *Biblische und babylonische Gottesidee*, 111; Langdon, *Semitic*, 46; see W. J. Fulco, *The Canaanite God Rešep* (AOS Essay 8; New Haven, Conn.: American Oriental Society, 1976) 1–32.

76. *KTU* 1.14.I.18–19; 1.15.II.6. In the parallel lists of bilingual names of gods from Ugarit, Reshep is paired with Nergal.

netherworld, war, and even metalworking, but there is too little material to draw any final conclusions.[77]

Biblical literature describes worship of the moon in the Judean religious tradition.[78] This lunar deity was assumed to have been the Mesopotamian deity Sin.[79] Scholars guessed that the name of the Syro-Palestinian moon-god was *Yareah*, since *yrḥ* was the word for 'moon'.[80] The existence of a god with that name was confirmed in the Ugaritic texts, but aside from his presence at a wedding and a drinking feast, not much information was added to what was already known about him. Some scholars, of course, feel that he was a fertility-god, but there are no data on which to base this interpretation.[81]

Finally, the god of the sea, *Yam*, was not treated as a deity prior to the discovery of the Ugaritic narratives, in which he plays an active, though ambiguous, role.[82] Nor has the existence of an individual god Yam been accepted without question. Margalit has argued that Yam was nothing more than the alter-ego of the god Mot.[83] This position arises from the long tradition of viewing Yam and Mot solely as antagonists of Baal.[84] There is, however, no reason to assume Yam was anything other than an individual deity, marked by brash self-interest and greed; these traits marked not only the Yam of Ugarit's myths, but also the "Sea" found in the Egyptian narrative fragment (which may or may not have any relationship to Yam).[85]

77. See the survey by Diethelm Conrad, "Der Gott Reschef," *ZAW* 83 (1971) 157–183; and the recent theory of Stephanie Dalley, "Near Eastern Patron Deities of Mining and Smelting in the Late Bronze and Early Iron Ages," in *Report of the Department of Antiquities, Cyprus, 1987* (Nicosia: Zavallis, 1987) 61–66.

78. 2 Kgs 23:5; Jer 8:1–2; Josh 10:12.

79. Langdon, *Semitic*, 46; Wood, *Religion of Canaan*, 74.

80. Ibid., 75–76; Paton, "Canaanites," 180.

81. McKay, *Religion in Judah*, 38.

82. The ambiguity comes from the broken state of the tablets on which the myth dealing with Yam was written; on the reconstruction of the myth, see del Olmo Lete, *Mitos y leyendas*, 90–92; and Gibson, *Canaanite Myths and Legends* (2d ed.; Edinburgh: T. & T. Clark, 1977) 2–3. For the relationship of the passage to the "Baal Cycle" as a whole see Gibson, "Theology," 204–6.

83. Margalit, *Matter of Life and Death*, 54 n. 2.

84. Gordon, "Canaanite Mythology," 200–202; del Olmo Lete, *Mitos y leyendas*, 68.

85. Cross, *Canaanite Myth*, 113–14; E. F. Wente, "Astarte and the Insatiable Sea," in *The Literature of Ancient Egypt: An Anthology of Stories, Instructions, and Poetry* (new ed.; ed. W. K. Simpson; New Haven, Conn.: Yale University Press, 1973) 134–35. It might also be noted that Bassile Aggoula, "Divinités phéniciennes dans un passage du *Fihrist* d'Ibn al-Nadim," *JA* 278 (1990) 5–7, believes that Yam survived as a distinct deity to the end of Syro-Phoenician religion, appearing in Arabic sources as *al-bahr*.

THE GODS IN OFFICE

The deities treated above (deities for whom sufficient information is available) had definite spheres of authority. They were responsible not only for aspects of nature or major portions of the cosmos but also for the care and control of particular city-states and nations. The "active" gods of this second level had a large amount of control over the universe and the beings, divine and mortal, who existed on lower levels of the hierarchy.[86] It was the second level that actively controlled the order of the world; the gods who inhabited this level were, in turn, responsible to El and Asherah, on the first level. The active deities were the gods who ran the universe, and in so doing clashed with each other over the use and abuse of power.

The Problem of *mlk*

The titles that were assigned to the deities of the second level reflected their status as rulers.[87] The use of the title *mlk* for more than one god has created a certain amount of confusion within the scholarly community. This title, which has consistently been translated 'king', was assigned in the Ugaritic texts to at least four deities.[88] El remained the *mlk* to whom others owed allegiance, but Baal, Mot, and Athtar were all entitled *mlk* as well.[89] The two most common theories concerning the use of this title for several deities are based on a misunderstanding of *mlk* that effectively limits "kingship" to a single deity. There is one school of thought that argues that El was once the king of the pantheon but that he was replaced by a new king, Baal.[90] On the other hand, several scholars have decided that El was the older, inactive king (an "otiose deity," he is usually called)

---

86. An important responsibility of these deities was to organize others to do the work in their sphere of influence. They appear with their personal messengers, whom they order about, and with authority to command lower-level deities (note Baal and Kothar-wa-Hasis). It has been suggested that the deities had their own armies, or at least their own retinue of serving divinities (Marjo Korpel, *Rift in the Clouds*, 498–99). However, this aspect of the active gods will be dealt with in the following chapters, where the artisan-gods and the messengers are described.

87. A modification of this section was published as: Handy, "A Solution for Many *MLKM*," *UF* 20 (1988) 57–59.

88. Gordon, *UT, s.v.* "*mlk*," 19.1483/p. 433 and "king": *mlk*/p. 533; Aistleitner, *WUS*, *s.v. mlk = König*; del Olmo Lete, *Mitos y leyendas*, 579, *s.v. mlk = rey*.

89. *KTU* 1.3.V.32; 1.6.VI.28; 1.2.III.18, respectively.

90. Kapelrud, *Baal in the Ras Shamra Texts*, 133; Cassuto, *Anath*, 59.

who turned active control over to a younger and more dynamic deity, Baal, also called *mlk*.[91] The conflict between Baal and Yam (and to a lesser extent, Mot) has been understood as a struggle for *the* kingship.[92] More recently there has been a notion, though not articulated, that somehow these various office-holders must have functioned together in one system.[93]

The problem lies not with the word *mlk*, but with the connotations of the term 'king'. The verbal root *mlk* means 'to rule'.[94] It does not mean to be the *sole* ruler. In the ancient Near Eastern political world, it was common for a series of rulers (any of whom might be called *mlk* 'king') to form a hierarchy within an empire. The city-states of Syria–Palestine had long been subject to the rulers of Egypt or to Hittite kings, even before the arrival of the Assyrians, Babylonians, Persians, Greeks, or Romans.[95] The king of a local city-state remained a "king," even though he served under the authority and at the discretion of the king of the empire. The title used for the king of the empire could quite literally have been "king of kings."[96] Therefore, *mlk* was a title used not only on more than one level of the hierarchy of an empire, but even of several people on the same level simultaneously.[97] Baal, Yam, and Mot ruled as kings over particular realms within the universe (storms, the sea, and the Netherworld) alongside each other, much as in Greek mythology Zeus, Poseidon,

---

91. Werner Schmidt, *Königtum Gottes in Ugarit und Israel* (BZAW 80; Berlin: Alfred Töpelmann, 1961) 52–54; Albright, *Yahweh and the Gods*, 120; Gray, *Legacy*, 155; Jirku, *Mythus der Kanaanäer*, 71.

92. Gordon, "Canaanite Mythology," 191; Pfeiffer, *Ras Shamra and the Bible*, 53–54; Ringgren, *Religions of the Ancient Near East*, 146.

93. Caquot and Sznycer, *Ugaritic Religion*, 12; Patrick Miller, "Aspects of the Religion of Ugarit," in *Ancient Israelite Religion* (ed. Miller, Hanson, and McBride; Philadelphia: Fortress, 1987) 60; M. H. Pope, "Status of El at Ugarit," *UF* 19 (1987) 224–28.

94. BDB, KB, *UT*, *WUS*, *s.v.* מלך/*mlk* as verbal root; also del Olmo Lete, *Mitos y leyendas*, 578.

95. For the city-state of Ugarit, see Michael C. Astour, "Ugarit and the Great Powers," in *Ugarit in Retrospect: Fifty Years of Ugarit and Ugaritic* (ed. Gordon D. Young; Winona Lake, Ind.: Eisenbrauns, 1981) 5–26.

96. The title "king of kings" denotes universal rule. It is first attested as a royal title for the Assyrian King Tukulti-Ninurta I (1244–1208 B.C.E.), *šar šarrāni* (Ernst Weidner, *Die Inschriften Tukulti-Ninurtas I. und seiner Nachfolger* [AfO Beiheft 12; Osnabrück: Biblio, 1970] 18, commentary for line 3). The recognition of several simultaneous kings may be seen in the Karatepe inscription (*KAI* 26.A.III.12 [= *TSSI* 3.50]), where the phrase *mlk bmlkm* occurs.

97. All city-state rulers could call themselves the *mlk* of their own territory, even though all of them together would have reigned under the *mlk* of their empire. In turn, under the city-state *mlkm* ruled mayors (*ḫazannū*) of the "daughter cities" of the city-states.

and Pluto ruled simultaneously.[98] At the same time, of course, El ruled as *mlk* over all three.[99]

Other titles used for the gods carry the same meaning as *mlk*. In the Ugaritic narratives alone a variety of words are used to designate rule by the gods. Athtar is called ᶜ*rẓ*, which may be translated 'tyrant', and Yam is called *zbl*, usually translated 'prince', but both titles apparently were intended to mean 'ruler'.[100] Both Baal and Yam were entitled *ṭpṭ*, which has often been translated 'judge' but should be understood as a designation for a ruler, parallel to *mlk* 'king'.[101] It is probable that *mlkt hšmym* 'Queen of heaven' was used in the same fashion as *mlk*, as a title for more than one goddess, though the information on this term is insufficient to reach a final conclusion at this time.[102] What is clear is that these gods were considered rulers (*mlk*, *ṭpṭ*, ᶜ*rẓ*, *zbl*, *mlkt*) in their respective spheres in the same way that human rulers (also entitled *mlk* and *mlkt*) of the city-states were rulers over their dominions. Though they served a king on a higher level, all of these deities could legitimately be called "king." The title *mlk* cannot be used to prove that one deity ruled over another in the divine realm any more than it can be used to prove that one king ruled over another in the case of city-state monarchs, in the human realm.

98. Del Olmo Lete, "La estructura del panteón ugarítico," in *Salvación en la palabra: Targum-Derash-Berith: En memoria del professor Alejandro Diez Macho* (ed. D. León; Madrid: Ediciones Cristiandad, 1986) 271–72, and n. 15; Brubacher, "Canaanite God of Death," 13 n. 1; Walter Burkert, *Greek Religion* (; Cambridge, Mass.: Harvard University Press, 1985) 136.

99. Gibson, "Theology," 208–9.

100. *KTU* 1.6.I.54–55; on ערץ as 'tyrant', see KB, keeping in mind that τύραννος originally referred to a king who placed himself on the throne and had no connotation of evil conduct; see LSJ, *s.v.* τύραννος. *KTU* 1.2.III.16; *zbl* is also used as a title for Baal and Yareah (del Olmo Lete, *Mitos y leyendas*, 544).

101. René Dussaud, "Les Combats sanglants de ᶜAnat et le pouvoir universel de El (V AB et VI AB)," *RHR* 118 (1938) 151 n. 8; Gray, *Legacy*, 87; see *UT, s.v. ṭpṭ*, and KB, *s.v.* שׁפט.

102. M. Delcor, "Le Culte de la 'Reine du ciel' selon Jer 7,18; 44,17–19,25 et ses survivances," in *Von Kanaan bis Kerala: Festschrift für Prof. Mag. Dr. Dr. J. P. M. van der Ploeg O. P. zur Vollendung des siebzigsten Lebensjahres am 4. Juli, 1979: Überreicht von Kollegen, Freunden und Schülern* (ed. W. C. Delsman et al.; AOAT 211; Kevelaer: Butzon & Bercker/Neukirchen-Vluyn: Neukirchener Verlag, 1982) 110, 119; Saul M. Olyan ("Some Observations concerning the Identity of the Queen of Heaven," *UF* 19 [1987] 164–65) writes that several goddesses in the second millennium B.C.E. were given the title. This is probably true for the first millennium as well; however, Olyan argues that the title was restricted in the first millennium B.C.E. to the goddess Astarte while acknowledging that this conclusion is uncertain (p. 174). Ackerman ("And the Women Knead Dough," 110–11) surveys possible goddesses and concludes that the queen of heaven could be Astarte, or maybe a syncretistic deity (pp. 116–17), which is unlikely.

Spheres of Authority

The deities of the second level had their own specific realms to control. These realms were territorial, natural, or even abstract. Moreover, one particular deity may have controlled both territorial and natural or abstract spheres simultaneously. The patron deity of Ugarit appears to have been Baal.[103] But he was responsible for the well-being of a number of other city-states in Syria–Palestine.[104] Other deities also were responsible for individual cities or minor realms.[105] In the capacity of patron deity of a particular earthly realm, a god was responsible for choosing the human ruler (another level of official entitled *mlk*) who served as the regent for the gods among the human residents of the region.[106] The mortal king was viewed as an underling of the patron deity and could be removed by the god if proper care of the territory was not maintained.[107] If the ruler behaved properly, the god was expected to provide for the well-being of the population by means of bountiful crops, basic necessities, and a well-equiped military force:

> And so in my days every goodness was to the Danunians, and
> satiety, and well-being, and I filling the silos (?) of Pahar, and
> I making horse over horse and shield over shield and army
> over army because of Baal and the gods
> (*KAI* 26.A.I.5–8 = *TSSI* 3.46).

The patron deity was expected to fight to protect his or her city-state from invasion from other powers (and, one assumes, other cities' patron deities); thus, in a war that was going poorly, it was understood that a proper petition, through the specific (and extreme) ritual of child sacrifice, would cause the patron deity to remove the army storming the gates of the besieged city:

> My horse to Baal we will consecrate,
> A vow to Baal we will fulfill,

---

103. Patrick Miller, "Aspects of Religion of Ugarit," 60; Dagon may also have served as a patron deity to the city of Ugarit, but little is known of his cult at Ugarit.

104. See, for example, the inscriptions from Zenjirli and Karatepe (*KAI* 214 and 26 = *TSSI* 2.6, 3.46).

105. See *KAI* 181 on Chemosh of Moab; also Judg 11:24. Philo of Byblos assembled a number of stories regarding the assignment of jurisdiction to the various deities: I.10.31–35, 38.

106. *KAI* 214.2–3; 1 Sam 9:16–17; 16:1–13.

107. 1 Sam 15:24–29; 1 Kgs 11:9–13; often found on inscriptions and sarcophagi are warnings that the gods have been requested to remove future rulers from their thrones should they be so rash as to efface these items; *KAI* 26.A.III.12–IV.1 (= *TSSI* 3.50–53); *KAI* 1.2 (= *TSSI* 3.14).

A son to Baal we will consecrate,
A *hitpa*-ritual we will fulfill,
A libation to Baal we will pour out;
The holy of Baal, we will go up,
We will walk the path of the house of Baal,
And Baal harkens to your shouts,
He throws the strong from your gate,
The strong from your city wall (*KTU* 1.119.29–36).[108]

In short, the patron deity of a political unit on earth was responsible for all aspects of the well-being of that state.

In addition to human realms, the level-two deities had realms in the world of nature. For some deities these realms corresponded to physical areas of the universe. Yam was god of the sea, Mot of the underworld. Other deities corresponded to natural phenomena. Shemesh and Shapshu were sun-deities; Yareah was the god of the moon. Other deities' spheres passed into the realm of abstraction. Reshep appears to have been a god of disease, while Anat was a goddess of warfare. In the natural realm, the deity was expected to perform the function that was his or her responsibility, so that the universe continued to operate properly.

Baal may be used as an example. When he ceased to exist by falling prey to Mot, the world was thrown out of kilter. The narrative at this point in the story describes both what Baal would have been doing were he alive and what was happening to the world because he was removed from this position. First, El saw in a dream the world as it should have been, with Baal alive.

The heavens rain oil,
The wadis run with honey,
And I know Victorious Baal is alive,
That "Prince" Baal of the Earth exists (*KTU* 1.6.III.6–9).[109]

Then El requested Anat to describe to Shapshu the state of the earth in the absence of Baal.

The springs of the fields are dry, oh Shapshu!
The springs of the fields of El are dry!

---

108. Note also the sacrifice made by the King of Moab as recounted in 2 Kgs 3:26–27, where it may be assumed that the deity he sacrificed to was Chemosh, though the text does not mention the name of the god; see Gerald L. Mattingly, "Moabite Religion and the Mesha[c] Inscription," in *Studies in the Mesha Inscription and Moab* (ed. Andrew Dearman; Archaeology and Biblical Studies 2; Atlanta: Scholars Press, 1989) 218.

109. The last line is often read as one long title for the god Baal: "Prince, Lord of Earth." See, for example, Ginsberg, "Ugaritic Myths," 140; Gibson, *Canaanite Myths and Legends*, 77; and del Olmo Lete, *Mitos y leyendas*, 228.

Baal stops the springs of the cultivated field.
Where is Victorious Baal;
Where is "Prince" Baal of the Earth? (*KTU* 1.6.IV.12–16).[110]

Baal brought the rains needed for the maintenance of life on earth. When he fulfilled this duty the earth was bountiful, but when he did not provide rain, both the divine and mortal worlds were disrupted. When Danil was reacting to the death of his son Aqhat at the hands of Anat, he prayed for the cosmos to suffer for this act, and he requested that the punishment be carried out by Baal withholding rain.

Baal will fail for seven years,
Eight, the Mounter of the Clouds.
Neither dew nor rain,
Neither flow of the deeps,
Nor benign voice of Baal (*KTU* 1.19.I.42–46).[111]

The various active deities had the power and resources to maintain their realms in an adequate fashion, whether their realms were political or natural. When the deities failed to carry out their proper functions, for one reason or another, the entire system ceased to function properly. The spheres of control most extensively described in the extant narratives are those of Baal, Anat, and Mot, but it is not unreasonable to assume that many other deities were thought to rule in similar fashion.

The active deities attained their positions by appointment from the highest level of bureaucratic authority. Asherah chose them and El installed them in their offices.[112] To hold a position, it was necessary for a god to remain in good standing with El, lest he remove him or her from office, as Mot was reminded by Shapshu:

Hear, prithee, oh God Mot!
How do you battle with Victorious Baal?
How will Bull El, your father, not hear you,
Will not pull up the support of your seat,
Will not overthrow the throne of your reign,
Will not shatter the sceptre of your rule? (*KTU* 1.6.VI.23–29).

The various deities were expected to act under the direction of the highest authority. Major undertakings, such as the construction pro-

---

110. For the meaning of *štk*, see van Zijl, *Baal*, 210–11.
111. For the meaning of *sr^c*, see del Olmo Lete, *Mitos y leyendas*, 633 ('flujo').
112. The activities of these two deities were described in the last chapter. Note the narrative concerned with the attempt to install Athtar on Baal's throne, *KTU* 1.6.I.43–65.

ject for Baal's house, needed to be cleared through El before the deities were allowed to commence activity.[113] El also appears to have been able to call on the various gods to aid him in projects of his own. Thus, Athena/Anat, as the goddess of war, was brought into battle by El in Philo of Byblos's history, just as he used both Anat and Shapshu to deliver his command in the Ugaritic narrative.[114] When the "storm-god" was faced with a delicate situation, it was to El that he turned for advice in the narrative fragment of Elkunirsha.[115] Thus, the deities had a great deal of autonomy, authority, and power. At the same time, they were expected to serve the interests of the organization headed by their superiors.

The Enigmatic Assembly

Like the people in the great centers of ancient Near Eastern empires around them, the people of Syria–Palestine perceived their deities as coming together at various times in an assembly.[116] Unfortunately, the narratives from Syria–Palestine, though relatively numerous, do not present a clear picture of the membership, purpose, or procedure of the divine assembly.[117] Various names are given to the organization of assembled deities in these sources.[118] Yet, the sources do not

113. *KTU* 1.3.IV.47–V.5; 1.4.I.4–8; 1.4.IV.20–V.19.

114. Philo of Byblos I.10.18; *KTU* 1.6.III.22–6.IV.24 (where the tablet breaks off).

115. Elkunirsha myth fragment, Goetze, "Hittite Myths, Epics, and Legends," in *ANET* (3d ed.; ed. J. B. Pritchard; Princeton: Princeton University Press, 1969) 519.

116. For Mesopotamia, see T. Jacobsen (*Treasures of Darkness: A History of Mesopotamian Religion* [New Haven, Conn.: Yale University Press, 1976] 86–91), who has worked a theoretical tradition backward from the mythological tales of the meeting of the gods to an assumed formation of a human assembly in the prehistoric periods of the area; see also his "Primitive Democracy in Ancient Mesopotamia," *JNES* 2 (1943) 159–72 (reprinted in *Toward the Image of Tammuz*, 157–70). This assembly may be seen in action in the *Enuma Elish* III.131–IV.34 and VI.165–VII.144, among other passages. For Egypt see Pierre Montet, *Eternal Egypt* (New York: New American Library, 1964) 219–21, on the assembled deities who greeted the dead; and Rosalie David, *A Guide to Religious Ritual at Abydos* (Warminster: Aris & Phillips, 1981) 92, on the coronation of the king and the assembled deities. The Ennead (generally numbered as nine gods) acted as a ruling council in the story of "Horus and Seth" (Lichtheim, *Ancient Egyptian Literature*, 2.214–23). For the assembled deities in the Hittite tradition, see O. R. Gurney, *The Hittites* (Harmondsworth: Penguin, 1954) 181, 184–87.

117. E. T. Mullen (*The Divine Council in Canaanite and Early Hebrew Literature* [HSM 24; Chico, Cal.: Scholars Press, 1980] 111–284) reviews the passages that deal with the gods in assembly.

118. Ugaritic texts supply *phr mᶜd* (*KTU* 1.2.I.20, 31) and *ᶜdt ilm* (*KTU* 1.15.II.7, 11); biblical terms include עדת־אל (Ps 82:1), קהל־קדשים or קהל־רב (ps 89:6, 22:26), and סוד קדשים (Ps 89:8); the assembly mentioned in the Deir ᶜAllā fragments is called the *mwᶜd* (J. Hoftijzer and G. van der Kooij, eds., *Aramaic Texts from Deir ᶜAlla* [DMOA 19; Leiden:

tell whether the mere congregation of divine beings was presumed to constitute a formal deliberative assembly of deities, or whether there was a difference between a banquet of riotous gods and a meeting of deities for deliberation.[119] Some suppositions regarding the divine assembly as it is found in the surviving narratives may be posited; however, these observations are tenuous, pending a discovery of further source materials.

The members of the assembly included at least the gods of the second level of deities, the active gods. In the Ugaritic passages portraying the assembly of the gods, aside from El, the gods who were named as being in attendance at such an assembly included Baal, Astarte, (possibly) Anat, and Kothar-wa-Hasis. Unfortunately, it is not possible to determine whether these divinities were mentioned because they belonged to the assembly of gods or because they were characters needed for the narrative being related. Was the assembly made up of the gods who controlled portions of the universe, natural phenomena, and abstract principles (that is, the active gods), or did it extend to the level of the artisan deities? Did Kothar-wa-Hasis's presence at the assembly make him a member or merely an attendant for some other god who was a member? Mullen considers one list of divine names to be *the* list of gods in the divine assembly, but it is far from clear whether the author intended to list the gods of the assembly. Indeed, the theory seems quite impossible, since the last entry on the list reads: "[And the ass]embly of ʾEl/the gods (and) its retinue."[120] At the very least the list includes two groups of gods, one of which formed the "assembly of the gods" and another which formed the "retinue" of those deities in the assembly. So, the question is, were the deities named in the list (a very small group) all assembly-members, or did some of them fall into the category of "retinue"? The reconstructed name of Kothar-wa-Hasis appears on the short list, but was he an assembly member or part of the retinue? The fragment is not very helpful. It may be said with certainty that the assembly did not consist of all known deities; the central ruling councils of gods in neighboring pantheons restricted the number of gods in their divine assemblies.[121] The number of deities known

---

Brill, 1976] 173, no. I.8; this line equals J. Hackett, *Balaam Text from Deir ʿAllā* [HSM 31; Chico, Cal.: 1980] 25, no. I.6).

119. Compare *KTU* 1.114 and 1.2.I.19–47, and both with 1.16.V.10–32 (broken context).

120. Mullen, *Divine Council*, 179.

121. The Egyptian Ennead, which appears with various numbers of gods constituting it, was a very small fraction of the known Egyptian pantheon (David, *Guide*, 170); and the seven divine final arbitrators of the Mesopotamian assembly were a far cry from the huge Mesopotamian pantheon (Jacobsen, *Treasures of Darkness*, 86).

from Ugarit would have swelled a council meeting to an unwieldy size if the gods were all members.[122] The basis of and limits on membership in the divine council remain elusive.

There is slightly more information concerning the purpose of the divine assembly. From the Ugaritic narratives it can be seen that one aspect of the assembled deities was constant: they feasted.[123] This is not to argue that the assembly was not important as a deliberative council, but the gods apparently gathered to do whatever they needed to do over a fine repast. The fact that Yam sent his messengers before the assembled gods to request the submission of Baal demonstrates the importance of the acquiescence of El and the assembled gods for the activities of Yam. It was the great feast thrown by Baal on the completion of his temple expansion that legitimated the new, improved cult site. Both Kirta and Danil gave feasts so that the gods would come as a group to consider the rulers' searches for their respective proper heirs.[124] It may be inferred, though it has not been demonstrated, that the assembly of the gods in Syria–Palestine met to work out the actual rule of the universe among the various deities.

The assembly also served as a source of information for the human realm. From the gathered deities in their assembly, information from the divine realm could be given to human messengers (or "prophets") to be related to the mortal world.[125] Humans could be made privy to the divine assembly either by being allowed to see it in action, as in the case of Micaiah, or by means of a dream instigated by the gods, as in the case of Balaam.[126] In both of these cases the gods planned actions to be taken with regard to the earth and the humans dwelling on it and then communicated with the human world by means of the assembly and a human messenger. Beyond serving as a line of communication downward toward mortals, the divine assembly also joined with the human congregation in worshiping the

---

122. Johannes C. de Moor gives some idea of what the size of the pantheon must have been. In addition, there are Hurrian gods attested for Ugarit, which raises the question as to their status: did they have a part in the assembly of deities or were they only "visiting dignitaries"? ("The Semitic Pantheon of Ugarit," *UF* 2 [1970] 187–228).

123. Loewenstamm ("Trinkburleske," 71) noted this regular feature. The tendency toward drinking assemblies and dining councils appears to have been well established in the ancient Near Eastern religious traditions: Jacobsen, *Treasures of Darkness*, 86; Lichtheim, *Ancient Egyptian Literature*, 2.217; and Gurney, *Hittites*, 184.

124. *KTU* 1.15.III.12–16; 1.17.I.16–23. That the gods in general were interested in finding proper royal heirs was noticed early in Ugaritic studies: Julian Obermann, *How Daniel Was Blessed with a Son: An Incubation Scene in Ugaritic* (JAOSSup 6; Baltimore: American Oriental Society, 1946).

125. H. Wheeler Robinson, "Council of Yahweh," *JTS* 45 (1944) 151–57; Mullen, *Divine Council*, 209–26.

126. 1 Kgs 22:19; Deir ʿAllā I.1.

head of the gods, who also was the head of the assembly, El.[127] Together with the human devotees, these deities sang the praise of their
ultimate ruler.[128] This suggests that the assembly was both a governing body and a religious community.

The clearest narrative about the procedure of the divine assembly
is the story of Micaiah's audience in heaven. Yahweh (= El) wished to
destroy the king of Israel during a battle, so the assembly of the
"host of heaven" was called to work out a plan toward this end.

> And he said, "Therefore, hear the word of Yahweh; I saw
> Yahweh enthroned upon his throne and all the host of heaven
> standing beside him on his right and on his left. And Yahweh
> said, 'Who will seduce Ahab that he will go up and fall at
> Ramoth Gilead?' And this one said this and that one said that.
> And the spirit came out and stood before Yahweh and said, 'I
> will seduce him.' And Yahweh said, 'How?' And he said, 'I
> will go out and I will be a lying spirit in the mouth of all his
> prophets.' And he said, 'You will seduce and you will succeed;
> go and do so!' And now, behold Yahweh set a lying spirit in
> the mouth of all these prophets of yours; Yahweh has spoken
> evil against you. (1 Kgs 22:19–23).[129]

Though the Bible calls the assembled beings צבא השמים, it is widely
understood that these were the gods who made up the heavenly
court in Judah and Israel.[130] The host was called together by Yahweh
(= El) in this narrative, though El was not the only god who could call
together the assembly; in fact, even the humans Kirta and Danil are
portrayed in the Ugaritic legends as bringing the divine assembly to-

---

127. Zeph 2:11; Ps 89:6–9, 97:7, 138:1–2, 148:1–4; it is most likely true that the gods
would have joined in singing the praises of any one of their own members should it
have been the feast day of the specific deity.

128. Luis Alonso Schökel, *Treinta salmos: Poesía y oración* (2d ed.; Madrid: Ediciones
Cristiandad, 1986) 432. The denizens of heaven and the congregations of earth form a
single congregation. This vision of ritual remains a part of modern liturgical belief:
Timothy Ware, *The Orthodox Church* (New York: Penguin, 1964) 270.

129. The exact date of the composition of the passage is unknown. It appears in a
context that in its current form cannot be dated before the end of the Babylonian
Exile and may reflect preexilic, exilic, or even postexilic theological speculation about
the divine assembly in Judah (or Israel, if the tale is taken from Northern Kingdom
traditions).

130. John Gray, *I & II Kings: A Commentary* (2nd rev. ed.; OTL; Philadelphia: West-
minster, 1970) 452; Edwin C. Kingsbury, "The Prophets and the Council of Yahweh,"
JBL 83 (1964) 283; and Tryggve N. D. Mettinger, "YHWH SABAOTH: The Heavenly
King on the Cherubim Throne," in *Studies in the Period of David and Solomon and Other
Essays* (ed. Tomoo Ishida; Winona Lake, Ind.: Eisenbrauns, 1982) 109–11.

gether.[131] The assembly is presented in the Micaiah passage as made up of members who, in the course of dealing with the problem before them, disagreed with each other. The highest authority sought the members' advice and accepted it; he did not command an action of his own devising that he expected them to carry out without dissent. It is clear, however, that the responsibility for carrying out the task was not Yahweh's, but belonged to the spirit (רוח) who thought up the ruse. The authority to perform the action was placed in the mouth of Yahweh, who pronounced the success of the mission before it was undertaken, and it was Yahweh who was credited with the successful ruse, though it was devised and carried out by another. The assembly in this story was called to confer on a specific matter related to the governance of the world.

The presentation of the divine assembly at the beginning of Job portrays the assembly as a group that met regularly on a set day to report to the highest authority. In this story the deities were expected to report to God (= אלהים) on the appointed day.[132]

> And the day came when the sons of God came to present themselves before Yahweh, and the Adversary also came among them. And Yahweh said to the Adversary, "From where have you come?"
>
> And the Adversary answered Yahweh and said, "From roving about the earth and walking around on it!"
>
> And Yahweh said to the Adversary, "Have you paid attention to my servant Job, because there is none like him on earth, a good and upright man, fearing God and turning from evil?"
>
> And the Adversary answered Yahweh and said, "Is it without cause Job fears God? Have you not fenced around him and around his house and around all which is his? You have blessed what his hand has done and his holdings have increased in the land. But should you now stretch out your hand and touch all which he has then certainly he will bless[133] you to your face."

---

131. See n. 115 above; Baal invited the gods to his house for food and drink (*KTU* 1.4.VI.44–46).

132. Marvin H. Pope, *Job: Introduction, Translation and Notes* (3d ed.; AB 15; Garden City, N.Y.: Doubleday, 1973) 9; Norman C. Habel, *The Book of Job: A Commentary* (OTL; Philadelphia: Westminster, 1985) 88–89.

133. 'Bless' should certainly be taken as a euphemism for 'curse' in this case (Pope, *Job*, 8). On the 'sons of God' (בני האלהים) as the gods of the divine assembly, see Jesús-Luis Cunchillos Ylarri, "Los bᵉne haʾelohîm en Gen. 6,1–4," *EstBib* 28 (1969) 31.

And Yahweh said to the Adversary, "Behold, everything
which is his is in your hand, only to himself do not stretch out
your hand!
    And the Adversary went out from before Yahweh
(Job 1:6–12).

In this passage the only member of the divine assembly that is given
a personality of any kind has no name, only a title (הַשָּׂטָן). This appears to demonstrate that the gods filled offices, had distinct responsibilities, and could be referred to solely by office title, which the
authors expected the audience to understand.[134] Yahweh, however,
was in control of the gods; it was from Yahweh that the Adversary
received authority to harass Job. But specific limitations were placed
on the god by Yahweh, and the Adversary did not exceed those limits. In this passage the individual deity was authorized by the highest authority to carry out a particular duty and then was turned
loose to do the commissioned work the best he could on his own.[135]

The assembly of the gods seems to have been made up of deities
who had a certain amount of autonomy, authorized by the presiding
deity. The assembly met both at set intervals and at times called by
El, various deities, or even humans for specific events. The business
of the assembly apparently included governance of both the heavenly and earthly realms, as well as religious and festive occasions.[136]

MALFUNCTIONING

If a bureaucracy were characterized by perfectly smooth relationships among its office holders, efficiency and decorum would be its
chief characteristics (see pp. 10–11). Unfortunately, this hardly ever

---

134. Robert Gordis (*The Book of God and Man: A Study of Job* [Chicago: University of
Chicago Press, 1965] 70) puts an even more positive interpretation on הַשָּׂטָן by using
the title "the prosecuting attorney"; however, the fact that this is a title rather than a
proper name is clear; see also Pope, *Job* (9–11).

135. The pantheon structure reflected in the preface to Job has been discussed in
Lowell K. Handy, "The Authorization of Divine Power and the Guilt of God in the
Book of Job: Useful Ugaritic Parallels," *JSOT* 60 (1993) 116–18.

136. It is highly unlikely that the primary function of the assembly was thought of
as military. Not only does the assembly of gods not appear to be portrayed as a military entity, but the basis for the military theory is suspect. Patrick Miller ("El the Warrior," *HTR* 60 [1967] 416), without adequate reason, equated the σύμμαχοι of Philo of
Byblos's history (I.10.23) with the divine assembly and concluded that the work of the
council of the gods in Syria–Palestine was military in nature. Unfortunately, Mullen
(*Divine Council*, 184) accepted this equation and proceeded to define the assembly
solely in military terms (pp. 185–212). There is no evidence from the narratives from
Syria–Palestine for understanding the divine council as an army unit.

is the case. The clash of individuals over personality, favors, status, and greed for possessions and power brings friction to an organization, friction to the point of open hostility. The active gods in the Syro-Palestinian pantheon comprised an organization of individual deities who should have acted together but often were at odds with each other. They exemplified both Brech's "difficult personality" and the "exempt" individuals, defined by Kanter (see nn. 1–8 above) as those whose behavior is tolerated because they are deemed too important to alienate.[137] The deities of this second level had great power and were self-interested, often greedy for more power, yet deemed so necessary for the proper functioning of the universe that they could indulge in improper behavior with a fair amount of impunity. Their malfunctioning set up the rather wild vision of the divine world that appears in the mythology of Syria–Palestine.

The most blatant example of abusive behavior accepted by the highest authority without punishment was displayed by the goddess Anat. Her character, as pictured by the Syro-Palestinians in the extant literature, was violent, vindictive, vengeful, self-absorbed, and insolent; in short, Anat was a "spoiled" goddess. In her personality two lines of human hierarchical malfunctioning converged to provide a very colorful if decidedly unsettling vision of a deity. On the one hand, Anat was a necessary divinity. She controlled warfare that was thoroughly without mercy, a sort of frenzied annihilation.[138] It was necessary that such a goddess be on the side of El and Asherah, should the situation demand it.[139] She was, therefore, indispensable as a patron goddess of all-out war. This clearly marked her as "exempt" in terms of bureaucratic treatment. At the same time, Anat was presented as the daughter of El, whom he knew very well but with whom he was extremely lax. This relationship is clearly presented in the exchange between the two deities when she came to El seeking the enlargement of Baal's house.

And Maiden Anat responded:
"Inside of your house, Oh El,

---

137. Brech, *Organisation*, 67; Kanter, *Men and Women*, 37.

138. The two most ferocious scenes in the extant Ugaritic literature are both concerned with the behavior of Anat. In one she is presented reveling in the corpses of slaughtered soldiers, treading on their corpses as on grapes for wine and adorning herself with the severed pieces of their anatomy (*KTU* 1.3.II.5–35). In the other passage she slew the god Mot four times over in a most violent manner (*KTU* 1.6.II.30–37). See Samuel E. Loewenstamm, "The Ugaritic Fertility Myth: The Result of a Mistranslation," *IEJ* 12 (1962) 87.

139. See Philo of Byblos I.10.18, though it is necessary to remember that the text may have been influenced by Greek sources.

Inside of your house do not rejoice,
Do not rejoice in the height of your palace.
Will I not seize them in my right hand?
[   ] in my great long arm?
I [   ] your pate;
I will cause your gray hair to fall with blood,
Gray hair of your beard with flowing gore!"
El answered in the seven inner-chambers,
In the eight closed anterooms:
"I know you, daughter, that you are inflexible,
That there is not among goddesses your contempt!
What do you want, Maiden Anat?"
And Maiden Anat answered:
"Your word, El, is wise;
Your wisdom throughout eternity;
Your word is fortunate life. . . . " (*KTU* 1.3.V.19–31).[140]

Anat clearly was not awed by El's status. She was offensive and threatened violence against El if he did not comply with her desires. In this particular case it is also clear that El was not frightened or cowed by his daughter.[141] Anat did not get what she wanted and had to resort to using the access afforded by Asherah, the Queen Mother, to pressure El into conceding to Baal's house construction. Anat in this single exchange tried both threat and flattery, but El knew her and was not disposed to make his decision based on either her sweet or sour behavior. Anat recognized the authority El held and abided by his decision. On the other hand, El was capable of allowing her to behave in a reprehensible manner when she wanted the bow of Aqhat so much that she wished to kill him to obtain it. El responded to the stereotyped threat with this speech:

I know you, daughter, that you are inflexible;
And there is not among goddesses your contempt!
Leave, daughter!
Arbitrary is your heart;
You take what is in your liver;

---

140. The word *maiden* is used for *btlt* in place of the more commonly used *virgin* (del Olmo Lete, *Mitos y leyendas*, 531; Gibson, *Canaanite Myths and Legends*, 144; Walls, "The Goddess Anat," 142–43; etc.), because the English word *virgin* connotes more restricted behavior than one finds in the goddess Anat. See Jan Bergman, Helmer Ringgren, and M. Tsevat, "*Betûlah*" (in *TDOT* 2.338–43). The passage is severely broken just at the point of Anat's threat, which makes the reconstruction of the exact speech impossible.

141. As correctly noted by Mullen, *Divine Council*, 65, and Walls, "The Goddess Anat," 138.

You set up what is in your breast;
Whoever hinders you will indeed be struck down
  (*KTU* 1.18.I.16–18).[142]

By allowing Anat whatever she wanted, in spite of the fact that she obviously needed to have his permission to attain it, El allowed basic rules of morality to be suspended in order to fulfill her whims.

Her status, being exempt from moral rectitude, was made possible by malfunctioning at the highest level of authority. Anat behaved in a manner consistent with that of a spoiled child, a motif that appears in other literature from the ancient Near East.[143] Particularly relevant is the portrait of Ishtar in the *Gilgamesh Epic*, where, in her desire for revenge upon Gilgamesh, Ishtar sought permission to take violent action against him.[144] Ishtar, like Anat, received consent from her father to behave in a self-centered manner inconsistent with moral behavior. In the biblical narratives, this motif appears in the stories of King David's sons, who were so spoiled that rape, revolt, and even murder were all accepted by him.[145] The relationship between El and Anat was pictured through a literary motif that portrayed spoiled offspring of rulers (human and divine) who commit atrocities with the tacit, even explicit, consent of their parents. This is a form of nepotism at its worst.

While the goddess Anat exemplifies problems between the highest level and the next level of active deities evidenced by preferential treatment on one side and insolence toward authority on the other, the battles of Baal represented malfunctioning *within* the level of the active deities. Though the gods Yam, Mot, and Baal were given realms to rule simultaneously, as kings of the sea, netherworld, and sky/earth, they all were desirous of adding the territory of their fellow

---

142. The use of the word 'your' with 'heart' is conjectural, since the tablet is broken at this point. 'What is in your *liver*' is a literal translation of a phrase meaning 'whatever you desire'. The word *ḥnp* has been translated 'arbitrary', since the verbal root in Hebrew has connotations of ruthlessness, flattery, and pollution, which may be conveyed by the English word 'arbitrary'.

143. Meindert Dijkstra, "Some Reflections on the Legend of Aqhat," *UF* 11 (1979) 201.

144. The scene occurs in tablet VI of the epic. The threat that Ishtar made to Anu does not appear in the extant *Gilgamesh Epic* at all, since there is a sizeable break in the text at this point in the narrative. The threat that now appears in modern renditions of the tale has been reconstructed on the assumption that Ishtar's speech here would have been the same as the one she made in *Descent of Ishtar into the Netherworld* (R. Frankena, "Nouveaux fragments de la sixième tablette de l'épopée de Gilgameš," in *Gilgameš et sa légende* [ed. Paul Garelli; RAI 7; Paris: Klincksieck, 1960] 118), which is at best a wild guess. A different threat was made by the goddess in the Sumerian version (oral communication from Thorkild Jacobsen to Jeffrey H. Tigay, author of *The Evolution of the Gilgamesh Epic* [Philadelphia: University of Pennsylvania Press, 1982] 25 n. 9).

145. 2 Sam 13:1–22, 15:1–19:8, and 13:27–39.

rulers to their own holdings. Thus, they were examples of the problem of individual character flaws in office-holders. Yam was pictured in the Ugaritic texts as insolent toward the other gods and El, and his desire for attaining what belonged to others seems to have consume his existence, a character trait found as well in the god Sea in the Egyptian tale. Mot was portrayed as voracious and insatiable. Baal, on the other hand, was not drawn as a deity who grasped as much of the cosmos as he could, but, having been made ruler of the earth by El, was clearly shown to be a strong, virile dolt. Given this set of characters to work with, it is not surprising that the authors presented Anat as the deity who kept Baal's rule safe from other gods. Baal may have been a strong warrior, but Anat had the brains, knowledge, and brashness to use her strength, whereas Baal blundered rashly. Thus the rulers of the universe were certain to clash with each other, not only over territorial rights, but also simply out of differences in their personalities.

The discord among the active deities was reflected in their behavior as patron deities of their respective city-states and nations. The gods could carry their battles into the human realm by ordering their subordinates, the mortal rulers, to carry on wars for them against other gods' human regents. As an example, a portion of the Mesha inscription illustrates the connection between the rivalry of the gods and the war between kings.

> And Chemosh said to me, "Go! Seize Nebo from Israel!" And I went in the night and I fought against it from sunrise until noon, and seizing it, then I destroyed it, 7000 men and boys, women and girls, and female booty, because I had declared a Holy War for Ashtar-Chemosh. And I took away from there the [rams ?] of Yahweh and I dragged them before Chemosh. But the King of Israel had built Jahaz and he stayed there while fighting me. Yet, Chemosh drove him out from before me. I took from Moab 200 men, all the best, and I besieged Jahaz and I seized it to add it on to Dibon
> (*KAI* 181.14–21).[146]

---

146. On the translation 'from' in 'Seize Nebo *from* Israel', see Francis I. Andersen, "Moabite Syntax," *Or* 35 (1966) 105. See also *KAI* 2.176. But note E. Lipiński, "Etymological and Exegetical Notes on the Meša^c Inscription," *Or* 40 (1971) 334. On 'female booty', see Judg 5:30 and Stanislav Segert, "Die Sprache der moabitischen Königs Inschrift," *ArOr* 29 (1961) 244. Women were regularly taken as booty in war. On the item taken to Chemosh from before Yahweh, here understood as 'rams', see Lipiński, "Etymological and Exegetical Notes," 335. For *rsh* as the 'best' men, see Segert, "Moabitischen Königs Inschrift," 267: *Häuptling*.

In this inscription the war between Mesha and the King of Israel was portrayed as a battle between Chemosh and Yahweh. It is not clear, due to a lacuna in the text, what was to be taken from before Yahweh and brought before Chemosh, but whatever it was, it represented the rivalry between the two gods and specifically the supremacy of one over the other.[147] This was not just a territorial skirmish on the part of human beings; in the theology of the Syro-Palestinian world Chemosh and Yahweh were engaged in a determined attempt to add the other god's territory to his own possessions. To add insult to injury, the devotees of Chemosh took something away from Yahweh and presented it to their god. Warfare on earth as a plane of warfare among the gods may be seen in several sources, so this aspect of the malfunctioning of patron deities is well attested.[148]

A certain amount of antagonism could also arise between one deity and the rest of the divine realm as a unit. Yam was defiant against the entire assembly of the gods in his pursuit of Baal for his slave.[149] In this admittedly broken narrative, Yam seems to have threatened the pantheon due to his desire to own Baal. Baal, on the other hand, appears to have been antagonistic toward the other gods as a group.[150] This enmity between the gods in general and the god Baal is alluded to on a couple of occasions in the Ugaritic narratives, but it is never explained.

When Anat announced the death of Baal to El, she declared:

Now Asherah and her children will rejoice!
The goddess and the gang of her relatives,
For dead is Victorious Baal!
For destroyed is "Prince" Baal of the Earth!
    (*KTU* 1.6.I.39–42).

While Asherah was mentioned immediately after this statement, there was no sign of joy on her part, only El's command to her to find

147. Edward Lipiński suggests the item would have been a sacrifice removed from one god and turned over to another ("North Semitic Texts from the First Millennium BC," in *Near Eastern Religious Texts Relating to the Old Testament* [ed. Walter Beyerlin; OTL; Philadelphia: Westminster, 1978] 239 n. i). He had already guessed that the item should be a ram (see previous note).

148. *KAI* 26.A.I.1–4; *KTU* 1.14.II.32–15.I.8; Josh 5:13–6:5.

149. *KTU* 1.2.I.

150. D. Nielsen (*Ras Šamra Mythologie und biblische Theologie* [AKM 21/4; Leipzig: Deutsche morgenländische Gesellschaft, 1936] 108) had already noticed the apparent split, which he explained: "Baᶜal ist ein Fremder und kein ᶜAširat-Sohn." He interpreted the difference in the gods as due to different points of origin for two groups of deities in the pantheon, one coming from North-Semitic areas and one from Old Arabian cultures. Pope (*El in the Ugaritic Texts* [VTSup 2; Leiden: Brill, 1955] 92–94) saw this conflict in terms of a battle between Baal and the forces of El.

a replacement to fill the vacant position (which she did). This suggests that the statement made by Anat was composed to fit her character as the surly war goddess, for what she declared would be the response of the gods to the death of Baal was nothing less than that they would sing a victory song, reciting the fact that he was dead.[151] The gods did not rejoice, Asherah was not pictured as being glad, and El was clearly saddened. Yet, it was reasonable for Anat, the brash and violent warrior, to sing of a death in a victory song.

While it cannot be shown that Asherah and the gods had a particular grudge against Baal, it is clearer that Baal could display extreme antipathy toward the gods.

> Baal seized the children of Asherah,
> The big ones he struck with a club,
> The small ones he struck with a mace,
> The insignificant ones he dragged to the earth
>   (*KTU* 1.6.V.1–4).[152]

Unfortunately, this passage comes immediately after a long break in the text and is followed by Baal sitting down on his throne. Why Baal was striking the gods is unclear; it may have had something to do with this particular narrative and may not be an example of general antipathy at all. Therefore, the precise nature of the supposed continual enmity between Baal and the rest of the pantheon of Syria–Palestine is unknown and perhaps nonexistent.

Sometimes, refusal to obey the gods or El as highest authority was clearly a matter of self-interest. When Yam demanded Baal for his slave by sending messengers to the assembled deities, Baal sought something from the assembled gods (perhaps support, perhaps protection) but did not receive it. Even so, he waited for the decree of El before acting, but unfortunately for him, El's response to Yam was not in Baal's favor:

> Your slave (is) Baal, oh Yam!
> Your slave (is) Baal, River!

151. On victory songs and their use of joyful language over the death of enemies, see Eissfeldt, *Old Testament*, 99–101. On the possibility of Anat as a singer of victory chants, see Charles Virolleaud, "Un Nouveaux chant de poème d'Alein-Baal," *Syria* 13 (1932) 124.

152. The two weapons (*ktp* and *ṣmd*) cannot be identified with certainty, though they clearly were " 'armas' especiales empeadas en los combates divinos y de las que tenemos un ejemplo en KTU 1.2 IV 11 ss" (Gregorio del Olmo Lete, *Interpretación de la mitología cananea: Estudios de semántica ugarítica* [FCB 2; Valencia: San Jerónimo, 1984] 79). No consensus has been reached on the meaning (or even the word division) of *dk ym* (or: *d kym*, ibid., 80; or: *dkym*, de Moor, *Myth of Baʿlu*, 227); although it is quite uncertain, de Moor's translation has been used here because it denotes size. The Hebrew root צער corresponds to Ugaritic *ṣġr*.

The Son of Dagon (is) your prisoner!
He will carry your tribute like the gods;
He will carry like a god your gifts!
    (*KTU* 1.2.I.36–38).[153]

Whatever was going on in the scene, which is not really very clear, was not to Baal's advantage.[154] It was only at this point in the narrative (when it became clear that obeying authority and peers meant losing his position) that Baal took action on his own. Though the activity was violent and contrary to the decree just made by El, it is also clear that it was not taken against El or the assembled deities but only against Yam, the object of immediate concern for Baal. Self-preservation appears to have been a strong impulse among deities, as it is among humans, and it could lead to the breaking of rules within a system.

Just as the gods were capable of misconduct, so also there were ways to reprimand them and punish their misbehavior. No doubt the strongest sentence that could be inflicted on a deity for improper conduct was death.[155] A lesser sentence was removal of a god from his or her allotted position in the divine hierarchy, and related to this was the threat of such removal.[156] Gods might attack each other over incidents of real or perceived moral turpitude, or they might be called on to punish another offending deity.[157] Thus the proper functioning of the organization as whole could be enforced from above (highest authority) or by peers on the level of the active gods and might even be requested by persons on lower levels of the organization, such as humans. The need for corrective behavior reflects standard bureaucratic malfunctioning and portrays the contemporary theological understanding of the pantheon.

153. In line 38 the extant *w* has been read as a *k*, parallel to the line above it (in fact, the tablet may have a *k* here due to the confusion often arising from the similar writing of these two letters; see emendation suggested in *KTU* notes). The phrase *bn qdš*, which follows in the same line, may be read in several ways ('child of the Holy One', 'Holy Son/Child', 'one of the Holy', etc.), but it means 'god'.

154. Van Zijl (*Baal*, 324) has noted that there is some ambiguity as to what the battle between Baal and Yam was supposed to be about. Without knowing the context for the dispute, the motivation for the actions of Baal remains uncertain.

155. Note that Anat slew Mot for killing Baal (*KTU* 1.6.II.30–37); Yahweh condemned the gods to death (Ps 82:7, both Yahweh and the gods being called אלהים); and El slew Uranos for abusing his wife (El's mother) in Philo of Byblos I.10.29.

156. Incidents involving Baal, Mot, Yam, and Athtar were discussed above and in the last chapter.

157. Baal attacked Yam (*KTU* 1.2.IV.15–27); Anat slew Mot (*KTU* 1.6.II.30–37); and Baal was called on to help Danil by avenging the death of his son Aqhat at the hands of Anat (*KTU* 1.19.I.38–48).

Chapter 5

Artisan Deities

There was a clearly discernible, though not well attested, level of deities in the pantheon of Syria–Palestine below the major active gods and above the messengers.[1] There is only one well-presented example of a deity from this divine level in the narratives from Syria–Palestine, but other possible representatives appear in lists of gods from Philo of Byblos's history. These deities had specialized areas of competence, which means that they were called on by the gods of the higher levels of the hierarchy to aid them in carrying out their own endeavors. The knowledge of the artisan gods was restricted to their own fields, but their knowledge in those fields far surpassed that of the gods for whom they worked. The artisan gods were used by the higher-level deities to do the actual work of carrying out the rule of the universe. Like human specialists, the artisan gods enjoyed a certain amount of forbearance at the hands of the higher-level deities, who recognized and depended on their superior capabilities.

THE OFFICE

The bureaucratic level of the artisan gods appears to correspond to the lowest level of management or the highest level of labor. On these levels in corporate bureaucracies, individual authority is not clearly defined. Lines are blurred between those who give orders with full authority and those who accept orders without authority.

---

1. Mark S. Smith ("Kothar wa-Hasis, the Ugaritic Craftsman God" [Ph.D. diss., Yale University, 1985] 22–26, 463) sets Kothar-wa-Hasis on a level between Baal and the messengers; see also his "Divine Travel as a Token of Divine Rank," *UF* 16 (1984) 359.

Individuals at this level might be called specialists or "functional managers," who

> have a responsibility towards higher management for the effective performance of the service concerned, but at the same time they have no immediate or direct authority over the people in the organisation who carry out the tasks of the enterprise and use, or are involved in, this service in so doing. Any specialist may have subordinates of his own, within his own field and within his own immediate jurisdiction: his relations with these are of the . . . "direct" type. . . . His own relations with his own immediate superior are of the same type. But his relations with all other executives or personnel in the organisation are of the "indirect" category. He is the purveyor of a certain service and his "advice" carries the full sanction of higher management and so must be accepted by all other managers whom it concerns.[2]

Individuals on this level of an organization work at the request of, or in the service of, higher levels of management, and in this regard are seen as working for the individuals on the higher levels. On the other hand, those who hold offices in the specialized fields are recognized as unique to the organization. They have a status somewhat outside a strict hierarchical structure because they may be called in to aid managerial personnel in more than one line of authority within the organization. They themselves do not belong to one particular line of authority in the organization, nor are they answerable solely to one boss. Rather, their unique capacities may be used by any of the managers. When they serve under the authority of individuals in one line of the bureaucratic hierarchy, they receive authority for one particular task from the managerial staff of that line of the hierarchy. Thus, while their competence is recognized, their authority within the structure of the hierarchy comes not from their own office but from those for whom they work.

The expertise of the individuals holding office at this level is considered above reproach. While managers are expected to control an entire section of the organization's hierarchy, the specialist concentrates on one particular aspect of work to be mastered. For the managerial personnel to call in the specialist is to acknowledge that the specialist has a better grasp of the immediate situation and the methods for dealing with it. At the same time, the manager does not relinquish control of the hierarchy to the specialist but merely adds the specialist to the sphere of authority under his or her line of control for the time during which the project lasts. The specialist is

2. Edward F. L. Brech, *Organisation: The Framework of Management* (London: Longmans, Green, 1957) 15. Such people have what is known as "specialist responsibility" (p. 13).

given control of the particular sphere of activity in which special competence is needed by the organization. The authority for this control comes at the discretion of those who usually have control of that section of the organization.

THE GODS

The level of the artisan gods is defined clearly only by the deity Kothar-wa-Hasis, who appeared as a major character in two situations described in the Ugaritic mythological narratives. The material from Philo of Byblos also contains a minimum amount of information about other deities who seem to have belonged to this level of the divine beings. They did not make the most important decisions in the universe but only helped the higher levels of the divine realm carry out their programs. For this reason they did not appear in the narratives as major characters and did not have large parts to play in the myths. This leaves modern scholars with very little data on which to base an accurate reconstruction of this bureaucratic level. Aside from the well-attested Kothar-wa-Hasis, there are a few other divinities who possibly belong to this category, though so little is known about them that they may be placed in this level of the divine hierarchy only with great caution and a bit of trepidation.

Kothar-wa-Hasis

At the turn of the twentieth century Kothar-wa-Hasis was, for all intents and purposes, unknown. It is possible that the deity called Χουσώρ who appears in the history related by Philo of Byblos is the same as "Kothar" in the double name "Kothar-wa-Hasis," which appears in the Ugaritic narratives.[3] However, no particular interest was taken in this deity, except that Philo of Byblos ascribed the discovery of iron, the ability to work with metal, and special skills in using various fishing and sailing paraphernalia to him.[4]

With the discovery of the mythological texts from Ugarit, the god Kothar-wa-Hasis was recognized as a deity with special abilities in metallurgy and construction. Yet, for some time after the discovery

---

3. Philo of Byblos I.10.11 (from Eusebius *Prep. Gospel*). See H. L. Ginsberg, "Two Religious Borrowings in Ugaritic Literature," *Or* 9 (1940) 39; M. Dahood, "Ancient Semitic Deities in Syria and Palestine," in *Le Antiche divinità semitische* (ed. S. Moscati; SS 1; Rome: Centro di studi semitici, 1958) 81; and Mark S. Smith, "The Magic of Kothar, the Ugaritic Craftsman God, in KTU 1.6. VI 59–60," *RB* 91 (1984) 379.

4. Lewis Bayles Paton, "Sanchuniathon," in *Encyclopedia of Religion and Ethics* (ed. J. Hastings: Edinburgh: T. & T. Clark, 1908–1922) 11.179.

of the name *Kothar-wa-Hasis* in the Ugaritic narratives, it was assumed that this name referred to two deities.[5] Even when it was recognized that a single god lay behind the double name, it was sometimes assumed that Kothar-wa-Hasis belonged to "a mythological race of dwarfs who were artificers and who possessed superior horses and chariots in their stables."[6]

When publication of the mythological narratives from Ugarit began, Kothar-wa-Hasis was seen as one of the main antagonists fighting the god Baal.[7] In this view, Kothar-wa-Hasis was thought to be the son of Yam and therefore engaged in fighting against Baal.[8] It became clear, however, that Kothar-wa-Hasis was, instead, the craftsman deity who produced the weapons by which Baal was able to vanquish the real antagonist, Yam.[9] The Ugaritic narratives provided ample evidence that Kothar-wa-Hasis was a craftsman and builder, since he not only produced the weapons for Baal, but also built the temple that was requested for Baal.

The information forming the basis of modern descriptions of Kothar-wa-Hasis has been multiplied because of an ever-increasing number of ancient Near Eastern deities who are posited to have been some sort of variant of Kothar-wa-Hasis. One example is Χουσώρ, who appears in Philo of Byblos and in a quotation attributed to Mochos of Sidon in the writings of the last of the Platonic academicians, Damascius, where the Χουσώρ is noted as one of the first beings at creation.[10] Ea has been interpreted by some to be the

5. Charles Virolleaud, "Un Nouveau chant du poème d'Aleïn-Baal," *Syria* 13 (1932) 124.

6. William Foxwell Albright, "Dwarf Craftsmen in the Keret Epic and Elsewhere in North-West Semitic Mythology," *IEJ* 4 (1954) 3. The horses in Albright's theory come from a citation in Herodotus's *Histories* 2.37, which could only be related to Kothar-wa-Hasis through an unlikely coincidence.

7. Charles Virolleaud, "La Révolte de Košer contre Baal: Poème de Ras-Shamra (III AB, A)," *Syria* 16 (1935) 29.

8. Ibid., 30 n. 1.

9. T. H. Gaster (*Thespis: Ritual, Myth, and Drama in the Ancient Near East* [New York: Norton, 1961] 164–67) sees the battle in terms of a common mythology found in many cultures, for which there may be no actual connection, but the place of Kothar-wa-Hasis as a helper to Baal is certain. See also Cyrus H. Gordon, "Canaanite Mythology," in *Mythologies of the Ancient World* (ed. S. N. Kramer; Garden City, N.Y.: Doubleday, 1961) 193–94.

10. Felix Jacoby (ed.), *Die Fragmente der griechischen Historiker* (Leiden: Brill, 1958) 784 F 4. An English translation appears as Appendix II in H. W. Attridge and R. A. Oden, *Philo of Byblos, The Phoenician History: Introduction, Critical Text, Translation, Notes* (CBQMS 9; Washington, D.C.: Catholic Biblical Assoc., 1981) 103. The text does not, in fact, have Χουσώρ create heaven and earth by opening an "egg," as has been suggested by A. I. Baumgarten, *"Phoenician History" of Philo of Byblos: A Commentary* (Études préliminaires aux religions orientales dans l'empire Romain 89; Leiden: Brill, 1981) 158 n. 104.

Mesopotamian deity equivalent to the Ugaritic Kothar-wa-Hasis because of a pair of god-list tablets found at Ras Shamra (one in Akkadian, one in Ugaritic). However, the name *Kothar* on the Ugaritic
tablet was totally reconstructed in a break in the tablet, so there is
actually no reason to assume that the scribes of Ugarit viewed the
two deities as equivalent.[11] The evidence that the Egyptian deities
Ptah and Thoth were viewed as variants of Kothar-wa-Hasis is no
more convincing than that for Ea.[12] Several other deities have also
been suggested as parallels to or variations of Kothar-wa-Hasis, but
none very successfully.[13] A certain amount of confusion may be due
to the attestation in the extant Ugaritic myths themselves of two
homelands for Kothar. He is clearly referred to as having lived outside of Syria–Palestine, but his dwelling is said to be both in Egypt
and on some island in the eastern Mediterranean.[14] This, of course,
only adds to the speculation that Kothar-wa-Hasis was a deity renowned for exceptional craftsmanship, known to scholars from some
other civilization of the time; however, there is no substantiable evidence on which to base the speculation.

11. Ibid., 166. The Ugaritic tablets that have been cited in an attempt to show that
the gods Ea and Kothar-wa-Hasis were considered the same deity are published in
Jean Nougayrol, "Textes suméro-accadiens des archives et bibliothèques privées d'Ugarit," *Ugaritica* 5 (1968) 45, 51 (see line 15). For the Ugaritic tablet, see Charles Virolleaud, "Les Inscriptions cunéiformes de Ras Shamra," *Syria* 10 (1929) plate 70, no. 17. Note
that part of only a single sign, perhaps *h*, is visible.

12. On Ptah, see William Foxwell Albright, "The Early Alphabetic Inscriptions
from Sinai and their Decipherment," *BASOR* 110 (1948) 17; repeated in idem, *From the
Stone Age to Christianity: Monotheism and the Historical Process* (2d ed.; Garden City, N.Y.:
Doubleday, 1957) 216; and *Yahweh and the Gods of Canaan: A Historical Analysis of Two
Contrasting Faiths* (Garden City, N.Y.: Doubleday, 1968; repr. Winona Lake, Ind.: Eisen-
brauns, 1978) 222–25, which is the source for the equation made by Attridge and
Oden, *Philo of Byblos*, 104 n. 6. The identification of Ptah and Kothar-wa-Hasis (or
Χουσώρ) has roots in the last century. See Gaster (*Thespis*, 164), who labels this identification "bizarre." On Thoth, the progression Taautos = Thoth = Hermes = Hermes Tris-
megistos = Kothar-wa-Hasis would have to be accepted; see Philo of Byblos I.9.24; and
Baumgarten, *Phoenician History*, 69, 227. The equation of Thoth and Hermes rests upon
the similar service rendered to superior gods in the realm of weaponry (Philo of Byblos I.10.18); see M. S. Smith, "Magic of Kothar," 379. This latter equation of deities remains quite dubious. See Baumgarten, *Phoenician History*, 73 n. 30, where he notes the
unlikely equation made by L. R. Clapham in a Harvard dissertation.

13. Kothar-wa-Hasis is related to Tammuz by William Foxwell Albright, *Archaeology and the Religion of Israel* (Baltimore: Penguin, 1942) 82. He is the father of Adonis
according to J. P. Brown, "Kothar, Kunyras, and Kythereia," *JSS* 10 (1965) 202. Dahood
("Ancient Semitic Deities," 81–82) relates the deity to Hephaistus in Greece, Vulcan in
Rome, and Mummu (an attendant of Ea!) in Babylon. On the whole question of Kothar
at Ebla, see W. G. Lambert, "Old Testament Mythology in Its Ancient Near Eastern
Context," in *Congress Volume: Jerusalem, 1986* (ed. J. A. Emerton; VTSup 40; Leiden:
Brill, 1988) 141–43.

14. Gaster, *Thespis*, 163–64.

The Χουσώρ of Philo of Byblos's history was one of two brothers who discovered the working of iron but was himself noted for two abilities. One ability was facility with words, which included the capacity for casting spells and prophesying.[15] Whether or not there is evidence in the Ugaritic narratives that Kothar-wa-Hasis had magical abilities is a debated issue.[16] If such evidence does exist, it is certainly minor and of less importance than the evidence for his capacity as a skilled craftsman. Χουσώρ was also renowned for his fishing and sailing abilities; however, the evidence from Ugarit that Kothar-wa-Hasis was active in fishing or sailing is even less convincing.[17]

It has been suggested that the narratives of Ugarit reflect a time when there was only one artisan god in the pantheon of Syria–Palestine, while Philo of Byblos wrote at a time when sources reflected the division of the various skills of Kothar-wa-Hasis among different deities.[18] So little mythological material survives from Ugarit or any other Syro-Palestinian civilization that one cannot state with assurance whether Kothar-wa-Hasis was considered the sole artisan god in an earlier period. There are many gods attested at Ugarit whose roles are unknown. Therefore, any theory of progression toward a multiplicity of deities in the skilled-labor trades is questionable. What is clear from the Ugaritic narratives is that Kothar-wa-Hasis was considered a skillful deity on whom other deities were dependent. His primary skill was construction, whether of weaponry, furniture, or temples.

The "Technogony" of Philo of Byblos

In the *History of the Phoenicians* by Philo of Byblos, there is one extended section that deals with gods who either discovered or invented devices for civilized life. James Barr has aptly called this section the "technogony."[19] This section of the history presents a series of pairs of gods, each of which is related to a human craft, but not

15. Philo of Byblos I.10.11.

16. Attridge and Oden, *Philo of Byblos*, 84 n. 66; Baumgarten, *Phoenician History,* 166; M. S. Smith, "Magic of Kothar," 377–80.

17. See Baumgarten, *Phoenician History,* 167.

18. F. Løkkegaard, "Some Comments on the Sanchuniaton Tradition," *ST* 7 (1954) 62. If it is true that Kothar appears in al-Nadim's *Fihrist* (Basile Aggoula, "Divinités phéniciennes dans un passage du *Fihrist* d'Ibn al-Nadim," *JA* 278 [1990] 7), it may imply that an artisan deity simply held a place among a number of other deities who specialized in particular fields of work; it is doubtful that, at an early period, one god was responsible for doing all of the work.

19. James Barr, "Philo of Byblos and His 'Phoenician History,'" *BJRL* 57 (1974) 22; Philo of Byblos I.10.7–14.

much more information than that is given.[20] Because Philo of Byblos presented all the deities as though they were humans, it is necessary to remember that a relationship between a deity and a discovery made by one of Philo's humans cannot be demonstrated to have been a part of the mythological world of the Phoenicians.[21] The Greek stories tell nothing about these gods that would help to link them with the pictures of the gods drawn from the Syro-Palestinian mythological narratives, so nothing is known about the real relationships between the deities mentioned and objects invented by humans.

Since the Χουσὼρ who has consistently been identified with Kothar-wa-Hasis appears in the technogony section, it is often assumed that the other "humans" named must also have had specific, perhaps otherwise unknown, Syro-Palestinian deities behind them.[22] This theory cannot be substantiated. Some deities known from Syro-Palestinian sources do make appearances in Philo of Byblos, but the inventions connected with them in the *History of the Phoenicians* may have no connection at all with the usual understanding of these gods in Syria–Palestine. The god ṣdq, for example, has usually been regarded as a deity related to righteousness, as the name implies.[23] And even though Philo of Byblos explains the name as meaning (in Greek) δίκαιον, which conforms to the normal understanding, the apparent conclusion to be drawn from the narrative text is that he was actually a god of salt.[24] There might have been some connection between ṣdq and salt in some unrecovered mythological text, but it is impossible to assume that just because a god appeared in the "technogony," he or

20. Barr ("Philo of Byblos," 62–63) has graphed the various gods and the discoveries or inventions attributed to them.

21. The difficulty of discerning the supposed deities who appear in the guise of mortal history is pointed out by Baumgarten (*Phoenician History*, 140); he suggests that the attempt must be made to determine the sphere of divine activity that led to connecting the god with the object of culture mentioned. This approach may or may not result in accurate conclusions about Syro-Palestinian theology. The difficulty of making these interpretations cannot be overemphasized. The "discoveries" may have been related to a deity in almost any fashion: perhaps they were related to myths told about the gods; they might have been emblems used to refer to the gods; or perhaps the item appeared in a tale about a god only tangentially (even one long forgotten by the time of Philo of Byblos). It is impossible to know for certain.

22. Patrick D. Miller, Jr. ("Fire in the Mythology of Canaan and Israel," *CBQ* 27 [1965] 258) finds real gods where Attridge and Oden (*Philo of Byblos*, 81 n. 53), with more proper caution, refrain.

23. Løkkegaard, "Some Comments," 62; Michael C. Astour, "Some New Divine Names from Ugarit," *JAOS* 86 (1966) 282; Roy A. Rosenberg, "The God Ṣedeq," *HUCA* 36 (1965) 162–63; Mario Liverani, "ΣΥΔΥΚ e ΜΙΣΩΡ," in *Studi in onore di Edoardo Volterra 6* (Milan: Giuffrè, 1971) 58.

24. Philo of Byblos I.10.13; a relationship between justice and salt has been suggested by Baumgarten (*Philo of Byblos*, 176).

she had to be "the god of" the aspect of civilization as related to the deity by Philo of Byblos. In the case of Χουσώρ, there may be a real relationship between the known Syro-Palestinian god and his description in Philo of Byblos. With ṣdq, however, there is a known Syro-Palestinian deity, but the "description" in Philo of Byblos does not appear to relate to the known deity. It is quite tenuous to posit such gods as "Light," "Flame," and "Fire," however, on the basis of the writings of Philo of Byblos. This means simply that the references to gods in the "technogony" do not provide much information that can be used with certainty.

Too little of the mythological world has been preserved in Philo's comments about the inventors and discoverers to recreate the character of the gods supposedly appearing in these texts. Indeed, it is unclear to what extent he conflated various traditions in order to create a systematic view of the origins of civilization in early Phoenician culture. Certainly Philo was influenced by the things that interested the Greek audience for whom he prepared the text. The discovery of fire, construction, sailing, or the use of salt might have stimulated Greek curiosity, whereas other discoveries, more important to the Phoenicians but less interesting to the Greeks, may not have been included. Both the works of Baumgarten and of Attridge and Oden deal with the gods individually in an attempt to determine what, if any, Syro-Palestinian deity might be lurking beneath the Greek text. The fact that the two studies disagree on the conclusions points out the nebulous state of knowledge regarding these gods. It takes a Kierkegaardian leap-of-faith to assume that each of Philo's individuals corresponds to a Phoenician deity. Philo's text may be used as only a list of names, some Semitic, some Greek, which may or may not correspond to Phoenician gods who dealt in specialized fields.

The only artisan god who was actually given narrative exposition in the history of Philo of Byblos was the god Taautos, who was equated with Egyptian Thoth and Greek Hermes.[25] This Hermes was credited with raising the troops of El to a fighting fury by means of magic spells.[26] Moreover, he was credited with inventing writing as well as the religious symbols for use in the cults of the various gods.[27] Like the god Kothar-wa-Hasis in the texts from Ugarit of a millennium earlier, Philo of Byblos's Hermes knew how to deal with metals, in this case iron rather than silver and gold. Yet Hermes and Athena (= Anat) were only advisors to El about the fashioning of

25. Philo of Byblos I.10.14.
26. Ibid., I.10.18.
27. Ibid., I.10.36–37.

weaponry. Unlike Kothar-wa-Hasis, Hermes did not make the armaments for his superior; El made his own weapons. Yet, as an artisan god, Hermes/Taautos served his superiors at their request and in pursuit of their aims. He was a specialist.

Marginal Deities

In the Legend of Kirta, El created a goddess for the express purpose of delivering King Kirta from a mortal malady that no existing deity was capable of curing.[28] The creation of Shatiqatu is tied solely to the immediate situation of the narrative, namely, saving Kirta's life.[29] This particular goddess appears to meet the requirements stipulated above for being on the level of divine hierarchy of the artisan gods. The goddess had a clearly defined area of specialization in which she is quite competent, since the king did indeed recover. In the passage itself the goddess does only what she was requested to do and nothing more, but the narrative is much too short to determine whether or not she was envisaged as having volition of her own. Shatiqatu appears nowhere else in the texts from Ugarit, neither in narrative nor ritual sources, so all that exists with which to define her is a single literary composition. It is possible either that Shatiqatu was a recognized, though minor, deity in a Syro-Palestinian cult, or that she was a literary invention concocted for the plot development of this particular legend. In either case, it would be reasonable to assume that she was presented in a manner deemed plausible to the contemporary audience.

A similar deity appears in biblical narratives, though no proper name is given to the god. The story of the creation of the image of the deity, as the story now appears, leaves the divine nature of the seraph out of the narrative:

> And Yahweh said to Moses, "Make for yourself a seraph and put it on a standard so it will happen that all who are bitten, as they look at it will live." And Moses made a snake of bronze and he put it on a standard so whenever "the" snake bit a man he would look at the bronze snake and he would live (Num 21:8–9).

---

28. *KTU* 1.16.V.10–VI.14.

29. The name of the goddess, *šᶜtqt*, appears to be related to her duty of chasing away the symptoms of Kirta's illness; the name seems to be a *šin*- stem of the verb *ᶜtq* ('she causes to pass'). The vocalization has been taken from G. del Olmo Lete, *Mitos y leyendas de Canaan segun la tradicion de Ugarit: Textos, versión y estudio* (FCB 1; Madrid: Ediciones Cristiandad, 1981) 320.

That the passage refers to the institution of a cult for a healing deity can be seen in the passage that recounts the later destruction of the cultic image.[30] Hezekiah had the bronze snake removed when it was being treated like a divine image:

> He removed the sanctuaries, and he shattered the stelae, and he cut down the asherah, and he crushed the bronze snake which Moses had made, for until those days the Israelites had burned food offerings to it; and it was named Nehushtan (2 Kgs 18:4).

The fact that the bronze snake was worshiped in the cult with burnt offerings clearly demonstrates that it was considered the representation of a deity.[31] As in the narrative from Ugarit concerning Shatiqatu, the biblical bronze snake deity was ordered by a superior deity, Yahweh, in a particular instance requiring a highly specialized skill from the divine world.[32] It may be nothing more than a coincidence that both the seraph and Shatiqatu were created specifically for the cure of deadly ailments. In the case of the seraph, Yahweh appears to have been an authoritative deity who knew which god was needed in the situation at hand. The passage assumes that Yahweh did not himself act to cure the people bitten by snakes but delegated that power to the lower deity. It is not certain that the god represented by the bronze snake was supposed to have been created at that particular time, as was Shatiqatu for Kirta's illness, but the creation of the image of the god, and, one suspects, the cult worship as well, was the effective medium for healing the snake bites. The text clearly presumes that the god was capable of effecting a cure.

One other biblical text may contain a reference to an artisan god. In 2 Kgs 1:1–8 the god Baal-Zebub (בעל זבוב) does not actually appear, but the references to him in the pericope imply not only that

30. John Gray, *I & II Kings: A Commentary* (2d ed.; OTL; Philadelphia: Westminster, 1970) 670; Rudolf Kittel, *Die Bücher der Könige: Übersetzt und erklärt* (Göttingen: Vandenhoeck & Ruprecht, 1900) 278–79; Adolphe Lods, *Israël des origines au milieu du VIIIe siècle* (Paris: Renaissance du livre, 1930) 469; H. H. Rowley, "Zadok and Nehushtan," *JBL* 58 (1939) 136–37.

31. For the meaning of the verb קטר in the context of the worship of deities, see Diana Edelman, "The Meaning of *qiṭṭēr*," *VT* 35 (1985) 399, 404.

32. It should be noticed that the biblical passage does not give a proper name for the god, but only a pun on the image. Certainly the deity is associated with healing, whether related to Horon and Asclepius or not (John Gray, "The Canaanite God Horon," *JNES* 8 [1949] 32). See now the connection drawn between the Shatiqatu passage and this biblical narrative in Baruch A. Levine and Jean-Michel de Tarragon, "'Shapshu Cries Out in Heaven': Dealing with Snake-Bites at Ugarit (KTU 1.100, 1.107)," *RB* 95 (1988) 518.

the deity existed, but also that he was an effective deity.[33] Since King Ahaziah was sending his messengers to seek an oracle from the god, it is not at all clear whether Baal-Zebub was worshiped as a deity of healing or as a god of oracles.[34] Since he was considered a foreign deity, the passage implies that some local god would have sufficed for Ahaziah's needs (2 Kgs 1:3). Nothing is mentioned of Baal-Zebub that would explain his status in his own pantheon, so it is quite impossible to determine his relationship with other deities. It does seem, however, that Baal-Zebub dealt in a specialty, a skill so renowned in fact that rulers from beyond the god's regional borders consulted him. This suggests that he may have been an artisan god.

Another type of individual who appears to belong to the level of service to the cosmic organization is the "borderline" divinity. The king of any city-state within Syria–Palestine also served in a specialized capacity as the regent of the patron deity of that city-state.[35] The relationship between the living king and his patron deity was similar to the relationship of the artisan gods to the major active gods. Of more immediate interest to the divine realm, however, was the status of the human ruler who had died and passed into the realm of the divine. When human monarchs died, they were understood to be taking a place among the lesser deities.[36] This vision of the royal afterlife

33. The name *Baal-Zebub* may actually be the name of the deity; see Gösta W. Ahlström, *An Archaeological Picture of Iron Age Religions in Ancient Palestine* (Studia Orientalia 55/3; Helsinki: Societas Orientalis Fennicae, 1984) 122. On the literary and religious importance of flies, see Anne Draffkorn Kilmer, "The Symbolism of the Flies in the Mesopotamian Flood Myth and Some Further Implications," in *Language, Literature, and History: Philological and Historical Studies Presented to Erica Reiner* (ed. Francesca Rochberg-Halton; AOS 67; New Haven, Conn.: American Oriental Society, 1987) 175–80. It has often been assumed that the real name of the god must have been *bᶜl zbl* (Baal, the "Prince"), a name derived from Matt 10:25; see Kittel, *Die Bücher der Könige*, 182; or Gray, *I & II Kings*, 463. See now Arvid Tångberg, "A Note on Baᶜal Zĕbūb in 2 Kgs 1,2.3.6.16," *SJOT* 6 (1992) 296.

34. Gray (*I & II Kings*, 463) believes Baal-Zebub was a healing deity; however, Joseph Robinson (*The Second Book of Kings* [CBCNEB; Cambridge: Cambridge University Press, 1976] 18) notes that the god may have been sought out only for an oracle rather than for a cure. See also Mordechai Cogan and Hayim Tadmor, *II Kings: A New Translation with Introduction and Commentary* (AB 11; Garden City, N.Y.: Doubleday, 1988) 24–25.

35. On the human king as regent to the patron deity, see Bertil Albrektson, *History and the Gods: An Essay on the Idea of Historical Events as Divine Manifestations in the Ancient Near East and in Israel* (ConBOT 1; Lund: CWK Gleerup, 1967) 42–52; and Gösta Ahlström, *Royal Administration and National Religion in Ancient Palestine* (SHANE 1; Leiden: Brill, 1982) 2–3.

36. Several Ugaritic texts deal with these nebulous figures; *KTU* 1.20–22; 1.108; and especially 1.161. The number of scholars accepting the theory that human kings passed into some sort of honored divine afterlife continues to grow. See, for example,

meant that their status as rulers in the universe continued into the netherworld. The king, after his death, became a god (*il*) who retained the title *mlk*, while joining a collective group known as the *mlkm* or the *rp³im*.[37] It seems, despite the sparse material available for reconstruction of such a thesis, that no matter which patron deity any ruler served in life, the deceased *mlkm* all served the sun deity in the underworld.[38] Even as the living kings ruled their land, so it appears that the deceased kings remained in charge of their lands, receiving sacrifices from the living kings, who perhaps hoped to achieve the favor or aid of the deified former rulers.[39] Still, the information concerning these deities is too slight to create a full picture of their existence and, indeed, this vision of the royal afterlife may be erroneous.

THE GODS IN OFFICE

The primary responsibility of the artisan gods was performing their specialized tasks. They were the foremost authorities and the most skilled in their own fields of competence. For this reason they were called upon by other gods to perform whatever action was needed in their field. Kothar-wa-Hasis was called upon to provide weapons for Baal in his battle with Yam. Kothar-wa-Hasis not only did what he had been asked, but also delivered a speech in which he made it clear that he knew his work would fulfill the requirements of Baal's request.

> Surely I say to you,
> To "Prince" Baal,
> Again I say to Mounter of the Clouds:
> "Now, your enemy, oh Baal,
> Now, your enemy you will strike.

John F. Healey, "MLKM/RP³UM and the KISPUM," *UF* 10 (1978) 90–91; Manfried Dietrich and Oswald Loretz, "Totenverehrung in Mari (12803) und Ugarit (KTU 1.161)," *UF* 12 (1980) 381–82; Pierre Bordreuil and Dennis Pardee, "Le Rituel funéraire ougaritique RS.34.126," *Syria* 59 (1982) 121–28; Gregorio del Olmo Lete, "The 'Divine' Names of the Ugaritic Kings," *UF* 18 (1986) 83–95; and John F. Healey, "The Last of the Rephaim," in *Back to the Sources: Biblical and Near Eastern Studies in Honour of Dermot Ryan* (ed. Kevin J. Cathcart and John F. Healey; Dublin: Glendale, 1989) 39.

37. Healey, "MLKM/RP³UM," 89–91; del Olmo Lete, " 'Divine Names' of Ugaritic Kings," 91.

38. Or, at least, so Klaas Spronk, *Beatific Afterlife in Ancient Israel and in the Ancient Near East* (AOAT 219; Kevelaer: Butzon & Bercker/Neukirchen-Vluyn: Neukirchener Verlag, 1986) 162–63.

39. De Tarragon, *Culte*, 187; Dietrich and Loretz, "Totenverehrung," 381–82.

Now you will silence your foe!
You will take your eternal rule,
Your dominion forever and ever"
    (*KTU* 1.2.IV.7–10).

Indeed, Kothar-wa-Hasis treated the weapons he produced for Baal as though they were solely responsible for the success of the battle, regardless of Baal's prowess.

Your name; you are Yagrush!
Yagrush, drive out Yam!
Drive Yam out of his throne!
River out of the seat of his dominion!
Take off from the hand of Baal
Like an eagle from his fingers!
Beat the shoulders of "Prince" Yam,
Between the hands of Ruler River!
    (*KTU* 1.2.IV.11–15).[40]

In the same manner, Kothar-wa-Hasis made Baal's house a palatial temple, a building without flaw, and corresponding to Baal's wishes (*KTU* 1.4.V.44–VI.35). Similarly, in the history by Philo of Byblos, Hermes aided El in his battles:

Then Hermes, to the allies of Kronos, saying magical words,
produced a desire of battle against Uranos on behalf of Ge
    (Philo of Byblos I.10.18).

As with Kothar-wa-Hasis, Hermes' work was successful and was exactly what was requested by El.

One thing that is clear already from these passages is that the artisan gods work for other deities who had higher positions and greater power in the hierarchy. These artisan gods carried out the plans of the major active gods and the gods of highest authority.[41] The recognition on the part of superiors that the artisan gods had a better grasp of a particular skill did not give the artisan gods complete freedom over the projects. Kothar-wa-Hasis, when building the palace for Baal, suggested the inclusion of a window, but Baal did not want the window to be built, and Kothar-wa-Hasis did as Baal desired. Even so, Kothar-wa-Hasis knew that Baal would eventually come around to his position.

---

40. A similar, but quite distinct address is made to the weapon *Ayyamur* in lines 19–23.

41. As noted by M. S. Smith, "Kothar wa-Hasis," 24.

And Kothar-wa-Hasis answered:
"Listen, oh, Victorious Baal!
Understand, oh, Mounter of the Clouds!
Will I not set a window in the house,
A window in the middle of the palace?"
And Victorious Baal answered:
"You will not set a window in the house,
A window in the middle of the palace!"
   (*KTU* 1.4.V.58–65).

Clearly, Baal was the instigator of the project, and the superior position of Baal over the artisan god Kothar-wa-Hasis is evident in Baal's announcement of the completion of the refurbished abode.

Victorious Baal rejoiced:
"I built my house of silver!
My palace of gold!"
   (*KTU* 1.4.VI.35–38).

The building of the house for Baal is assumed to have been instigated by Baal, authorized by the highest authority in the pantheon, El, constructed by the artisan god most skilled in carpentry, Kothar-wa-Hasis, but "built" by Baal himself (the major active god who motivated the project). The artisan god was considered a helper to the active deity, who in turn was presumed to be the *real* builder.

This relationship may also be discerned among other deities posited as belonging to the artisan god level. Though Hermes helped and advised El, it was El who built the weapons and fought the war. "With the advice of Athena and Hermes, Kronos constructed of iron a sickle and a spear."[42] The stories of Moses' bronze snake and of El's creation of Shatiqatu both present deities who only did as they were told by their superiors in the divine realm. On the other hand, the artisan gods appear to have been on their own. The seraph did not need Yahweh to cure snake-bite; nor, it appears, did Shatiqatu need help from El to cure Kirta, once El had created her and established her to fulfill that purpose. In each case, though the task was carried out by the craft-god, attribution of the completion of the matter is credited to and recognized as the work of the superior deity for whom the artisan gods were requested to work. The skilled expertise of the artisan gods served the desires of other deities.

While Kothar-wa-Hasis appears to have worked by himself in procuring the two weapons for Baal in the Baal and Yam battle narrative, it is less clear whether he commanded a force of workers in

42. Philo of Byblos I.10.18.

building the palace for Baal. The texts may suggest that Kothar-wa-Hasis had a construction crew to carry out his instructions in building of the house for Baal. If *ḫrn* and *ᶜḏbt* refer to groups of suppliers and construction workers, then it appears that Kothar-wa-Hasis headed a large workforce in the construction of the palace.[43] It would have been these workers, then, who were sent to Lebanon for cedar and who carried out the construction of the palace.[44] They are given no individuality in the narrative and are only indirectly mentioned. If Kothar-wa-Hasis did in fact have a crew for his work-project assignment, the work itself was done by that crew but attributed to him. In this regard the artisan god was to his labor force as Baal was to the entire project. At both levels the head of the unit was credited with the accomplishment of that unit. While it is clear that the workers who served Kothar-wa-Hasis also served Baal while they were engaged in the construction of Baal's palace, it is not clear whether they were considered a constant part of a workforce under the leadership of Kothar-wa-Hasis. If they did form a "subset" of divinities under his control, this implies the existence of another level under the artisan gods.[45] It is also possible that the workers were assumed to be the human laborers who worked on the building of Baal's temple and that they were perceived as serving under the god Kothar-wa-Hasis; this detail, though quite important, is not clear in the narrative. No other deity who might fit into this level of the divine world is described well enough to be useful in testing this theory.

In a perfect, smoothly running version of the universal hierarchy, the artisan-god level of the bureaucracy would have been an efficient organizational group that oversaw the performance of the actual work required by the managerial levels of the organization. The members of this level were marked by a particularly acute capacity for specialized skills; their specialized knowledge was supreme. However, they worked for gods higher in the organization who determined the projects they were to complete. If the superior deities differed with an artisan god, it was the artisan god who gave way. While the artisan gods seem to have been independent of any particular deity, they could serve under any of their superiors. In turn, at least in the case of Kothar-wa-Hasis at Ugarit, there appear to

43. *KTU* 1.4.V.13–14, 29–30. See del Olmo Lete, *Mitos y leyendas*, 202–3, 554, 599; on the other hand, see Gibson, *Canaanite Legends*, 61, where the translations 'caravan' and 'wares' leave open the question of a work force.

44. *KTU* 1.4.VI.18–21. The "construction" of the palace/temple consisted of a series of days in which the house was fired as though in a kiln, *KTU* 1.4.VI.22–35.

45. If these "personages" do form a level of deities, they would correspond to the level of the messenger deities (gods who do only what they are told to do); see description in the next chapter.

have been others, either human or divine, who served under his governance to carry out the programs placed in the care of the artisan gods. In all known cases where the artisan gods appear in narrative texts, they are totally competent. Any minor problems can be attributed to orders given to the artisan gods by their superiors.

MALFUNCTIONING

The artisan gods did what they were supposed to do. However, there are two manifestations of malfunctioning expressed in the sources for these deities. The first of these is the fact that the artisan god could dissent from or contradict the superior for whom he or she worked. When Kothar-wa-Hasis suggested constructing a window for Baal's house, Baal rejected the suggestion. Even though Kothar-wa-Hasis knew that Baal would eventually turn to his position, he did what Baal told him to do. Yet, Kothar-wa-Hasis made it very clear to Baal that he was in disagreement with the orders given him.[46] In the end it was Baal who reversed himself on the question of the window:

> And Victorious Baal answered:
> "I will set, Kothar, today,
> Kothar, immediately;
> A window will be opened in the house,
> A window in the middle of the palace,
> And a breach of the clouds,
> According to the word of Kothar-wa-Hasis"
> (*KTU* 1.4.VII.14–20).

The fact that Kothar-wa-Hasis had his own opinion on the project and could dissent from the plans of his superior show that the artisan god had an independent will, uncontrolled by his immediate superior. Moreover, the deity could argue his position against the god who designed the project. The passage also demonstrates that the knowledge of the artisan god was considered to be greater than that of the managerial deity in matters of specialization. The superior gods could ignore the artisan gods' superior knowledge for reasons of their own; this, in itself, is an example of malfunctioning in an organization.

Closely related to the first type of malfunctioning is the second. Artisan gods had superior knowledge and did become slightly arrogant about it. After Baal relented and had Kothar-wa-Hasis build

---

46. *KTU* 1.4.V.58–65.

the window in his palace, Kothar-wa-Hasis taunted him about having told him he would change his position:

Laughing, Kothar-wa-Hasis
Raised his voice and shouted:
"Did I not say to you, to Victorious Baal:
'You will return, Baal, to my word'?"
(*KTU* 1.4.VII.21–25).[47]

The verbs ṣḥq and ṣḥ emphasize the insolent nature of the subordinate's address to Baal. There is no sign that Baal had any negative reaction to Kothar-wa-Hasis's remarks. This suggests that the deities on the artisan god level were allowed, not only to contradict their superiors but also to treat them with a certain amount of disrespect. This behavior was previously described for the higher levels of the bureaucracy, as, for example, in the attitude of Anat toward El. Apparently the "exempt" status enjoyed by the active deities extended to the artisan gods because of their positions as repositories of necessary knowledge and skill. Nonetheless, such behavior portrays an organization that was not functioning without problems. If the action taken by Kothar-wa-Hasis is representative of the way in which the deities on this level were allowed to misbehave, it may be true that the extent of "exempt" behavior was more curtailed for the artisan gods than for the more uncivil active gods; this fact then would be a distinguishing characteristic of the two levels. There was dissent even on this lower level, a sign that the purposes of the organization as set forth by the management were not carried out with wholehearted support from all deities.

There is an interesting aspect to the artisan god level of the divine hierarchy. These gods, as they are portrayed in the existing narratives, were always correct. Whatever they did was done properly. When they did something wrong it was because their superiors had ordered them to act contrary to their own intuitions. In such cases they were allowed to make their feelings known, but, being under orders, did as they were told. They were allowed to make fun of the less-intelligent orders of their superiors. They, in their individual spheres of authority, knew all, acted skillfully, and made no errors; and at the same time, they also put up with the clashes, plans, and occasional bungling of the higher gods.

---

47. This passage is clearly a taunt and not the fulfillment of prophecy. Divination is not one of the attested attributes of Kothar-wa-Hasis, contra M. S. Smith's opinion ("Kothar wa-Hasis," 461).

Chapter 6

Messenger Deities

The lowest level of deity in the Syro-Palestinian pantheon was that of the messenger god. While the higher levels of divine personnel were responsible for determining the activities of the universe and for seeing to it that these activities were carried out, the lowest level of the divine hierarchy was made up of numerous deities who appear to have had their own names but who acted in a manner that has made it difficult to distinguish them from one another. They were used by the higher gods to carry messages from one deity to another. In performing this function the messengers delivered the text of their superiors' speeches without amplifying the content, adding their own comments, or in any way inserting themselves into the job. Though it is true that gods at other levels of the divine hierarchy were allowed a certain amount of misbehavior due to their specialized functions, which were necessary for the smooth operation of the universe, the messengers were apparently not extended the same right. The messenger deities did what they were told to do, and they did nothing else; they existed solely to serve the higher levels of the pantheon.

THE OFFICE

The level of messenger god corresponds to the stereotypical notion of labor in corporate bureaucracies. In the "pure type" of bureaucracy that Weber posited, labor exists as a group "oriented to the instructions of a managerial agency."[1] The labor force does not own the means of production, a characteristic it shares with the managerial levels; but, unlike management, it does not have access to the

---

1. Max Weber, *Theory of Social and Economic Organization* (New York: Free Press, 1947) 219.

decision-making process of the organization.[2] The members of labor do only what is ordered by the managers; they are "but parts of a mechanism" beyond their control.[3] This is the one level that is not allowed to diverge from the plans of the higher levels of the organization. Furtheremore, there is no special treatment for the members of labor by those with organizational authority, since personnel at the labor level may be replaced with other individuals without the organization suffering a loss of specialized skills or knowledge. In this respect, labor forms the group Kanter has labeled "nonexempt."[4] Labor does not dissent, it does not contradict its superiors, it never acts on its own, and it has no independent authority beyond that conferred upon it by its superiors. Labor formed the very bottom of the divine hierarchy; therefore, there is no evidence of personnel serving under the messengers. By definition, then, messengers, as members of the lowest level, lacked independent authority.

In actual performance in an organization, however, labor personnel do not generally act as a passive machine. Individuals in the workplace play as important a part in labor's service as they do on the level of management. Laborers (both as individual laborers and as an organizational level) do not merely perform the actions ordered by those above; dissent, malcontent, incompetence, rebellion, and misunderstanding may all cause deviations from the plans devised by the managers.[5] Moreover, it is not uncommon for ideas arising among labor to be taken into account in the decision-making processes of the managerial levels of corporations. In practice the level of labor is as complicated as any of the managerial levels.

However, when reading the texts dealing with the Syro-Palestinian mythological world, one can see that the messengers of the divine realm were portrayed in a manner consistent with examples of "ideal" labor rather than as examples of "real" labor. While *human* messengers in ancient Near Eastern cultures were supposed to act only on the orders of their superiors, they did not act in total compliance with this ideal.[6] In theory, a messenger lacked independence

---

2. Karl Marx, *Capital: A Critique of Political Economy* (ed. Frederick Engels; New York: Modern Library, 1906) 391; as with Weber, who also sees labor as being without control over the organization (*Theory of Organization*, 219, 331), Marx posits an "ideal" hierarchical type (belonging to nineteenth-century Europe).

3. Marx, *Capital*, 205.

4. Rosabeth Moss Kanter, *Men and Women of the Corporation* (New York: Basic Books, 1977) 39.

5. Ibid., 149–51.

6. The ideal messenger acts as an extension of the sender; this is spelled out in an Akkadian letter from Ugarit, RS 11.730.8–16, translated by Sally W. Ahl, "Epistolary

from his employer and acted as an extension of the one who sent him, carrying messages in the words of the sender, without change or delay.[7] Reality was clearly a different matter. Theft, untrustworthiness, escape, tardiness, and ineptitude all played a part in the function of real human messengers in the ancient Near Eastern world.[8] Human messengers known to the authors of the Ugaritic narratives would have displayed the malfunctioning of their trade. The *deities* in the office of divine messenger, however, corresponded to the "pure type" of messenger. Unlike any other level of the divine hierarchy, gods belonging to the messenger level did not exhibit conflicts and mistakes.

Labor, as it appears reflected in the messenger gods, was the level of the hierarchy that served the managerial levels without causing trouble. The work force was in effect merely an extension of the personnel who planned the activities of the organization. Without having opportunity to express individuality or the ability to dissent from the organization's plans, labor was passive and obedient, merely doing the work required by the higher levels in the organization.

THE GODS

The main sources of information about the messenger gods are the narrative tablets from Ugarit and the books of the Bible.[9] The gods of this level are a particularly nondescript group, not portrayed in any depth as individuals. Since the deities are usually presented as conveying messages from one to another (or to humans), they appear something like animated "letters" in the texts. The divine beings of this level showed no individual volition, at least not until late in the first millennium B.C.E. when, in the Jewish tradition, "angels" were

---

Texts from Ugarit: Structural and Lexical Correspondences in Epistles in Akkadian and Ugaritic" (Ph.D. dissertation, Brandeis University, 1973) 200. It is this ideal vision of the messenger that is reconstructed by John T. Greene, *The Role of the Messenger and Message in the Ancient Near East* (BJS 169; Atlanta: Scholars Press, 1989).

7. W. F. Leemans, *The Old-Babylonian Merchant: His Business and His Social Position* (Studia et documenta ad 3; Leiden: Brill, 1950) 35; and A. D. Crown, "Messengers and Scribes: the ספר and מלאך in the Old Testament," *VT* 24 (1974) 366.

8. CAD, *s.v.* ṣuḫāru. On ṣuḫāru, see André Finet, "Le ṣuḫārum à Mari," in *Gesellschaftsklassen im Alten Zweistromland und in den angrenzenden Gebieten* (ed. D. O. Edzard; RAI 18; PhHKA 75; Munich: Bayerischen Akademie der Wissenschaften, 1972) 65–72. For messengers in general, see Samuel A. Meier, *The Messenger in the Ancient Semitic World* (HSM 45; Atlanta: Scholars Press, 1988) 168–79.

9. For a complete list of the biblical passages that deal with the מלאכים, see Jesús-Luís Cunchillos Ylarri, "Étude philologique de *mal'ak*: Perspectives sur le *mal'ak* de la divinité dans la bible hébraïque," in *Congress Volume: Vienna, 1980* (ed. J. A. Emerton; VTSup 32; Leiden: Brill, 1981) 30 n. 1.

the sole remaining denizens of the divine populace recognized as serving the highest authority in heaven. At that time, "angels" began to be ascribed very distinct individual characteristics, and one entire faction of the messenger level was portrayed as rising in a futile revolt against supreme power.[10] However, in the ancient Syro-Palestinian sources the pantheon is presented as a functioning organization, with the messenger deities acting as "ideal" labor, presented in the literature with evidence neither of the individual wills of the deities of other divine levels, nor of any independent action beyond their superiors' instructions.

מלאכים

The מלאכים ('messengers', or 'angels', as they have generally been referred to in Western religious literature) have been known for a long time. In fact, belief in the existence of "angels" has never passed out of Jewish, Christian, or Islamic religious traditions.[11] For the scholarly study of these divine messengers, the primary source continues to be the biblical narratives. By the early 1900s two main theories concerning the origins of these heavenly beings were posited. One group insisted that belief in "angels," a belief now present in the biblical texts, must have originated in a lower form of faith that had its origin in the cultures surrounding and prior to Israel.[12] According to this theory,

10. The later traditions of a revolt by some of the angels against Yahweh include in their narratives some of the stories in the Bible that originally related material about the gods (בני האלהים) rather than about messengers. However, all biblical references that had originally presumed some form of divine being other than Yahweh at some time came to be read as referring to "angels." The tale of the "fallen angels" is usually connected to the "sons of gods" who appear in Gen 6:1–4. See *1 Enoch* 6–8 for what may be an early second-century B.C.E. rendition of the story. This passage is assumed to be a fragment of an even earlier work called the "Book of Noah"; see R. H. Charles, *The Apocrypha and Pseudepigrapha of the Old Testament in English* (Oxford: Clarendon, 1913) 2.163; and E. Isaac, "1 (Ethiopic Apocalypse of) Enoch (Second Century B.C.–First Century A.D.)," in *The Old Testament Pseudepigrapha* (ed. James H. Charlesworth; Garden City: Doubleday, 1983) 1.7. Note that the idea that angels could revolt, or act on impulse at all, was rejected by several Christian writers during the period of the early church, especially when confronted with texts interpreted to be about angels in the Old Testament; see L. R. Wickham, "The Sons of God and the Daughters of Men: Genesis VI 2 in Early Christian Exegesis," *OTS* 19 (1974) 135–39.

11. For surveys of "angels" in the three religious traditions, consult the following articles: Bernard J. Bamberger et al., "Angels and Angelology," in *EncJud* 2.956–77; T. L. Fallon et al., "Angels," in *New Catholic Encyclopedia* 1.506–16; and Sachiko Murata, "The Angels," in *Islamic Spirituality: Foundations* (ed. Seyyed Hossein Nasr; World Spirituality: An Encyclopedic History of the Religious Quest 19; New York: Crossroad, 1987) 324–44.

12. W. R. Smith, *The Religion of the Semites: the Fundamental Institutions* (New York: Schocken, 1972) 445–46.

belief in "angels" formed part of the less-knowledgeable system of beliefs that existed prior to the development of a pure monotheism. The retention of belief in these beings in the literature of the biblical books was seen as an example of the tenacity of ingrained religious ideas even when a superior religious vision had supplanted them.

The other theory, which has become the dominant theory of the twentieth century, held that the angels were a late creation of the Judean religion, manufactured to fill a void left by the cessation of belief in any gods other than Yahweh.[13] In this theory, belief in "angels" provided a theological position that allowed for nondivine yet supranatural beings to carry on the responsibilities previously understood to have been the duties of various Syro-Palestinian deities. When the belief in several gods was no longer recognized and only the one god, Yahweh, was believed to control all things, angels were perceived as obedient to and extensions of the one true god. These heavenly beings were not thought to have come from the native religious world of Syria–Palestine but to have developed in Jewish communities under the influence of Persian religion.

Both popular positions have presumed that the center of religious belief in angels was the Jewish religion and its descendants, Christianity and Islam.

The discovery of the Ugaritic texts did not markedly affect these theories concerning the origin of "angels." Even though there are messenger gods who appear in the Ugaritic narratives (including Yam's *mlakm*), which would seem to demonstrate that the theological creation of the מלאכים could not have been a "late Judean" innovation, the theory that they were invented at a late date to replace "gods" remains popular.[14] The narratives of the Ugaritic myths portray the messenger gods in the highly restricted function of being "living letters." All that these messengers did in the narratives was

---

13. W. O. E. Oesterley in Oesterley and Robinson, *History of Israel* (Oxford: Clarendon, 1932) 2.308–9 n. 4. B. D. Eerdmans ("On the Road to Monotheism," *OTS* 1 [1942] 121) suggests that all of the older personal gods became angels.

14. See Jesús-Luís Cunchillos Ylarri (*Cuando los ángeles eran dioses* [BibSal 14; Salamanca: Universidad Pontificia, 1976]), who has compiled the various strands of this theory; he concludes (pp. 158–59) that the various local Canaanite gods were redefined as angels at the time when Yahweh was seen as the supreme sole deity in "Israel." The perspective is succinctly stated by James L. Mays: "The theophany is introduced by a summons to 'the sons of God,' the divine beings who peopled the heavenly throne room in the mythopoetic vision of the Old Testament, a vision formed in the era of religious thought before there were angels" ("Psalm 29," *Int* 39 [1985] 62). See Manfred Weippert, "The Baalam Text from Deir ʿAllā and the Study of the Old Testament," in *The Balaam Text from Deir ʿAlla Re-evaluated: Proceedings of the International Symposium Held in Leiden 21–24 August 1989* (ed. Jacob Hoftijzer and G. van der Kooij; Leiden: Brill, 1991) 170.

memorize messages, go to the recipient, and repeat the text verbatim as it was presented to them.[15] The use of these messengers in the stories from Ugarit is restricted to the divine realm. When the gods sent messages to humans, they themselves appeared, whereas in the biblical texts, messengers function to allow Yahweh to confer with mortals without having to appear before them himself.

Labor-Gods?

In chapter 5, it was noted that Kothar-wa-Hasis may have had a crew of workers under his control when he was constructing the improved house for Baal. The existence of this crew is quite uncertain, but if the texts do refer to workers, and if they are divine and not human, they seem to fit on the same level as the messenger deities.[16] It must be remembered, however, that it is also possible that these crew members were not deities at all but human craftsmen who worked on the temple of Baal. In the mythological world view of the texts, these humans would have been assumed to be working under the direction of the divine artisan god, Kothar-wa-Hasis.

By the same token, if the construction workers were assumed to be divine, then they belonged to a category of deity subservient to the artisan god. There is little to determine the characteristics of these gods. It is clear in the passages that the work expected of them was done, and done well. On the other hand, they had no volition of their own but did only what was demanded of them by those who authorized the projects on which they worked. If they were deities, their representation in the mythological narratives is in the category of messengers, doing work for supervisors without dissent, complaint, or other signs of malfunctioning.

Seraphim

In the scene of Isaiah's call, there are creatures of the divine realm, called seraphim, standing as attendants to the enthroned Yahweh in the temple (Isa 6:2, 6).[17] Long treated as a subclass of angels in Jew-

---

15. Cunchillos Ylarri, "Étude philologique de *malᵓak*," 42, 50.

16. *KTU* 1.4.V.13–14, 29–30; 1.4.VI.18–21.

17. During the question session of my lecture at the Chicago Society of Biblical Research, Robert D. Haak suggested that I take into account the seraphim, who have been understood as on the same level as angels in the hierarchy. This lecture was later published as "Dissenting Deities or Obedient Angels: Divine Hierarchies in Ugarit and the Bible," *BR* 35 (1990) 18–35.

ish and Christian traditions, these beings appear in the Bible only in this passage. It is fairly clear that these beings were the guardians of the throne of God, and as such they functioned to impress visitors to the heavenly royal court, just as courtiers and palace guards would stand impressively about a human monarch's palace.[18] The fact that the noun used for these divinities is a word for poisonous snakes elsewhere in the biblical texts suggests that the guardians may in fact have been seen as serpentine beings.[19] This would be consistent with serpents used as royal symbols and heavenly guardians throughout the ancient Near and Middle East.[20] Being heavenly beasts, however, these seraphim had wings, indeed three pair, the same number of wings that Κρόνος is said to have had in Philo of Byblos, where the multiple wings are presumed to be symbolic of the god's eternal vigilance, mind, and perception.[21] This would not be an odd number of wings for the closest guards of the highest authority (since Κρόνος was presumed to be El in Philo's history). There may also be a play on the verb 'to burn' (שׂרף), and the seraphim (שׂרפים) may in fact be "fiery serpents."

In the single biblical text where these divinities appear, they clearly are standing guard at the throne of Yahweh. They are present at the ordination of Isaiah to his position as a prophet of God, but their speeches are clearly the speech of Yahweh's will, and their actions are God's actions, intended to purify Isaiah for the task ahead. In this respect, the seraphim did not act differently from other angels in the Bible. That they are not called מלאכים may suggest that their primary function was not the bearing of messages (as the "messengers" proper did), but some other function in the hierarchy. It appears reasonable to posit that they were the "palace guard" of the heavenly throne room, as it were, "angels" dressed up in fancy uniforms. Their

---

18. Otto Kaiser, *Isaiah 1–12: A Commentary* (OTL; Philadelphia: Westminster, 1972) 76.

19. Num 21:6, 8; Deut 8:15; Isa 14:29, 30:6.

20. H. Frankfort, *Kingship and the Gods: A Study of Ancient Near Eastern Religions as the Integration of Society and Nature* (Chicago: University of Chicago Press, 1978) 107, on the uraeus, called, curiously, "fiery snake"; Pierre Amiet, *Elam* (Auvers-sur-oise: Archée, 1966) 58, 310–11, 382, fig. 233:A–B, fig. 286:A–C; G. J. P. McEwan, "ᵈмuš and Related Matters," *Or* 52 (1983) 219; Veronica Ions, *Indian Mythology* (London: Hamlyn, 1967) 102. J. A. B. van Buitenen (ed. and trans., *The Mahabharata I: The Book of the Beginning* [Chicago: University of Chicago Press, 1973] 89) translates the description of the snakes guarding the divine drink of the Indian deities, found in *Mahabharata* 1.29: "shimmering like blazing fires," while their tongues, mouths, and eyes burn or flash with lightning, turning to ashes all upon whom they look. Note also Jacob Milgrom (*Numbers* [Jewish Publication Society Torah Commentary; Philadelphia: Jewish Publication Society, 1990] 459–60), who associates the seraphim with royal symbols in Egypt, but also with the seraph made by Moses in Num 21:9.

21. Philo of Byblos I.10.36–37 (from Eusebius *Prep. Gospel*).

status in the hierarchy, however, was the same as that of the messengers. They did what they were told and spoke only what they were ordered to speak by those higher up in the organization. Therefore, the seraphim should be seen as on the messenger level.[22]

THE GODS IN SERVICE

The deities of this level did not rule; they served, but on the divine plane. There are two major areas in which these deities are are represented as functioning in the extant sources. The activity portrayed most extensively is that of being a messenger of divine communications. The messenger gods also appear in narratives where they carried out jobs determined for them by deities on a superior level. In their activities, they served as extensions of the will of higher gods. Yet, they are presented as individual divine beings who happened to be under the control of other gods.

22. It is uncertain whether the cherubim, who figure so prominently in cult iconography in the Bible, functioned at this level, or were viewed as artisan gods specializing in "security," or perhaps were not even assumed to be deities. If they were deemed gods, they well may have been thought of as "angels in spiffy uniforms" who guarded the holy places and the throne of God. The one intelligible story that deals with a cherub as an individual (Gen 4:24) has Yahweh appoint the cherub to be a guard with a magic fiery sword over the entrance to Eden; see excursus by Nahum Sarna, *Genesis* (Jewish Publication Society Torah Commentary; Philadelphia: Jewish Publication Society, 1989) 375–76. The context for the reference in Ezek 28:14, 16 (for which much emendation of the text has been suggested) is unknown, though this cherub usually is related to the one in the Eden narrative: Kalman Yaron, "The Dirge over the King of Tyre," *ASTI* 3 (1964) 30; and J. H. van Dijk, *Ezekiel's Prophecy on Tyre (Ez 26,1–28,19): A New Approach* (BibOr 20; Rome: Pontifical Biblical Institute, 1968) 119–21; however, it is sometimes argued to be one of the temple cherubim: Robert R. Wilson, "The Death of the King of Tyre: The Editorial History of Ezekiel 28," in *Love and Death in the Ancient Near East: Essays in Honor of Marvin H. Pope* (ed. John H. Marks and Robert M. Good; Guilford, Conn.: Four Quarters, 1987) 215. The entire passage is a quagmire of textual difficulties, which explains the diversity of interpretations, but whoever is addressed as the "cherub" in Ezek 28:16 is presumed to have offended God: Knud Jeppesen, "You Are a Cherub, but No God," *SJOT* 1 (1991) 91; however, this is understood by most scholars to refer to the King of Tyre (ibid., 91, 94) or even to the high priest (Wilson, "Death of the King of Tyre," 216), but not to the cherub itself. Yaron ("Dirge over king of Tyre," 30–31) insists that cherubim never act on their own, though it is impossible from the amount of data available to be certain of that, since, as he suggests, there may well be a Phoenician mythological tradition behind the cherubim of which nothing is currently known (p. 51). The possibility that cherubim were seen as "heavenly animals" rather than "deities" in a formal sense must also be considered seriously. This solution would accord with the use of cherubim as beasts of burden for Yahweh in the temple (on the ark) and in Ezekiel's visions, chaps. 1–3 and 10 (chariot).

The Divinity of the Gods

Because the 'angels' of the Jewish tradition were not considered gods, it should first be demonstrated that the beings in the Ugaritic texts were in fact divine creatures.[23] The messengers in the Ugaritic texts are designated by several words, the meanings of most of which are unknown.[24] However, the word used for Yam's messengers in the mythological narrative is *mlak*, familiar from biblical מלאך.[25] It is in the narration of the activities of these messengers that the authors of the myths declare that the messengers are in fact gods. When Baal's messengers approached Anat with his message for her, the author declares, in the role of the omniscient teller of the story, that the personnel approaching the goddess were gods: 'Lo, Anat saw the gods' (*hlm.ᶜnt.tph.ilm*).[26] In the mind of the author, these messengers were classified as *ilm*, 'gods'. Additional evidence for the divine nature of the messengers is found in the ritual texts at Ugarit where Asherah's messengers, *qdš* and *amrr*, appear.[27] The tablet contains the two names of her messengers along with other well-known deities of the Ugaritic pantheon.

The מלאכים of the biblical texts may well have been less than divine, but some passages imply that the nature of these beings as gods had not been entirely lost. In the Bible, the messengers usually are presented as subservient creatures who do only the will of Yahweh; however, there are some examples in which the distinction between Yahweh and messenger becomes confused. The conflation of Yahweh and 'angel' is nowhere more apparent than in the story of Moses meeting the deity:

23. It is widely recognized that the theology of the Old Testament does not accept the divine status of angels, since Yahweh alone is God: Walther Eichrodt, *Theology of the Old Testament* (OTL; Philadelphia: Westminster, 1967) 2.201; H. Ringgren, *Israelite Religion* (trans. D. E. Green; Philadelphia: Fortress, 1966) 100; Oesterley and Robinson, *History of Israel*, 2.308–9.

24. The words *ᶜnn*, *ǵlm*, and *tᶜdt* are all used for these messenger deities in the same sense as *mlakm*, yet the exact meaning of the terms, not to mention the question of whether they had slightly different connotations reflecting their positions, elludes certainty; see del Olmo Lete, *Mitos y leyendas de Canaan Segun la tradicion de Ugarit: Textos, vesión y estudio* (FCB1; Madrid: Ediciones Cristianad, 1981) 602, 607, and 637, for the variety of interpretations that have been suggested and see notes cited there for further sources.

25. Thus: "Yam sent messengers" = *mlakm.ylak.ym*; KTU 1.2.I.11. See E. T. Mullen, *The Divine Council in Canaanite and Early Hebrew Literature* (HSM 24; Chico, Cal.: Scholars Press, 1980) 210.

26. KTU 1.3.III.32; their status is noted by K. Merling Alomia, "Lesser Gods of the Ancient Near East and Some Comparisons with Heavenly Beings of the Old Testament" (Ph.D. dissertation, Andrews University, 1987) 237.

27. KTU 1.123.26.

> And a messenger [מלאך] of Yahweh appeared to him in a
> flame of fire from the midst of the bush; and he looked, and
> wow, the bush was burning with fire but the bush was not
> consumed. And Moses said, "Wow! I will turn and look at this
> great spectacle to know why the bush is not burned." And
> Yahweh saw that he turned to look, and God [אלהים] called to
> him from the midst of the bush, and he said, "Moses! Moses!"
> And he said, "Here am I!" (Exod 3:2–4).

The shift from messenger to god has sometimes been understood as
an odd confusion in the text.[28] It has sometimes been argued that the
phrase מלאך יהוה ('angel of Yahweh', as it is usually translated) is a
technical term for the manifestation of Yahweh and therefore means
the god in person rather than a messenger sent by the deity.[29]

The relationship between Yahweh and the messengers is also ambiguous in the story of Abraham and his visitors at Mamre.

> And he raised his eyes and he looked and indeed there were
> three men [אנשים] standing over against him; when he saw
> them he ran to greet them from the opening of the tent and he
> bowed down to the ground (Gen 18:2).

There is nothing particularly interesting in this scene, yet, at the end
of the visit, as the three "men" are ready to depart, the narrative
takes a strange turn:

> And Yahweh [יהוה] went away as soon as he finished speaking
> to Abraham, and Abraham returned to his place. And the two
> messengers [מלאכים] went to Sodom in the evening
> (Gen 18:33–19:1).

While the three visitors appear at the beginning as men, they depart
as Yahweh and two messengers. The pair of messengers have in fact
been sent by Yahweh with instructions to destroy Sodom (Gen
19:13). A close relationship is maintained between the messengers
and Yahweh; the messengers, whether speaking from burning
bushes or demolishing wicked cities, are assumed to reflect Yahweh's
intentions. At no point, however, does the biblical material define the
מלאכים, who function as messengers, as "gods."[30] The careful use of

---

28. Martin Noth, *Exodus: A Commentary* (OTL; Philadelphia: Westminster, 1962) 40.

29. Samuel Rolles Driver, *The Book of Exodus* (CBSC; Cambridge: Cambridge University Press, 1918) 19; Gerhard von Rad, *Old Testament Theology* (New York: Harper &
Row, 1962) 1.285–87.

30. Although "angels" have been consistently studied by analyzing characters from
the biblical texts who in fact are called "gods," in this study the מלאכים are not considered just another definition of אלהים. The terms בני אלהים, בני אלים, בני עליון, and קדשים

the messengers in the Bible certainly reflects a desire on the part of the biblical authors to present Yahweh as the only "god" and to exclude messengers from this status.[31] It is true, however, that the angels are understood as presenting the words and actions of Yahweh as though he himself were presenting them.

The Work of the Messenger Deities

The primary function of the messenger deities in the narratives from Ugarit was to deliver messages from one deity to another.[32] Their entire existence, as presented in the surviving Ugaritic literature, consisted of a highly restricted series of actions, all related to the conveyance of divine communication. The messenger gods, no matter who sent them on their mission, are presented in stereotyped actions, using predictable verbs.[33] Though the gods were given individual names and thus apparently individual characters, their behavior was quite indistinguishable. The gods of the upper levels in the bureaucracy seem to have had their own personal messengers. Baal sent his word out by the pair of messenger deities named *gpn w ugr*, who may well have been servants solely of Baal.[34] Asherah had at least one messenger, *amrr*, and possibly two others, *qdš* and *dgy*.[35] The Ugaritic narratives often picture the messengers as having been sent out in pairs.[36]

---

all refer to deities in general, but may or may not include the messenger class. The heavenly צבאות may well include all the gods of heaven, including the messenger gods (Ps 33:6), but the word is also used explicitly to refer to forbidden gods (which would not necessarily include the messenger gods: Deut 17:3, 2 Kgs 17:16). It is assumed that the biblical texts used the word מלאך when the messenger deities were intended; other terms often used for divine beings may not refer to the messenger deities at all. There is also no reason to assume a relationship between the angels and the stars; Eichrodt, *Theology of OT*, 2.196; W. Herrmann, "Die Frage nach Göttergruppen in der religiösen Vorstellungswelt der Kanaanäer," *UF* 14 (1982) 95.

31. No matter what the historical progression of religious beliefs may have been in Judah or Israel, the biblical texts present a picture of the religious world in which Yahweh is the sole recognized deity for Judah and Israel; von Rad, *Theology*, 1.210–212; Eichrodt, *Theology of OT*, 1.220–27; Bernhard Lang, *Monotheism and the Prophetic Minority: An Essay in Biblical History and Sociology* (SWBAS 1; Sheffield: Almond, 1983) 50.

32. Cunchillos Ylarri, "Étude philologique de *malʾak*," 40, 42, 50.

33. Ibid., 39. The verbs are limited to *leave, arrive, turn, respond,* and *notice;* del Olmo Lete, *Mitos y leyendas,* 52.

34. *KTU* 1.3.III.36. See H. L. Ginsberg, "Baal's Two Messengers," *BASOR* 95 (1944) 25; R. Good, "Cloud Messengers?" *UF* 10 (1978) 436–37.

35. *KTU* 1.3.VI.10–11. See Edward Lipiński, "Envoi d'un messager (V AB, F, 7–11)," *Syria* 50 (1973) 37.

36. Alomia, "Lesser Gods of the Ancient Near East," 236.

It should be noticed that the messengers simply became the messages they were ordered to convey.[37] They became the words of the deity who sent them, repeating a message verbatim and engaging in no other activities. The reader knew that the texts were delivered verbatim because the narrative often recounts the message both when the sending deity relates it to the messenger gods and then again as the messengers deliver it to the deity to whom it was directed.[38] The same messengers might then be requested to take a message back to the god who first sent them. This was done without complaint, it seems, because the messengers were acting as extensions of their divine superior. Again, the response was sometimes repeated at both ends of the mission.[39]

The messages delivered were in the form of letters. Ugaritic epistles began with a three-part heading, though the order of the individual parts differed in each letter. The standard letter began with the following series.[40]

> 1. *l* + proper name   to so and so
> 2. *rgm*   say!
> 3. *tḥm* + proper name/title   a/the message of so-and-so

When Baal directed the messenger deities to carry a message to Anat, he explained the manner of approaching the goddess:

> Like servants then enter;
> At the feet of Anat bow and fall,
> Bow down, honor her,
> And say to Maiden Anat [*rgm l btlt ᶜnt*],
> Recite to the relation of peoples
> A message of Victorious Baal [*tḥm aliyn bᶜl*],
> A word of the victorious of heroes
>   (*KTU* 1.3.III.8–14).[41]

All the formal aspects of the letter heading were present in the messengers' deliveries. The messengers, however, were not responsible for the content of the missives; they merely recited the words composed by the superior deities.[42]

---

37. Cunchillos, "Étude philologique de *malʾak*," 40.

38. See, for example, *KTU* 1.2.I.17–19 and 33–35.

39. For example, Mot sent a message back to Baal by Baal's own messengers (*KTU* 1.4.VII.52 [ending in a broken tablet]–1.5.II.12). Thus, the two superior deities communicated through the messengers as if by letter (Cunchillos, "Étude philologique de *malʾak*" 42, 50).

40. See, for example, letters *KTU* 2.12.1–5, 2.13.1–4, 2.10.1–3.

41. The definitions of *ǧlm*, *ymmt*, and *limm* are quite uncertain; however, the intention of the passage is unrelated to the meanings of these particular words.

42. Alomia, "Lesser Gods of the Ancient Near East," 231.

The function of the messenger deities was determined by the role they played in the lives of the gods of the upper levels of the hierarchy. The messenger deities had no independent say regarding their own actions. The deities who sent them out with their messages used them for long-distance communication so that they did not have to make the trips themselves.[43] In this way higher-level deities made appointments, worked out differences, and set up forays to visit El. The messenger gods themselves had no part in the communication that was taking place; they merely conveyed the information promptly, willingly, and correctly.[44]

In the extant narratives from Ugarit, the *mlakm* 'messengers' restricted their services to the divine realm. They are not depicted as mediators between the gods of the higher levels and the human world. When the gods in the Ugaritic narratives communicated with people, they did it directly. Communication between the gods in *De Dea Syria* and their devotees was also direct, through the statues representing the gods in their temples.[45] The *mlakm* in the Ugaritic texts appear to have been personnel of the gods, but it is impossible to know whether they were also sent by gods to deal with humans. In any case, the messengers appeared in Ugarit solely as a means of communication.

Even though there was only one recognized deity in the narratives of the Bible, he also used messengers for communication. Obviously, as a single deity, he would not use messengers to deal with other gods, but the biblical מלאכים *were* sent by Yahweh to deliver messages to mortals. Yahweh was perfectly capable of speaking directly to humans and did so in many biblical texts.[46] In some cases, however, he communicated with the human world by means of the מלאכים. Three times a messenger was sent to women with a divine word concerning their future, unborn children.[47] A messenger might also be sent to stop action already in progress.[48] Sometimes the word of God

---

43. E. Lipiński, "Envoi d'un messager (V AB, F, 7–11)," *Syria* 50 (1973) 37; del Olmo Lete, *Mitos y leyendas*, 39.

44. Alomia ("Lesser Gods of the Ancient Near East," 234, 240) stresses the two former characteristics. It should be noted that these messengers appear to be quite adept at what they do.

45. *De Dea Syria* relates tales of deities appearing directly to humans (pp. 15 and 19) and describes oracles by the statue of Apollo (p. 36). In the *Report of Wenamun* the deity seized a page boy and proclaimed a message through him (Hans Goedicke, *The Report of Wenamun* [JHNES; Baltimore: Johns Hopkins University Press, 1975] 53). This event is recorded as having occurred in Byblos circa 1100 B.C.E. (p. 11).

46. See, for example, Gen 17:1–2 (Abraham); Exod 19:3–6 (Moses); 1 Sam 3:11–14 (Samuel); 1 Kgs 3:5 (Solomon); Isaiah 6 (Isaiah); Jeremiah 1 (Jeremiah); Ezekiel 1–3 (Ezekiel).

47. Gen 16:7–12, 21:17–18; Judg 13:3.

48. Gen 22:11; Num 22:21–35.

brought by the messenger was to the effect that the person should in-stigate some action.[49] A messenger speaking in each of these situa-tions was to be listened to as though he were the mouth of Yahweh. In several of the passages it is explicitly stated that not only was Yah-weh speaking, but Yahweh was also present.[50] So certain were the people that the word of a divine messenger was true that a false prophet who claimed his message was delivered to him by a messen-ger was taken for a true prophet on the basis of this claim alone.[51]

Like the messengers of the Ugaritic pantheon, the biblical מלאכים did exactly what they were told to do. They delivered messages without complaint, promptly, and correctly. Like the Ugaritic mes-senger deities, they had no independent volition but only carried out the will of Yahweh, who commanded them. The words of the messengers were, in fact, the words of Yahweh. By virtue of their position as messengers of higher authority, they were subservient to the rest of the heavenly world.

Unlike the Ugaritic *mlakm*, the biblical מלאכים also engaged in ac-tivities unrelated to the carrying of messages. In certain biblical nar-ratives the מלאכים displayed the same unwavering loyalty to Yahweh in carrying out particular jobs that they did in delivering messages. Yahweh was the source of all activity carried out by the messengers; no other gods existed to make use of them. Something that was done by one of the messengers, therefore, was in effect done by Yahweh. A variety of tasks were delegated to these minor divine personnel. Examples of messenger tasks mentioned in the Bible are: protecting individuals from various dangers, executing punishment for im-proper behavior, acting as leaders to the nation of Israel, and even finding a wife for one of the patriarchs.[52] These stories demonstrate that the messengers who were members of the divine realm in Judah were considered more than mere bearers of information. They also acted as agents of the one god. This fact may reflect the theological stance of the authors of the Bible, that Yahweh alone was deity but because of his majesty, mundane acts needed to be handled by lesser personnel.[53] The messengers, as obedient and loyal servants of Yah-weh, could act in his name.

Within the wider cultural sphere of influence of Syria–Palestine, delivering messages is the only activity attributed to messenger dei-

---

49. Exod 3:2, 2 Kgs 1:3.

50. Gen 16:13, 31:11–13; Exod 3:4; Judg 6:11–18, 13:22.

51. 1 Kgs 13:18.

52. Protection: Gen 16:7–13, 21:17; 2 Kgs 1:3, 15; 19:35; 2 Chr 32:21; Zech 1:9–14; Ps 34:8, 91:11; Job 33:23. Punishment: Gen 19:13; 2 Sam 24:15; 1 Chr 21:12; Ps 35:5, 78:49. Leading: Exod 14:19, 23:20, 23, 32:34, 33:2; Judg 2:1. Wife service: Gen 24:7, 40.

53. Ringgren, *Israelite Religion*, 310–11.

ties. But, in the pantheons of the Syro-Palestinian city-states, there were deities belonging to other levels who handled such tasks, even though these gods disobeyed their superiors' orders, something that the "angels" in the Bible did not do. It is quite possible that messenger deities did engage in activities other than the transfer of communications between gods. For example, the workers on Baal's palace may have been considered divine rather than human, for they displayed the attributes of the messengers: competence, obedience, acquiescence, and prompt compliance.[54] But because of the small amount of source material available for reconstruction of this level of the divine world in Syria–Palestine, it is unclear whether the *mlakm* and similar gods were thought to perform duties other than bearing correspondence.

The messenger deities have been shown to be the servant personnel of the divine realm.[55] Their primary purpose was to transfer messages from the deities of a higher level in the divine bureaucracy, either to other gods or to the human world. Other tasks may have been assigned to them, but the authority for their actions came from their superiors in the divine realm. The beings are presented as willing, obedient, competent, and prompt servants, who did what they were told to do and nothing more. There was a total lack of dissent by gods of this level. The messenger gods did not contradict their superiors, nor did they make suggestions regarding the management of the universe or their own conduct. This level was not consulted about decisions carried on in the higher levels of the cosmic hierarchy. It was the duty of the messenger gods to do exactly what they were told to do and to do it well. They are portrayed as extensions of the deities who told them what to do. This was the lowest level of the divine hierarchy in Syria–Palestine. There were no gods subordinate to the messenger deities. Nor did the messenger deities have any authority of their own, except by the grace of their superiors. Messengers were expected to obey the wishes of other deities and to acknowledge their lowly position in the hierarchy.[56]

MALFUNCTIONING

In the narratives from Ugarit there is no real evidence of malfunctioning among the messenger deities, although the messengers sent by Yam to the assembled gods did make insulting demands on behalf of their master, Yam. But even in this instance, they were

54. *KTU* 1.4.V.13–14, 29–30; 1.4.VI.18–21.

55. Called at times "slaves," designating their low servant status; Alomia, "Lesser Gods of the Ancient Near East," 238.

56. M. S. Smith, "Divine Travel as a Token of Divine Rank," *UF* 16 (1984) 359.

merely carrying out the demands of their master.[57] It may be that such actions were disruptive and insubordinate, but the source of the disruption and insubordination was not the messenger but the superior who prompted them to behave in this manner. This means that the messengers did act in a fashion appropriate to their position in the divine hierarchy. Aside from this single instance, messengers in the Ugaritic texts acted like ideal "letters," repeating verbatim the notices entrusted to them.

This cannot be said of the messenger in the biblical tradition. It is true that the Bible itself presents messengers (מלאכים) as loyal and dutiful servants of Yahweh, but traditions stemming from the biblical accounts of the "angels" do include major malfunctioning. The one instance in the Bible that, according to some, shows the untrustworthy nature of "angels" does not in fact display any malfunctioning on the part of the messengers; instead, the text highlights the unworthiness of mortals.

> If in his servants he does not trust
> And with his messengers [מלאכים] he finds fault,
> How much less the inhabitants of clay houses
> Whose foundation is in dust;
> They are crushed before a moth! (Job 4:18–19).

This is not a passage about misbehaving "angels," since the question that was asked in the preceding discussion was whether any human could be more just than God (Job 4:17). The answer given is that even the personnel of heaven (the מלאכים) fall short of the perfection of Yahweh. This being the case, no human can possibly claim to be more just than Yahweh and base the claim in reality. The reference to the messengers in this passage is for comparison and is not, as is sometimes claimed, a reference to the "fallen angels."[58] The text points out that the messengers were beings lower than Yahweh, a fact that would have been presupposed in a divine hierarchical system; nothing in the passage suggests that they were particularly disobedient.

No doubt it was because the messenger deities were totally obedient to their superior gods in the pantheon that the Judean religious circles who posited Yahweh as the sole deity allowed them to be retained. Any other gods, from any other level of the divine hierarchy, were capable of dissenting from their superiors and their peers.

---

57. *KTU* 1.2.I.11–20, 30–35. Gordon, "Canaanite," pp. 191–192; Gray, *Legacy*, 24. The content of the message sent by Yam is clear, but the question of whether the messengers were told to disregard proper etiquette before the divine assembly remains; Mullen, *Divine Council*, 125.

58. Pope, *Job: Introduction, Translation and Notes* (3d ed.; AB 15; Garden City, N.Y.: Doubleday, 1973) 37 n. 18.

This meant that several gods might create a universe in which conflicting divine purposes were the normal state of existence. If the theology of Judea was to posit a world in which only one deity set the agenda, it was necessary that there be no other gods capable of resisting the will of that one god. Major active deities had been the primary rulers of the earthly realm; they clearly had been perceived as having their own purposes, which created conflicts within their level of the divine world as well as with the purposes of the highest authority, El. Even the artisan gods were allowed a certain amount of autonomy and could disagree with their superiors. Alone among the gods, messengers could not act without the express authority of gods higher in the organization. There was no threat of dissension within the level of messenger gods.

Therefore, a religious group desiring a single deity with absolute control of the universe and a "staff " in heaven could retain the level of the messenger deities without allowing for any divine dissent from the authority of the one ruling god. This appears to be what happened when Judean religion reduced its pantheon to Yahweh. In fact, the pantheon was reduced to two levels of divinities: Yahweh, the highest authority (also called אל), and the messenger gods, who had no independent authority. This ensured that Yahweh was both the sole source of all authority in the cosmos and that he had royal servants to carry out the ordering of the universe.[59]

In the Jewish religious literature of the late first millennium B.C.E. and the early centuries C.E., a distinct shift may be seen in the role of the messengers of the divine world. No longer considered deities, the messengers took on aspects of a perfect bureaucracy under the care of God. Rank upon rank of angels controlled the universe in the name of Yahweh.[60] Yet, the cosmos did not appear to be functioning as though

---

59. On the shift from many gods to a single deity and its effect on the status of the messenger gods, see my "Realignment in Heaven: An Investigation into the Ideology of the Josianic Reform" (Ph.D. diss., University of Chicago, 1987) 324–25.

60. *Jub.* 2:2 lists ranks of angels. This text appears to derive from sometime in the second century B.C.E., though the dating of the text is at best tentative; see O. S. Wintermute, "Jubilees (Second Century B.C.)," in *The Old Testament Pseudepigrapha* (ed. James H. Charlesworth; Garden City: Doubleday, 1985) 2.43–44. Of course, *1 Enoch* 20:1–8 and 40:1–10 also describe this heavenly host of angels. A journey through heaven, with its vast multitudes of angels charged with various duties in the ten heavens, is related in *2 Enoch* 3–22; however, the suggested dates for this composition range from late in the first century B.C.E. to the early second millennium C.E. See Francis I. Andersen, "2 (Slavonic Apocalypse of) Enoch (Late First Century A.D.)," in *The Old Testament Pseudepigrapha* (ed. James H. Charlesworth; Garden City: Doubleday, 1983) 1.95; Ringgren, *Israelite Religion*, 311. See now Saul M. Olyan, *A Thousand Thousands Served Him: Exegesis and the Naming of Angels in Ancient Judaism* (Texte und Studien zum Antiken Judentum 36; Tübingen: Mohr, 1993), esp. pp. 31–69, 118, where the rise of these angelic ranks is shown to derive from the exegesis of written texts.

it were a well-ordered system in the care of one beneficent god who had no dissenting attendants in the universe. However, the possibility of assigning the blame for discord in the cosmos to gods other than Yahweh was unacceptable in the Jewish view of the universe. If the malfunctioning aspects of life appeared to derive from the heavenly realm, the malfunctioning would have to have its origin in Yahweh, unless the traditional belief in obedient angels were modified.

The later belief that the heavenly realm was made up solely of Yahweh and numerous "angels" at his beck and call was projected backward, supporting the assertion that the divine realm always has been made up only of Yahweh and his messengers. This view was the one that became dominant in the Jewish tradition, as well as in Christianity and Islam. As a result, passages in the Bible originally referring to gods of the higher levels of the pantheon had to be interpreted as narratives about messengers.[61] This was the only possible way to read such texts as Gen 6:1–4 without having to acknowledge the existence of gods other than Yahweh.[62] In this way the behavior patterns of the major active gods, which prior to the reduction of the pantheon would not have been attributed to messenger-level deities came to be attributed to the divine personnel called מלאכים.

Once the shift of attributes was made, the messengers could be seen as dissenting from and rebelling against Yahweh. The evils of the world could then be attributed to "angels" who were in rebellion against God. A number of biblical passages, foremost among them Gen 6:1–4, could be brought into alignment with this interpretation and an entire mythological tradition developed concerning these "fallen angels."[63] The disobedient angels not only were seen as being in conflict with the will of Yahweh, but also became almost a mirror-image of the divine realm. The ambiguous figure of "the adversary" in Job, Zechariah, and 1 Chronicles became the leader of angels in revolt and defiance against Yahweh.[64] This "fallen" angel became the antithesis of Yahweh in heaven and the source of all evil, carried

---

61. This theological shift is discernible even in the translation of the Hebrew Bible into Greek; see John G. Gammie, "The Angelology and Demonology in the Septuagint of the Book of Job," *HUCA* 56 (1985) 5–7.

62. The texts dealing with the "corrupt" angels, as seen in Gen 6:1–4, are attested as early as the early second century B.C.E.; John J. Collins, "The Place of Apocalypticism in the Religion of Israel," in *Ancient Israelite Religion* (ed. P. D. Miller, P. D. Hanson, and S. D. McBride; Philadelphia: Fortress, 1987) 541. See *1 Enoch* 6:1–8, 64:1–2, 69:1–15; *Jub.* 5:1–4; and Josephus *Ant.* 1.3.1.

63. On the tradition of the fallen angels, see Julian Morgenstern, "The Mythological Background of Psalm 82," *HUCA* 14 (1939) 75–120; and the short summary by Arthur Marmorstein, "Fallen Angels," *s.v.* "Angels and Angelology," *EncJud* 2.966–68.

64. Job 1:6–12, 2:1–7; Zech 3:1–2; and 1 Chr 21:1 (but, see the parallel narrative in 2 Sam 24:1).

out through his own gang of messengers ("fallen angels"), who became known generally as "demons."[65]

This trajectory of malfunctioning beings among the ranks of messenger gods may be followed in historical Jewish and Christian religious thought, a development of theological belief concerning the levels of the divine world that may be traced in extant texts. What happened to the level of messengers in the rest of the Syro-Palestinian religious world as this shift was taking place in Jewish tradition is not known. The messengers possibly continued their existence as loyal and obedient deities of the lowest level, but until more material is available, the position of the messenger deities in Syria–Palestine in the first millennium C.E. remains unknown.

What can be learned about malfunctioning in the pantheon view of Syria–Palestine regarding the messengers is clear. As long as there were levels of gods within a divine hierarchy, the messenger gods formed a level in which there was no malfunctioning. If in a narrative the messengers acted in a way that differed from the acceptable order of the cosmos, it was because they were given orders by deities on levels of the hierarchy capable of making decisions contrary to the proper governance of the universe. The messenger gods were less important than the gods who commanded them. This was not malfunctioning on the messenger's part. Rather, this was the normal state of a hierarchy in which the gods of the lowest level were to be obedient and trustworthy personnel at the bottom of the chain of authority. In sources in which it is clear that the messengers were viewed as being in revolt and even totally opposed to the ultimate authority, it is also apparent that the religious views of the community forced the messengers to assume the attributes of deities who belonged to higher levels of the pantheon. These communities also abandoned belief in a pantheon in favor of belief in a single deity who controlled the world. This was a theological position unnecessary for devotees of a hierarchical pantheon. It cannot be assumed that this shift in theology (messenger deities acquiring attributes of the higher levels of divinities) emerged in areas of Syria–Palestine outside of Jewish circles, nor even that it appeared in all segments of Judaism at the same time. In sum, in the pantheon, messengers belonged to the only level of deities that is pictured ideally. There was no malfunctioning, since messengers were the obedient servants of the authoritative deities.

65. See *1 Enoch* 6:7–8 and 69:2–15, where the leader is named Semyaz. In the long version of *2 Enoch* 7 and 29:4–6, the leader is named Satanail. Again, the Greek translation reflects contemporary theology by translating satan (השׂטן) as the devil (ὁ διάβολος) in Job (see Gammie, "Angelology and Demonology," 18). The view has a long historical tradition, reflected in literature such as Dante Alighieri's *Divine Comedy* and John Milton's *Paradise Lost*.

Chapter 7

Summary

The bureaucratic structure of the divine world in ancient Syria–Palestine, which has been described as a hierarchy with four levels, reflects only the texts that have been discovered and that are susceptible to coherent reading and interpretation. There is good reason to believe that the hierarchy in heaven was considered by the people of Syria–Palestine to be comprised of many levels, probably more than the four presented in this book. Within these levels, undoubtedly there were even more subtle layers and distinctions. The hierarchical levels delineated in this work are based on the deities for whom there is significant information. Unfortunately, the vast amount of mythological material from Syria–Palestine that once existed was the only means by which a detailed picture of the divine bureaucracy could possibly be reconstructed, and that material is now lost.

No clear distinction between levels of the gods can be confirmed without more information. If available, we may guess that such information would reveal the exact functions of members of the various levels and the original boundaries of the hierarchical levels. With the current data, however, only general distinctions can be posited. At the same time, there appears to have been no clear distinction between the hierarchy of the divine realm and the hierarchy of the mortal world. That is, the universe came together in a single cosmic bureaucracy.

COSMIC HIERARCHY

While this study concentrates on the mythological vision of the rule of the universe at the divine level, the Syro-Palestinian perception of the cosmos also included human rule, which was incorporated into the theology along with bureaucratic divine rule. At the top of the organization was the ultimate divine authority for all of the cosmos, while at the bottom were human slaves. The fourfold hierarchy of the divine realm may be diagramed as follows, with one example provided for each level:

Authoritative Deities	El
Active Deities	Baal
Artisan Deities	Kothar
Messenger Deities	*gpn w ugr*

That this social stratification reflected a model familiar from human society is to be expected. It does in fact correspond very closely to the fourfold hierarchy of ancient Near Eastern society as proposed by Diakonoff, which may be diagramed similarly:

Aristocracy	King and rural bourgeoisie
Royal servants	Recipients of land grants for service: "governing class"
Royal laborers	Skilled craftsmen
Private slaves	Lowest human populace: not free[1]

Even though both diagrams represent theoretical social stratification based on limited data, it is noteworthy that the divine levels and the human social strata both represent the same social divisions. Highest authority in heaven rested with the ultimate divine ruling couple, El and Asherah, who corresponded to the human sphere's king and queen. The active deities were assigned areas to rule by the authoritative deity and retained them as long as they remained in loyal service to that god. Similarly, "royal servants" were allotted their own lands to govern on the human level.[2] The artisan gods and the royal laborers both represented free, skilled craftsman, while the

---

1. I. M. Diakonoff, "Structure of Near Eastern Society before the Middle of the 2nd Millennium B.C.," *Oikumene* 3 (1982) 94–98. Some may, with good reason, question the adequacy of these four levels to describe the society, but they are the levels (or divisions) recorded by the scribes. Diakonoff has placed levels two and three under the title "men of the king" (p. 97).

2. C. G. Libolt ("Royal Land Grants from Ugarit" [Ph.D. diss., University of Michigan, 1985] 39–40) notes that theoretically all land was granted by the king to his subordinates. This land could be recalled if the subordinate misbehaved. See A. F. Rainey, "Social Stratification of Ugarit" (Ph.D. diss., Brandeis University, 1962) 26. Note that in theory all of this land belonged to the patron deity, and the mortal king was merely acting on behalf of that patron deity (B. Albrektson, *History and the Gods: An Essay on the Idea of Historical Events as Divine Manifestations in the Ancient Near East and in Israel* [ConBOT 1; Lund: C. W. K. Gleerup, 1967] 45, 51).

messenger-gods and the human slaves provided, on their respective planes, personnel without independent volition.

While the two realms, divine and human, reflect each other, they also were considered to be portions of the same hierarchy. Among the ranks of those who ruled the universe were both gods and humans. Above all levels of universal rule were the deities of highest authority, El and Asherah. The mortal world was divided among deities of the second level, who governed cities and nations through their own subordinates, human kings and queens. These human rulers could, in turn, allocate land, or "daughter-cities," to their subordinates to rule.[3] The bureaucratic offices continued downward, since each level of human personnel owed position to superiors in both the human and divine worlds.

The bureaucracy of the daughter-cities also reflected the various levels seen in the divine realm. The local mayor, or *ḫazannu*, owed the right to his position to the will of the ruler of the central city-state.[4] Under the mayor were other officials, who were to oversee various aspects of the maintenance of the district. These officials were given the title *rb*, which expressed the fact that each official was the main person in charge of his specialized field.[5] Yet, beneath the orders of the *rb* were those who actually did the work. At the bottom of society were the slaves, who served their owners without rights or dispute, at least in theory. Thus, the "boss of the shepherds," a title found at Ugarit (*rb nqdm*), would have under his command a group of shepherds. Perhaps one of the shepherds owned a slave, so that in the rural social organization the fourfold hierarchy would be reproduced at the lowest end of the cosmic hierarchy:

ḫazannu	mayor of the daughter-city
rb	"boss" of a particular profession
ᶜm	"people" = free population
ᶜbd	slaves

Each of the various layers of rule in the cosmic scheme is reconstructed in this study through texts left by authors instructed in the scribal schools, so where a pattern has emerged, I have assumed it stemmed from the world view of the scribal schools. All levels of the

---

3. Rainey, "Social Stratification," 16–1, 26–27; M. Heltzer, *The Rural Community in Ancient Ugarit* (Wiesbaden: Reichert, 1976) 5.

4. Ibid., 80; H. W. F. Saggs, *The Greatness That Was Babylon* (New York: New American Library, 1962) 247–48; Ahlström, *Royal Administration and National Religion in Ancient Palestine* (SHANE 1; Leiden: Brill, 1982) 22–23.

5. Heltzer, *Rural Community*, 32.

universe came together, in their thinking, in one cosmic system. A chain of authority was produced that extended downward from the king of gods through levels of bureaucratic personnel, divine and human, to culminate in the lowest human member of the hierarchy, the slave. The rulers at the higher end of the bureaucracy were all entitled *mlk*, whereas the lower-level personnel each had a distinct title. This universal hierarchy may be illustrated by diagramming the relationship between the ultimate authority, El, and a slave belonging to a seaman (see chart, p. 173).[6] The idea that there are levels of control in heaven that extend downward through ranks of deities to the human level was not unique to the world of Syria–Palestine. Evidence for hierarchical rule of the cosmos is found in writings from the Hellenistic and Roman periods in the Mediterranean area.[7] Deriving from Syro-Palestinian origins, Jewish and Christian traditions in the Roman Empire envisioned a universe ruled by ranks of "angels."[8] The structure made room for the minor (and major) inconsistencies between the ideal of world order and the reality of life. Indeed, in the gnostic view of the universe, the levels of rulers were all demonic; thus the whole world was seen as being under the control of not just inept, but evil, bureaucrats.[9] Wherever an empire made up of numerous local governments was found, the basic form of the universal bureaucratic pantheon was also found. The governmental structure of the empire could be extended upward to an ultimate "emperor," who ruled the entire universe as a mortal emperor should rule an earthly kingdom.

A REFLECTION OF THE AUTHORS

All narrative information about the divine world as seen by the people of Syria–Palestine came from the minds of the authors of the mythological tales, which means that the tales represent the beliefs

---

6. *Rb malaḫḫē* is attested at Ugarit (ibid.); see also Gordon, *UT*, 447.

7. In the cults of the Near East in Roman times, the hierarchy of heaven could be made up of gods from several different nations and include "angels" (J. Teixidor, *The Pagan God: Popular Religion the Greco-Roman Near East* [Princeton: Princeton University Press, 1977] 14–15). Greek and Roman religious circles found the hierarchy a fine structure in which to include all the known cults, putting their favorite at the top of the system (R. MacMullen, *Paganism in the Roman Empire* [New Haven: Yale University Press, 1981] 79–83).

8. Already in the Christian book of Revelation (2:1), angels were assigned to all the individual churches. Perhaps the fullest account of angels in bureaucratic power, however, comes from the fifth or sixth century C.E. in *3 Enoch* 7–10.

9. Kurt Rudolph, *Gnosis: The Nature and History of Gnosticism* (San Francisco: Harper & Row, 1983) 67–70.

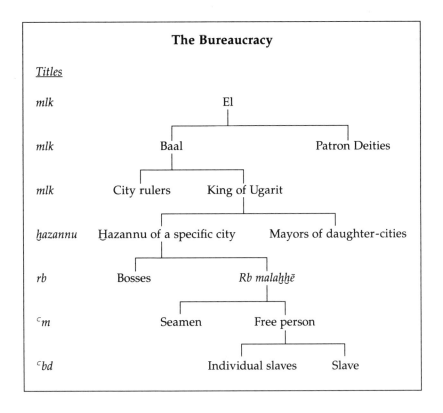

of a very restricted portion of the population, due to the fact that the ability to read and write was not universal in ancient Near Eastern civilizations. Those who could write had gone through the scribal schools and so had incorporated the values and views of that system. The myths they then composed reflected their vision of the cosmos, a vision that reflected scribal school teachings.

The scribal schools were geared toward the education and placement of competent people in various jobs necessary for the proper functioning of the state, cult, and commerce. Those who went to the schools sought to attain positions of some importance in the bureaucratic hierarchy of the city-states. Part of the goal of their education was to understand the workings of the state and the role they would play in that system. The educational curriculum of the scribal schools was based on a systematic vision of the society in which it existed. It is safe to assume that the levels of the divine hierarchy found in the mythological texts were those promulgated by the vision of the world present in the scribal school system and introduced to other people on the same bureaucratic level as the scribes.

If the mythological bureaucracy of the gods looks very much like the bureaucratic structure of society in the city-states of Syria–Palestine, it is because the many tablets discovered that deal with daily governance were tallied by scribal school graduates who had sat side by side with the scribal authors of the myths. Both the scribal talliers and the authors of the myths had been versed in the "true" nature of society during their school days. Their presentation of the hierarchy of heaven reflected the world in which they lived. They were part of the bureaucratic system. They were urban. They were recognized as adept by their superiors and were particularly conscious of the fact that they worked for the ruler. They were educated and, more importantly, aware of their own education, in contrast to people below them in the social system and even people who held superior positions, both of whom lacked education. The gods, as described by these scribes, functioned in a world very similar to their own.

It is likely that the scribes saw themselves as belonging to the level of society Diakonoff has called "royal laborers." These people worked for land owners; they also worked for the rulers themselves. Perhaps their vision of themselves may be seen in their presentation of the level of artisan gods. In the mythological narratives, the two highest levels of deities demonstrated a great deal of malfunctioning. The ruling gods were often dumb, insensitive, abusive of their own power, reckless with their subordinates, insubordinate with their superiors, and occasionally just plain wrong. The deities of these highest levels are pictured with all the foibles of the human bureaucrats that the scribes must have served. The messenger gods, on the other hand, are presented as stereotypes of the lowest laborers in the palace. The representations of these divinities are of an ideal personnel, because they neither thought nor dissented. They, unlike their human counterparts, functioned perfectly, just as a scribe would think such underlings ought to act.

The artisan gods, on the other hand, are described neither as brutally realistic masters, nor as brainless servants. In fact, they are presented as having been brilliant. They knew everything within their own field of competence. All the heavenly gods needed their help and acknowledged their superiority in their specific fields. Artisan gods did not make mistakes; their superiors made mistakes and then ordered them to carry out the faulty orders. No matter how much the artisan god protested the error, he knew his place and did what he had been told, fully aware that the stupid command of the superior would become apparent and the wise advice of the artisan god would be followed in the end. Such knowledgeable deities suffered through the rule of their less knowledgeable superiors because that is the way bureaucracy works. It does not require a great stretch of imagination to propose that the scribal authors of the mythological tales saw themselves as the Kothar-wa-Hasis figures, having to take orders from the virile, if inept, Baal. They worked for human rulers who had gained office by service to the king, and they had to put up with orders from people who had not gone to scribal school and did not know how things "really were," according to "the book." In drawing the divine counterpart for themselves, these scribes were able to demonstrate their own brilliance and express the recognition that they felt they should have been receiving.

The bureaucracy envisioned for the divine realm was not an ideal representation of a perfect hierarchy. The scribes were not the personnel who made great decisions in ruling the "land," but rather the level of bureaucracy that had to carry out the day-to-day work of carrying out the decisions made by higher authorities. The universe could be run better than it was being run, and the myths reflect this fact.[10] However, this vision of the universe was the vision of the scribal schools. To what extent other segments of society accepted particular aspects of this vision is unknown. This leads full circle back to the original questions: how much of the material in these sources was "required" or "dictated" by the civilization, and how much creativity was allowed the individual authors? Was there a difference between the beliefs of the people and the writings of the scribes? If the culture was defined by the scribal level of the hierarchy and the narratives were written by scribal authors, was there any real distance between the latter and the former? At present there is no way to know. It is important, however, always to remember that the sources originated in urban, bureaucratic, educated, and (probably) male circles and that the color of the culture was affected by the lens through which it was seen.

SUMMARY

The sources for recreating a vision of the divine world of Syria–Palestine are insufficient for the job. The extant materials do not adequately explain the divine governing system as the people in that culture understood it. Any information unearthed in the future could change the vision of the Syro-Palestinian pantheon drastically, just as in the past, new information has continually changed the picture.

---

10. One suspects from reading the mythological narratives that the artisan gods would have run the universe much better if they had been given a chance. This may be a reflection of the aspirations of the scribes who were writing the texts.

Assuming that the existing narrative material must have come from the stylus of scribal school graduates, I have proposed that the mythological world portrayed in the extant narratives should be understood in the light of the world in which those scribes functioned. Theirs was a bureaucratic system in which offices were filled by competent personnel who functioned in a series of hierarchical levels. Four levels may be distinguished in the material from Syria–Palestine.

The first level was that of ultimate authority or highest authority. The gods on this level owned the universe and ensured that the functions of the lower levels were carried out. They were especially renowned for wisdom and the capacity to assign competent personnel to the lower levels; therefore, they were somewhat less active than the gods of the other levels, because their responsibility was primarily to see that the rest of the organization was working. In Syria–Palestine the deities of the first level were El (or his equivalents) and Asherah.

The gods of the second level were the active deities or the patron gods. They were the deities to whom authority to rule the various portions of the cosmos was given. They were placed in office by the highest authorities and functioned under their superiors' jurisdiction. Natural, political, and abstract spheres of influence were allotted to them. Baal, Anat, Mot, Shapshu, and a host of other deities filled these offices in the hierarchy. They did not necessarily get along with each other or the rest of the universe in general, but in theory they were able to handle their own areas within the cosmos.

The third level consisted of the artisan gods, who were highly specialized deities possessing the knowledge and skill required by the rest of the pantheon to carry out the purposes of the gods in positions of authority. These deities were considered to be superb in their own fields; they made no mistakes. The only problems for which they were responsible resulted from obeying orders rather than from their own decision-making abilities. Kothar-wa-Hasis was the only artisan god portrayed well in the sources.

The messenger-gods composed the fourth hierarchical level. They served their superiors but were allowed no say in any decisions. They did what they were told and nothing else. These gods had no independent volition beyond the carrying out of a specific task. Though they did have names, their personalities and actions are indistinguishable one from another. They are best known in the Bible as "angels".

Every level of the divine hierarchy had its counterpart in human society. While the first three levels shared with their human counterparts the malfunctioning typical of their positions in society, the messengers were portrayed in an ideal manner, unlike the human messengers of the ancient Near Eastern hierarchies. This view of the divine world is based on a scribal view of bureaucratic rule from the schools of Syria–Palestine. This bureaucratic vision of the cosmos must be considered in any attempt to understand the position and the behavior of deities described in the mythology of the Syro-Palestinian world.

Bibliography

Ackerman, Susan. "And the Women Knead Dough": The Worship of the Queen of Heaven in Sixth-Century Judah." Pp. 109–24 in *Gender and Difference in Ancient Israel*. Edited by Peggy L. Day. Minneapolis: Fortress, 1989.

_____. "The Queen Mother and the Cult in Ancient Israel." *Journal of Biblical Literature* 112 (1993) 385–401.

_____. *Under Every Green Tree: Popular Religion in Sixth-Century Judah*. Harvard Semitic Monographs 46. Atlanta: Scholars Press, 1992.

Aggoula, Basile. "Divinités phéniciennes dans un passage du *Fihrist* d'Ibn al-Nadim." *Journal Asiatique* 278 (1990) 1–12.

Ahl, Sally W. "Epistolary Texts from Ugarit: Structural and Lexical Correspondences in Akkadian and Ugaritic." Ph.D. dissertation, Brandeis University, 1973.

Ahlström, Gösta W. *An Archaeological Picture of Iron Age Religions in Ancient Palestine*. Studia Orientalia 55/3. Helsinki: Societas Orientalis Fennicae, 1984.

_____. *Aspects of Syncretism in Israelite Religion*. Translated by Eric J. Sharpe. Horae Soederblomianae 5. Lund: C. W. K. Gleerup, 1963.

_____. *Royal Administration and National Religion in Ancient Palestine*. Studies in the History of the Ancient Near East 1. Leiden: Brill, 1982.

Aistleitner, J. *Die mythologischen und kultischen Texte aus Ras Schamra*. Bibliotheca orientalis hungarica 8. Budapest: Kiadó, 1959.

Albrektson, Bertil. *History and the Gods: An Essay on the Idea of Historical Events as Divine Manifestations in the Ancient Near East and in Israel*. Coniectanea Biblica, Old Testament 1. Lund: C. W. K. Gleerup, 1967.

Albright, William Foxwell. "Akkadian Letters." Pp. 482–90 in *Ancient Near Eastern Texts Relating to the Old Testament*. 3d edition. Edited by James B. Pritchard. Princeton: Princeton University Press, 1969.

_____. *Archaeology and the Religion of Israel*. Baltimore: Penguin, 1942.

_____. "Dwarf Craftsmen in the Keret Epic and Elsewhere in North-West Semitic Mythology." *Israel Exploration Journal* 4 (1954) 1–4.

_____. "The Earliest Forms of Hebrew Verse." *Journal of the Palestine Oriental Society* 2 (1922) 69–86.

_____. "The Early Alphabetic Inscriptions from Sinai and Their Decipherment." *Bulletin of the American Schools of Oriental Research* 110 (1948) 6–22.

_____. *From the Stone Age to Christianity: Monotheism and the Historical Process*. 2d ed. Garden City, New York: Doubleday, 1957.

_____. "Some Remarks on the Song of Moses in Deuteronomy XXXII." *Vetus Testamentum* 9 (1959) 339–46.

_____. *Yahweh and the Gods of Canaan: A Historical Analysis of Two Contrasting Faiths.* Garden City, New York: Doubleday, 1968; reprinted, Winona Lake, Ind.: Eisenbrauns, 1978.

Alomia, K. Merling. "Lesser Gods of the Ancient Near East and Some Comparisons with Heavenly Beings in the Old Testament." Ph.D. dissertation, Andrews University, 1987.

Alonso Schökel, Luis. *Treinta salmos: Poesía y oración.* 2d ed. Madrid: Ediciones Cristiandad, 1986.

Alt, Albrecht. *Essays on Old Testament History and Religion.* Translated by R. A. Wilson. Garden City, New York: Doubleday, 1966.

Amiet, Pierre. *Elam.* Auvers-sur-oise: Archée, 1966.

Andersen, Francis I. "Moabite Syntax." *Orientalia* 35 (1966) 81–120.

_____. "2 (Slavonic Apocalypse of) Enoch (Late First Century A.D.)." Pp. 91–221 in *The Old Testament Pseudepigrapha*, volume 1. Edited by James H. Charlesworth. Garden City, New York: Doubleday, 1983.

Andreasen, Niels-Erik A. "The Role of the Queen Mother in Israelite Society." *Catholic Biblical Quarterly* 45 (1983) 179–94.

Andreski, Stanislav. *Max Weber's Insights and Errors.* London: Routledge & Kegan Paul, 1984.

"Arti-Facts, News, Notes, and Reports from the Institutes: Cultic Inscriptions Found in Ekron," *Biblical Archaeologist* 53 (1990) 232.

Astour, Michael C. "The Netherworld and Its Denizens at Ugarit." Pp. 227–38 in *Death in Mesopotamia.* Edited by Bendt Alster. Mesopotamia 8. Copenhagen: Akademisk, 1980.

_____. "Some New Divine Names from Ugarit." *Journal of the American Oriental Society* 86 (1966) 277–84.

_____. "Ugarit and the Great Powers." Pp. 3–29 in *Ugarit in Retrospect: Fifty Years of Ugarit and Ugaritic.* Edited by Gordon Douglas Young. Winona Lake, Indiana: Eisenbrauns, 1981.

Attridge, Harold W., and Robert A. Oden Jr. *Philo of Byblos, The Phoenician History: Introduction, Critical Text, Translation, Notes.* Catholic Biblical Quarterly Monograph Series 9. Washington, D.C.: Catholic Biblical Association, 1981.

Attridge, Harold W., and Robert A. Oden Jr. *The Syrian Goddess (De Dea Syria) Attributed to Lucian.* Society of Biblical Literature Texts and Translations 9. Missoula, Montana: Scholars Press, 1976.

Bamberger, Bernard J. et al. "Angels and Angelology." Pp. 956–77 in *Encyclopedia Judaica*, volume 2. Jerusalem: Keter, 1971.

Barnard, Chester I. *The Functions of the Executive.* Cambridge: Harvard University Press, 1951.

Barr, James. "Philo of Byblos and His 'Phoenician History.'" *Bulletin of the John Rylands University Library of Manchester* 57 (1974) 17–68.

Baudissin, Wolf Wilhelm Grafen. *Adonis und Esmun: Eine Untersuchung zur Geschichte des Glaubens an Auferstehungsgötter und an Heilgötter.* Leipzig: Hinrichs, 1911.

Bauer, Hans. "Die Gottheiten von Ras Schamra." *Zeitschrift für die Alttestamentliche Wissenschaft* 51 (1933) 81–101.

Baumgarten, Albert I. *The "Phoenician History" of Philo of Byblos: A Commentary.* Études préliminaires aux religions orientales dans l'Empire Romain 89. Leiden: Brill, 1981.

Bellah, Robert N. "Religious Evolution." *American Sociological Review* 29 (1964) 358–74.

Ben-Barak, Zafrira. "The Queen Consort and the Struggle for Succession to the Throne." Pp. 33–40 in *La Femme dans le proche-orient antique: Compte rendu de la XXXIIIe rencontre assyriologique internationale (Paris, 7–10 julliet 1986).* Edited by Jean-Marie Durand. Rencontre assyriologique internationale 33. Paris: Éditions recherche sur les civilisations, 1987.

————. "The Status and Right of the Gĕbîrâ," *Journal of Biblical Literature* 110 (1991) 23–34.

Bergman, Jan, Helmer Ringgren, and M. Tsevat. "Bᵉthûlāh." Pp. 338–43 in *Theological Dictionary of the Old Testament,* volume 2. Edited by G. Johannes Botterweck and Helmer Ringgren. Translated by John T. Willis. Grand Rapids, Michigan: Eerdmans, 1975.

Bermant, Chaim, and Michael Weitzman. *Ebla: A Revelation in Archaeology.* New York: Times Books, 1979.

Blau, Peter M. *The Dynamics of Bureaucracy: A Study of Interpersonal Relations in Two Government Agencies.* Chicago: University of Chicago Press, 1955.

Bloch-Smith, Elizabeth. *Judahite Burial Practices and Beliefs about the Dead.* Journal for the Study of the Old Testament Supplement Series 123. Sheffield: JSOT Press, 1992.

Bordreuil, Pierre, and Dennis Pardee. "Le Rituel funéraire ougaritique RS.34.126." *Syria* 59 (1982) 121–28.

Bowman, Charles Howard III. "The Goddess ᶜAnatu in the Ancient Near East." Ph.D. dissertation, Graduate Theological Union, 1978.

Branden, Albert van den. "La Triade phénicienne." *Bibbia e oriente* 23 (1981) 35–63.

Brech, Edward Franz Leopold. *Organisation: The Framework of Management.* London: Longmans, Green, 1957.

Bretschneider, Joachim. "Götter in Schreinen: Eine Untersuchung zu den syrischen und levantinischen Tempelmodellen, ihrer Bauplastik und ihren Götterbildern." *Ugarit-Forschungen* 21 (1991) 13–32.

Bright, John. *A History of Israel.* Philadelphia: Westminster, 1959.

Britan, Gerald M., and Ronald Cohen. "Toward an Anthropology of Formal Organizations." Pp. 9–30 in *Hierarchy and Society: Anthropological Perspectives on Bureaucracy.* Edited by Gerald M. Britan and Ronald Cohen. Philadelphia: Institute for the Study of Human Issues, 1980.

Brown, John Pairman. "Kothar, Kinyras, and Kythereia." *Journal of Semitic Studies* 10 (1965) 197–219.

Brubacher, Gordon Paul. "The Canaanite God of Death in the Myth of Baal and Mot." Ph.D. dissertation, Drew University, 1987.

Bryce, Glendon E. *A Legacy of Wisdom: The Egyptian Contribution to the Wisdom of Israel.* Lewisburg, Pennsylvania: Bucknell University Press/ London: Associated University Press, 1979.

Burkert, Walter. *Greek Religion.* Translated by John Raffan. Cambridge: Harvard University Press, 1985.

_____. *Structure and History in Greek Mythology and Ritual.* Sather Classical Lectures 47. Berkeley: University of California Press, 1979.

Caquot, André, and Maurice Sznycer. *Ugaritic Religion.* Iconography of Religions 15/8. Leiden: Brill, 1980.

Caquot, André, and Maurice Sznycer, editors. "Textes ougaritiques." Pp. 351–458 in *Les Religions du proche-orient asiatique: Textes babyloniens, ougaritiques, hittites.* Edited by René Labat et al. Le trésor spirituel de l'humanité. Paris: Fayard et Denoël, 1970.

Caquot, André, Maurice Sznycer, and André Herdner. *Textes ougaritiques, 1: Mythes et légendes.* Littératures anciennes du proche-orient 7. Paris: Du Cerf, 1974.

Caquot, André, Jean-Michel de Tarragon, and Jesús-Luis Cunchillos. *Textes ougaritiques, 2: Textes religieux et rituels, correspondance.* Littératures anciennes du proche-orient 14. Paris: Du Cerf, 1989.

Carroll, Robert P. *From Chaos to Covenant: Prophecy in the Book of Jeremiah.* New York: Crossroad, 1981.

Cassuto, U. *The Goddess Anath: Canaanite Epics of the Patriarchal Age.* Translated by Israel Abrahams. Jerusalem: Magnes, 1971.

Cazelles, Henri: "Essai sur le pouvoir de la divinité à Ugarit et en Israël." *Ugaritica* 6 (1969) 25–44.

Champollion-Figeac, Jacques Joseph. *Égypte ancienne.* L'Univers: Histoire et description de tous les peuples. Paris: Didot, 1839.

Charles, R. H. *The Apocrypha and Pseudepigrapha of the Old Testament in English.* 2 volumes. Oxford: Clarendon, 1913.

Clifford, Richard J. *The Cosmic Mountain in Canaan and the Old Testament.* Harvard Semitic Monographs 4. Cambridge: Harvard University Press, 1972.

_____. "Cosmogonies in the Ugaritic Texts and in the Bible." *Orientalia* 53 (1984) 183–201.

_____. "Phoenician Religion." *Bulletin of the American Schools of Oriental Research* 279 (1990) 55–64.

Cogan, Mordechai, and Hayim Tadmor. *II Kings: A New Translation with Introduction and Commentary.* Anchor Bible 11. Garden City, New York: Doubleday, 1988.

Collins, John J. "The Place of Apocalypticism in the Religion of Israel." Pp. 539–58 in *Ancient Israelite Religion.* Edited by Patrick D. Miller Jr., Paul D. Hanson, and S. Dean McBride. Philadelphia: Fortress, 1987.

Comte, Auguste. *Cours de philosophie positive.* 4th ed. Paris: Baillière et Fils, 1877.

Conrad, Diethelm. "Der Gott Reschef." *Zeitschrift für die Alttestamentliche Wissenschaft* 83 (1971) 157–83.

Coogan, Michael David. "Canaanite Origins and Lineage: Reflections on the Religion of Ancient Israel." Pp. 115–24 in *Ancient Israelite Religion.* Edited by Patrick D. Miller Jr., Paul D. Hanson, and S. Dean McBride. Philadelphia: Fortress, 1987.

_____. *Stories from Ancient Canaan.* Philadelphia: Westminster, 1978.

Cook, Stanley A. *The Religion of Ancient Palestine in the Light of Archaeology.* Schweich Lectures 1925. London: Oxford University Press, 1930.

Cowley, A. *Aramaic Papyri of the Fifth Century B.C.* Oxford: Clarendon, 1923.

Cross, Frank Moore Jr. *Canaanite Myth and Hebrew Epic: Essays in the History of the Religion of Israel.* Cambridge: Harvard University Press, 1973.

_____. "The Evolution of the Proto-Canaanite Alphabet." *Bulletin of the American Schools of Oriental Research* 134 (1954) 15–24.

_____. "The Origin and Early Evolution of the Alphabet." *Eretz Israel* 8 (1967) 8*–24*.

Cross, Frank Moore Jr., and David Noel Freedman. *Studies in Ancient Yahwistic Poetry.* Society of Biblical Literature Dissertation Series 21. Missoula, Montana: Scholars Press, 1975.

Crown, A. D. "Messengers and Scribes: The ספר and מלאך in the Old Testament." *Vetus Testamentum* 24 (1974) 366–70.

Cumont, Franz. *Oriental Religions in Roman Paganism.* N.p.: Routledge, 1911. Reprint. New York: Dover, 1956.

Cunchillos Ylarri, Jesús-Luís. *Cuando los ángeles eran dioses.* Bibliotheca salamanticensis 14. Salamanca: Universidad Pontifica, 1976.

_____. "Étude philologique de *mal'āk*: Perspectives sur le *mal'āk* de la divinité dans la bible hébraïque." Pp. 30–51 in *Congress Volume: Vienna 1980.* Edited by J. A. Emerton. Vetus Testamentum Supplements 32. Leiden: Brill, 1981.

_____. "Le Dieu Mut, guerrier de El." *Syria* 62 (1985) 205–18.

_____. "Los b^ene ha'elohîm en Gen. 6,1–4." *Estudios biblicos* 28 (1969) 5–31.

Dahood, Mitchell J. "Ancient Semitic Deities in Syria and Palestine." Pp. 65–94 in *Le antiche divinità semitiche.* Edited by Sabatino Moscati. Studia semitici 1. Rome: Centro di studi semitici, 1958.

_____. "Ebla, Ugarit and Phoenician Religion." Pp. 45–57 in *La religione fenicia: Matrici orientali e sviluppi occidentali atta del colloquio in Roma, 6 marzo 1979.* Studia semitici 53. Rome: Consiglio nazionale delle ricerche, 1981.

Dalley, Stephanie. "Near Eastern Patron Deities of Mining and Smelting in the Late Bronze and Early Iron Ages." Pp. 61–66 in *Report of the Department of Antiquities, Cyprus, 1987.* Nicosia: Zavallis, 1987.

David, Rosalie. *A Guide to Religious Ritual at Abydos.* Warminster: Aris & Phillips, 1981.

Day, John. "Asherah in the Hebrew Bible and Northwest Semitic Literature." *Journal of Biblical Literature* 105 (1986) 385–408.

_____. *Molech: A God of Human Sacrifice in the Old Testament.* University of Cambridge Oriental Publications 41. Cambridge: Cambridge University Press, 1989.

Day, Peggy L. "Anat: Ugarit's 'Mistress of Animals'." *Journal of Near Eastern Studies* 51 (1992) 181–90.

_____. "Why Is Anat a Warrior and Hunter?" Pp. 141–46, 329–32 in *The Bible and the Politics of Exegesis: Essays in Honor of Norman K. Gottwald on His Sixty-Fifth Birthday.* Edited by David Jobling, Peggy L. Day, and Gerald T. Sheppard. Cleveland: Pilgrim, 1991.

Delcor, M. "Le Culte de la 'Reine du ciel' selon Jer 7,18; 44,17–19,25 et ses survivances." Pp. 101–22 in *Von Kanaan bis Kerala: Festschrift für Prof. Mag.*

Dr. Dr. J. P. M. van der Ploeg O. P. zur Vollendung des siebzigsten Lebensjahres am 4. Juli, 1979: Überreicht von Kollegen, Freunden und Schülern. Edited by W. C. Delsman et al. Alter Orient und Altes Testament 211. Kevelaer: Butzon & Bercker/Neukirchen-Vluyn: Neukirchener Verlag, 1982.

Delitzsch, Friedrich. *Babel and Bible: Two Lectures.* New York: Putnam's Sons/ London: Williams & Norgate, 1903.

Dever, William G. "Asherah, Consort of Yahweh? New Evidence from Kuntillet ꜤAjrûd." *Bulletin of the American Schools of Oriental Research* 255 (1984) 21–37.

_____. *Recent Archaeological Discoveries and Biblical Research.* Seattle: University of Washington Press, 1990.

Dhorme, Edouard. *Le Livre de Job.* Paris: Lecoffre, 1926.

Diakonoff, I. M. "The Structure of Near Eastern Society before the Middle of the 2nd Millennium B.C." *Oikumene* 3 (1982) 7–100.

Dietrich, Manfried, and Oswald Loretz. *"Jahwe und seine Aschera": Anthropomorphes Kultbilt in Mesopotamien, Ugarit und Israel—Das biblische Bilderverbot.* Ugaritisch-Biblische Literatur 9. Münster: Ugarit-Verlag, 1992.

_____. "Totenverehrung in Mari (12803) und Ugarit (KTU 1.161)." *Ugarit Forschungen* 12 (1980) 381–82.

_____. "Ugaritische Rituale und Beschwörungen." Pp. 299–357 in *Rituale und Beschwörungen II.* Texte aus der Umwelt des Alten Testaments 2/3. Gütersloh: Mohn, 1988.

Dietrich, Manfried, Oswald Loretz, and J. Sanmartín. *Die keilalphabetischen Texte aus Ugarit: Einschliesslich der keilalphabetischen Texte ausserhalb Ugarits: Teil 1 Transkription.* Alter Orient und Altes Testament 24. Kevelaer: Butzon & Bercker/Neukirchen-Vluyn: Neukirchener Verlag, 1976.

Dijk, H. J. van. *Ezekiel's Prophecy on Tyre (Ez 26,1–28,19): A New Approach.* Biblical et orientalia 20. Rome: Pontifical Biblical Institute, 1968.

Dijk, J. van. "ꜤAnat, Seth and the Seed of Prēꜥ." Pp. 31–51 in *Scripta Signa Vocis: Studies about Scripts, Scriptures, Scribes and Languages in the Near East Presented by J. H. Hospers by His Pupils, Colleagues and Friends.* Edited by H. L. J. Vanstiphout et al. Groningen: Forsten, 1986.

Dijkstra, Meindert. "Some Reflections on the Legend of Aqhat." *Ugarit Forschungen* 11 (1979) 199–210.

Dodge, Bayard, editor and translator. *The Fihrist of al-Nadim: A Tenth-Century Survey of Muslim Culture.* 2 volumes. Records of Civilization: Sources and Studies 83. New York: Columbia University Press, 1970.

Donner, H., and W. Röllig. *Kanaanäische und aramäische Inschriften.* 3 volumes. Wiesbaden: Harrassowitz, 1969–1973.

Drijvers, H. J. W. *The Religion of Palmyra.* Iconography of Religions 15/15. Leiden: Brill, 1976.

Driver, G. R. *Cannaanite Myths and Legends.* Old Testament Studies 3. Edinburgh: T. & T. Clark, 1956.

Driver, Samuel Rolles. *The Book of Exodus.* Cambridge Bible for Schools and Colleges. Cambridge: Cambridge University Press, 1918.

Driver, Samuel Rolles, and George Buchanan Gray. *A Critical and Exegetical Commentary on the Book of Job.* 2 volumes. International Critical Commentary 14–15. New York: Scribner's, 1921.

Du Mesnil du Buisson, Robert. *Études sur les dieux phéniciens hérités par l'Empire Romain.* Études préliminaires aux religions orientales dans l'Empire Romain 14. Leiden: Brill, 1970.

―――. "Origine et évolution du panthéon de Tyr." *Revue de l'histoire des religions* 164 (1963) 133–63.

Dussaud, René. "Les Combats sanglants de ᶜAnat et le pouvoir universel de El (V AB et VI AB)." *Revue de l'histoire des religions* 118 (1938) 133–69.

―――. *Les Découvertes de Ras Shamra (Ugarit) et l'Ancien Testament.* 2d ed. Paris: Geuthner, 1941.

―――. "Nouveaux reseignments sur la Palestine et al Syrie vers 2000 avent notre ère." *Syria* 8 (1927) 216–33.

―――. "Peut-on identifier l'Apollon barbu de Hiérapolis de Syrie?" *Revue de l'histoire des religions* 126 (1943) 128–49.

Edelman, Diana. "The Meaning of *Qiṭṭēr.*" *Vetus Testamentum* (1985) 395–404.

Edwards, M. J. "Philo or Sanchuniathon? A Phoenician Cosmology." *Classical Quarterly* 41 (1991) 213–20.

Edzard, Dietz Otto. *Hymnen, Beschwörungen und Verwandtes aus dem Archiv L.2769.* Archivi reali di Ebla, Testi, 5. Rome: Missione archeologica italiana in Siria, 1984.

Eerdmans, B. D. "On the Road to Monotheism." *Oudtestamentische Studiën* 1 (1942) 105–25.

Eichrodt, Walther. *Theology of the Old Testament.* 2 volumes. Translated by J. A. Baker. Old Testament Library. Philadelphia: Westminster, 1961–1967.

Eisenstadt, S. N. "Social Change, Differentiation, and Evolution." *American Sociological Review* 29 (1964) 375–86.

Eissfeldt, Otto. *Adonis und Adonaj.* Leipzig: Akademie, 1970.

―――. "Baᶜalšamēn und Jahwe." *Zeitschrift für die Alttestamentliche Wissenschaft* 57 (1939) 1–31.

―――. *El im ugaritischen Pantheon.* Berichte über die Verhandlungen der sächsischen Akademie der Wissenschaften zu Leipzig 98.4. Berlin: Akademie, 1951.

―――. *Das Lied Moses Deuteronomium 32 1–43 und das Lehrgedicht Asaphs psalm 78 samt einer Analyses der Umgebung des Mose-Liedes.* Berichte über die Verhandlungen der sächsischen Akademie der Wissenschaften zu Leipzig 104.5. Berlin: Akademie, 1958.

―――. *The Old Testament: An Introduction.* Translated by Peter R. Ackroyd. New York: Harper & Row, 1965.

―――. *Ras Schamra und Sanchunjaton.* Beiträge zur Religionsgeschichte des Altertums 4. Halle: Niemeyer, 1939.

Eliade, Mircea. *A History of Religious Ideas.* 3 volumes. Translated by Willard R. Trask, Alf Hiltebeitel, and Diane Apostolos-Cappadona. Chicago: University of Chicago Press, 1978–1985.

―――. *Patterns in Comparative Religion.* Translated by Rosemary Sheed. New York: New American Library, 1958.

Emerton, J. A. "New Light on Israelite Religion: The Implications of the Inscriptions from Kuntillet ᶜAjrud." *Zeitschrift für die Alttestamentliche Wissenschaft* 94 (1982) 2–20.

Erman, Adolf. *The Ancient Egyptians: A Sourcebook of Their Writings*. Translated by Aylward M. Blackman. New York: Harper & Row, 1966.

Evans, Geoffrey. "Ancient Mesopotamian Assemblies: An Addendum." *Journal of the American Oriental Society* 78 (1958) 114–15.

Falkenstein, Adam. Review of *Ur Excavations Texts VI: Literary and Religious Texts*, by C. J. Gadd and Samuel Noah Kramer. *Bibliotheca orientalis* 22 (1965) 279–83.

Fallon, T. L. et al. "Angels." Pp. 506–16 in *New Catholic Encyclopedia*, volume 1. New York: McGraw-Hill, 1967.

Ferrara, A. J. *Nanna-Suen's Journey to Nippur*. Studia Pohl: Series Maior 2. Rome: Pontifical Biblical Institute, 1973.

Finet, André. "Le *ṣuḫārum* à Mari." Pp. 65–72 in *Gesellschaftsklassen im Alten Zweistromland und in den angrenzenden Gebeiten: XVIII*. Rencontre assyriologique internationale. Edited by D. O. Edzard. Philosophische-historische Klasse Abhandlungen new series 75. Munich: Bayerischen Akademie der Wissenschaften/Beck, 1972.

Fisher, Loren R. "Creation at Ugarit and in the Old Testament." *Vetus Testamentum* 15 (1965) 313–24.

Fleming, Daniel E. "Baal and Dagan in Ancient Syria." *Zeitschrift für Assyriologie und Vorderasiatische Archäologie* 83 (1993) 88–98.

Fleming, David Marron. "The Divine Council as Type Scene in the Hebrew Bible." Ph.D. dissertation, Southern Baptist Theological Seminary, 1989.

Fohrer, Georg. *Geschichte der israelitischen Religion*. Berlin: de Gruyter, 1969.

Follet, René. "Sanchuniaton, personnage mythique ou personne historique?" *Biblica* 34 (1953) 81–90.

Frankena, R. "Nouveaux fragments de la sixième tablette de l'épopée de Gilgameš." Pp. 113–22 in *Gilgameš et sa légende*. Edited by Paul Garelli. Rencontre assyriologique internationale 7. Paris: Klincksieck, 1960.

Frankfort, Henri. *Kingship and the Gods: A Study of Ancient Near Eastern Religion as the Integration of Society and Nature*. Chicago: University of Chicago Press, 1978.

Frazer, James George. *Adonis, Attis, Osiris: Studies in the History of Oriental Religion*, volume 6: *The Golden Bough*. 3d ed. New York: Macmillan, 1935.

Freedman, David Noel. "Yahweh of Samaria and His Asherah." *Biblical Archaeologist* 50 (1987) 241–49.

Freilich, Donna. "Is There an Ugaritic Deity *Bbt*?" *Journal of Semitic Studies* 31 (1986) 119–30.

Friedman, Richard Elliott. "From Egypt to Egypt: Dtr[1] and Dtr[2]." Pp. 167–92 in *Traditions in Transformation: Turning Points in Biblical Faith*. Edited by Baruch Halpern and Jon D. Levenson. Winona Lake, Indiana: Eisenbrauns, 1981.

Fulco, William J. *The Canaanite God Rešep*. American Oriental Series 8. New Haven, Connecticut: American Oriental Society, 1976.

Gammie, John G. "The Angelology and Demonology in the Septuagint of the Book of Job." *Hebrew Union College Annual* 56 (1985) 1–19.

Gaster, Theodore H. *Thespis: Ritual, Myth, and Drama in the Ancient Near East*. New York: Norton, 1961.

Gawlikowski, M. "Les Dieux Palmyre." Pp. 2605–58 in *Aufstieg und Nieder-gang der römischen Welt* II:18.4. Berlin: de Gruyter, 1990.

Gese, Hartmut. "Die Religionen altsyriens." Pp. 1–232 in *Die Religionen altsyriens, altarabiens, und der Mandäer.* Edited by Hartmut Gese, Maria Höfner, and Kurt Rudolph. Die Religionen der Menscheit 10/2. Stuttgart: Kohlhammer, 1970.

Geus, C. H. J. de. *The Tribes of Israel: An Investigation into Some of the Presuppositions of Martin Noth's Amphictyony Hypothesis.* Studia Semitica Neerlandica 18. Amsterdam: Van Gorcum, 1976.

Gibson, J. C. L. *Canaanite Myths and Legends.* 2d ed. Edinburgh: T. & T. Clark, 1977.

_____. *Textbook of Syrian Semitic Inscriptions.* 3 volumes. Oxford: Clarendon, 1971–1982.

_____. "The Theology of the Ugaritic Baal Cycle." *Orientalia* 53 (1984) 202–19.

Ginsberg, H. L. "Baal's Two Messengers." *Bulletin of the American Schools of Oriental Research* 95 (1944) 25–30.

_____. "Two Religious Borrowings in Ugaritic Literature." *Orientalia* 9 (1940) 39–44.

_____. "Ugaritic Myths, Epics, and Legends." Pp. 129–55 in *Ancient Near Eastern Texts Relating to the Old Testament.* 3d ed. Edited by James B. Pritchard. Princeton: Princeton University Press, 1969.

Goedicke, Hans. *The Report of Wenamun.* Johns Hopkins Near Eastern Studies. Baltimore: Johns Hopkins University Press, 1975.

Goetze, Albrecht. "Hittite Myths, Epics, and Legends." Pp. 120–28 in *Ancient Near Eastern Texts Relating to the Old Testament.* 3d ed. Edited by James B. Pritchard. Princeton: Princeton University Press, 1969.

Good, R. "Cloud Messengers?" *Ugarit Forschungen* 10 (1978) 436–37.

Gordis, Robert. *The Book of God and Man: A Study of Job.* Chicago: University of Chicago Press, 1965.

Gordon, Cyrus H. "Canaanite Mythology." Pp. 181–218 in *Mythologies of the Ancient World.* Edited by Samuel Noah Kramer. Garden City, New York: Doubleday, 1961.

_____. "Ebla, Ugarit and the Old Testament." *Orient* 25 (1989) 134–68.

Gottwald, Norman K. *The Tribes of Yahweh: A Sociology of the Religion of Liberated Israel 1250–1050 B.C.E.* Maryknoll, New York: Orbis, 1979.

Grabbe, Lester L. "The Seasonal Pattern and the 'Baal Cycle.'" *Ugarit Forschungen* 8 (1976) 57–63.

Grant, Frederick C. *Hellenistic Religions: The Age of Syncretism.* New York: Liberal Arts, 1953.

Grant, Robert M. *Gods and the One God.* Library of Early Christianity 1. Philadelphia: Westminster, 1986.

Gray, John. "The Canaanite God Horon." *Journal of Near Eastern Studies* 8 (1949) 27–34.

_____. *I & II Kings: A Commentary.* 2d rev. ed. Old Testament Library. Philadelphia: Westminster, 1970.

_____. *The Legacy of Canaan: The Ras Shamra Texts and Their Relevance to the Old Testament.* 2d rev. ed. Vetus Testamentum Supplements 5. Leiden: Brill, 1965.

Grdseloff, Bernhard. *Les Débuts de culte de Rechef en Égypte.* Cairo: Institut français d'archéologie orientale, 1942.

Greene, John T. *The Role of the Messenger and Message in the Ancient Near East.* Brown Judaic Studies 169. Atlanta: Scholars Press, 1989.

Gurney, O. R. *The Hittites.* Harmondsworth: Penguin, 1954.

_____. *Some Aspects of Hittite Religion.* Schweich Lectures 1976. Oxford: Oxford University Press, 1977.

Güterbock, Hans Gustav. "The Hittite Version of the Hurrian Kumarbi Myths: Oriental Forerunners of Hesiod." *American Journal of Archaeology* 52 (1948) 123–34.

Habel, Norman C. *The Book of Job: A Commentary.* Old Testament Library. Philadelphia: Westminster, 1985.

_____. *Yahweh versus Baal: A Conflict of Religious Cultures.* New York: Bookman, 1964.

Hackett, JoAnn. *The Balaam Text from Deir ꜤAllā.* Harvard Semitic Monographs 31. Chico, California: Scholars Press, 1980.

_____. "Can a Sexist Model Liberate Us? Ancient Near Eastern 'Fertility' Goddesses." *Journal of Feminist Studies in Religion* 5 (1989) 65–76.

_____. "Response to Baruch Levine and André Lemaire." Pp. 73–84 in *The Balaam Text from Deir ꜤAlla Re-evaluated: Proceedings of the International Symposium Held at Leiden 21–24 August 1989.* Edited by Jacob Hoftijzer and G. van der Kooij. Leiden: Brill, 1991.

Hägg, Tomas. *The Novel in Antiquity.* Berkeley: University of California Press, 1983.

Hajjar, Youssef. "Divinités oraculaires et rites divinatoires en Syrie et en Phénicie à l'époque gréco-romaine." In *Aufstieg und Niedergang der Römischen Welt* II:18.4, pp. 2236–2320. Berlin: de Gruyter, 1990.

Halpern, Baruch. "Dialect Distribution in Canaan and the Deir Alla Inscriptions." Pp. 119–39 in *"Working with No Data": Semitic and Egyptian Studies Presented to Thomas O. Lambdin.* Edited by David M. Golomb. Winona Lake, Ind.: Eisenbrauns, 1987.

_____. *The First Historians: The Hebrew Bible and History.* San Francisco: Harper & Row, 1988.

Handy, Lowell K. "The Authorization of Divine Power and the Guilt of God in the Book of Job: Useful Ugaritic Parallels." *Journal for the Study of the Old Testament* 60 (1993) 107–18.

_____. "Dissenting Deities or Obedient Angels: Divine Hierarchies in Ugarit and the Bible." *Biblical Research* 35 (1990) 18–35.

_____. "Hezekiah's Unlikely Reform." *Zeitschrift für die Alttestamentliche Wissenschaft* 100 (1988) 111–15.

_____. "A Realignment in Heaven: An Investigation into the Ideology of the Josianic Reform." Ph.D. dissertation, University of Chicago, 1987.

_____. "A Solution for Many *MLKM*." *Ugarit Forschungen* 20 (1988) 57–59.

_____. "Sounds, Words and Meanings in Psalm 82." *Journal for the Study of the Old Testament* 47 (1990) 51–66.

Harmon, A. M., editor and translator. *Lucian.* 8 volumes. Loeb Classical Library. Cambridge: Harvard University Press/London: Heinemann, 1925.

Hauser, W. A. *The Fabulous Gods Denounced in the Bible: Translated from Seldon's "Syrian Deities."* Philadelphia: Lippincott, 1880.

Healey, John F. "The Last of the Rephaim." Pp. 33–44 in *Back to the Sources: Biblical and Near Eastern Studies in Honour of Dermot Ryan.* Edited by Kevin J. Cathcart and John F. Healey. Dublin: Glendale, 1989.

_____. "MLKM/RPᵓUM and the KISPUM." *Ugarit Forschungen* 10 (1978) 89–91.

_____. "The Sun Deity and the Underworld: Mesopotamia and Ugarit." Pp. 239–42 in *Death in Mesopotamia.* Edited by Bendt Alster. Mesopotamia 8. Copenhagen: Akademisk, 1980.

_____. "The Ugaritic Dead: Some Live Issues." *Ugarit Forschungen* 18 (1986) 27–32.

Heaton, E. W. *Solomon's New Men: The Emergence of Ancient Israel as a National State.* New York: Pica, 1974.

Hehn, Johannes. *Die biblische und die babylonische Gottesidee.* Leipzig: Hinrichs, 1913.

Heider, George C. *The Cult of Molek: A Reassessment.* Journal for the Study of the Old Testament Supplement Series 43. Sheffield: JSOT Press, 1985.

Heltzer, Michael. *The Internal Organization of the Kingdom of Ugarit.* Wiesbaden: Reichert, 1982.

_____. "Royal Economy in Ancient Ugarit." Pp. 459–96 in *State and Temple Economy in the Ancient Near East,* volume 2. Edited by Edward Lipiński. Orientalia Lovaniensia Analecta 6. Louvain: Department Oriëntalistiek, 1979.

_____. *The Rural Community in Ancient Ugarit.* Wiesbaden: Reichert, 1976.

Herbert, Edward, Lord of Cherbury. *De religione laici.* Edited and translated by Harold R. Hutcheson. Yale Studies in English 98. New Haven, Connecticut: Yale University Press, 1944.

_____. *De veritate.* Translated by Meyrick H. Carré. Bristol: Arrowsmith, 1937.

Herdner, Andrée. *Corpus des tablettes en cunéiformes alphabétiques découvertes à Ras Shamra–Ugarit de 1929 à 1939.* 2 volumes. Mission de Ras Shamra 10. Paris: Imprimerie Nationale/Geuthner, 1963.

Herrmann, Siegfried. *A History of Israel in Old Testament Times.* Translated by John Bowden. Philadelphia: Fortress, 1975.

Herrmann, W. "Die Frage nach Göttergruppen in der religiösen Vorstellungswelt der Kanaanäer." *Ugarit Forschungen* 14 (1982) 93–104.

Higgens, Elford. *Hebrew Idolatry and Superstition: Its Place in Folklore.* Reprinted, Port Washington, New York: Kennikat, 1971.

Hoffner, H. A., Jr. "The Elkunirsa Myth Reconsidered." *Revue hittite et asianique* 23 (1965) 5–16.

_____. *Hittite Myths.* Edited by Gary M. Beckman. Society of Biblical Literature Writings from the Ancient World 2. Atlanta: Scholars Press, 1990.

Hoftijzer, J., and G. van der Kooij, editors. *Aramaic Texts from Deir ᶜAlla.* Documenta et monumenta orientalia antiqui 19. Leiden: Brill, 1976.

_____. *The Balaam Text from Deir ᶜAlla Re-evaluated: Proceedings of the International Symposium Held at Leiden 21–24 August 1989.* Leiden: Brill, 1991.

Holland, T. A. "A Study of Iron Age Baked Clay Figurines, with Special Reference to Jerusalem: Cave 1." *Levant* 9 (1977) 121–55.

Holter, Knut. "Was Philistine Dagon a Fish-God? Some New Questions and an Old Answer." *Scandinavian Journal of the Old Testament* (1989/1) 142–47.

Honroth, W., O. Rubensohn, and F. Zucker. "Bericht über die Ausgrabungen auf Elephantine in den Jahren 1906–1908." *Zeitschrift für ägyptische Sprache und Altertumskunde* 46 (1909–1910) 14–61.

Hooke, S. H. "Traces of the Myth and Ritual Pattern in Canaan." Pp. 68–86 in *Myth and Ritual: Essays on the Myth and Ritual of the Hebrews in Relation to the Culture Pattern of the Ancient Near East.* Edited by S. H. Hooke. Oxford: Oxford University Press, 1933.

_____, editor. *The Labyrinth: Further Studies in the Relation between Myth and Ritual in the Ancient World.* London: SPCK, 1935.

_____, editor. *Myth and Ritual: Essays on the Myth and Ritual of the Hebrews in Relation to the Culture Pattern of the Ancient Near East.* Oxford: Oxford University Press, 1933.

Hörig, Monika. *Dea Syria: Studien zur religiösen Tradition der Fruchtbarkeitsgöttin in Vorderasien.* Alter Orient und Altes Testament 208. Kevelaer: Butzon & Bercker/Neukirchen-Vluyn: Neukirchener Verlag, 1979.

Hornung, Erik. *Conceptions of God in Ancient Egypt: The One and the Many.* Translated by John Baines. Ithaca, New York: Cornell University Press, 1982.

Hvidberg-Hansen, F. O. *La Déessee TNT: Une Étude sur la religion canaanéopunique: I Texte.* Translated by Françoise Arndt. Copenhagen: Gad's, 1979.

Ions, Veronica. *Indian Mythology.* London: Hamlyn, 1967.

Isaac, E. "1 (Ethiopic Apocalypse of) Enoch (Second Century B.C.–First Century A.D.)." Pp. 5–89 in *The Old Testament Pseudepigrapha.* Edited by James H. Charlesworth. Garden City, New York: Doubleday, 1983.

Jacobsen, Thorkild. "Primitive Democracy in Ancient Mesopotamia." *Journal of Near Eastern Studies* 2 (1943) 159–72.

_____. *Toward the Image of Tammuz and Other Essays on Mesopotamian History and Culture.* Harvard Semitic Studies 21. Cambridge: Harvard University Press, 1970.

_____. *The Treasures of Darkness: A History of Mesopotamian Religion.* New Haven, Connecticut: Yale University Press, 1976.

Jeppesen, Knud. "You Are a Cherub, but No God!" *Scandinavian Journal of the Old Testament* (1991) 83–94.

Jirku, Anton. *Der Mythus der Kanaanäer.* Bonn: Habelt, 1966.

Joines, Karen Randolph. *Serpent Symbolism in the Old Testament: A Linguistic, Archaeological, and Literary Study.* Haddonfield, New Jersey: Haddonfield House, 1974.

Kaiser, Otto. *Isaiah 1–12: A Commentary.* Translated by R. A. Wilson. Old Testament Library. Philadelphia: Westminster, 1972.

Kaiser, Werner et al. "Stadt und Tempel von Elephantine: Siebter Grabungsbericht." *Mitteilungen des Deutschen archäologischen Instituts Abteilung Kairo* 33 (1977) 63–100.

Kanter, Rosabeth Moss. *Men and Women of the Corporation.* New York: Basic Books, 1977.

Kapelrud, Arvid S. *Baal in the Ras Shamra Texts*. Copenhagen: Gad, 1952.

_____. "Baᶜal, Schöpfung und Chaos." *Ugarit Forschungen* 11 (1979) 407–12.

_____. *God and His Friends in the Old Testament*. Oslo: Universitetsforlaget, 1979.

_____. *The Ras Shamra Discoveries and the Old Testament*. Norman, Oklahoma: University of Oklahoma Press, 1963.

_____. "The Relationship between El and Baal in the Ras Shamra Texts." Pp. 79–85 in *The Bible World: Essays in Honor of Cyrus H. Gordon*. Edited by Gary Rendsburg et al. New York: KTAV, 1980.

_____. *The Violent Goddess: Anat in the Ras Shamra Texts*. Oslo: Universitetsforlaget, 1969.

Katz, Peter. "The Meaning of the Root קנה." *Journal of Jewish Studies* 5 (1954) 126–31.

Kaufman, Stephen A. "The Pitfalls of Typology: On the Early History of the Alphabet." *Hebrew Union College Annual* 57 (1986) 1–14.

Keel, Othmar. *The Symbolism of the Biblical World: Ancient Near Eastern Iconography and the Book of Psalms*. Translated by Timothy J. Hallett. New York: Seabury, 1978.

Keel, Othmar, and Christoph Uehlinger. *Göttinnen, Götter und Gottessymbole: Neue Erkenntnisse zur Religionsgeschichte Kanaans und Israels aufgrund bislang unerschlossener ikonographischer Quellen*. Quaestiones Disputatae 134. Freiburg im Breisgau: Herder, 1993.

Kilmer, Anne Draffkorn. "The Symbolism of the Flies in the Mesopotamian Flood Myth and Some Further Implications." Pp. 175–80 in *Language, Literature, and History: Philological and Historical Studies Presented to Erica Reiner*. Edited by Francesca Rochberg-Halton. American Oriental Series 67. New Haven, Connecticut: American Oriental Society, 1987.

Kingsbury, Edwin C. "The Prophets and the Council of Yahweh." *Journal of Biblical Literature* 83 (1964) 279–86.

Kirk, G. S. *Myth: Its Meaning and Functions in Ancient and Other Cultures*. Sather Classical Lectures 40. London: Cambridge University Press/ Berkeley: University of California Press, 1970.

Kittel, Rudolf. *Die Bücher der Könige: Übersetzt und erklärt*. Göttingen: Vandenhoeck & Ruprecht, 1900.

Klengel, Horst. "Die Palastwirtschaft in Alalaḫ." Pp. 435–57 in *State and Temple Economy in the Ancient Near East*, volume 2. Edited by Edward Lipiński. Orientalia Lovaniensia Analecta 6. Louvain: Department Oriëntalistiek, 1979.

Kloos, Carola. *Yhwh's Combat with the Sea: A Canaanite Tradition in the Religion of Ancient Israel*. Amsterdam: van Oorschot/Leiden: Brill, 1986.

Knudtzon, J. A. *Die El-Amarna-Tafeln*. 2 volumes. Vorderasiatische Bibliothek 2. Leipzig: Hinrichs, 1907–1915.

Korpel, Marjo Christina Annette. *A Rift in the Clouds: Ugaritic and Hebrew Descriptions of the Divine*. Ugaritisch-Biblische Literatur 8. Munster: Ugarit, 1990.

Kraeling, Emil G. *The Brooklyn Museum Aramaic Papyri: New Documents of the Fifth Century B.C. from the Jewish Colony at Elephantine*. New Haven, Conn.: Yale University Press, 1953.

Kramer, Samuel Noah. "Dumuzi's Annual Resurrection: An Important Correction to 'Inanna's Descent.'" *Bulletin of the American Schools of Oriental Research* 183 (1966) 31.

_____. "'Inanna's Descent to the Nether World' Continued and Revised." *Journal of Cuneiform Studies* 5 (1951) 1–17.

_____. *The Sacred Marriage Rite: Aspects of Faith, Myth, and Ritual in Ancient Sumer.* Bloomington: Indiana University Press, 1969.

Kupper, Jan-Robert. "Un Gouvernement provincial dans le royaume de Mari." *Revue d'assyriologie et d'archéologie orientale* 41 (1947) 149–83.

Lambert, W. G. "Goddesses in the Pantheon: A Reflection of Women in Society?" Pp. 125–30 in *La Femme dans le proche-orient antique: Compte rendu de la XXXIIIᵉ rencontre assyriologique internationale (Paris, 7–10 Juillet 1986).* Edited by Jean-Marie Durand. Rencontre assyriologique internationale 33. Paris: Éditions recherche sur les civilisations, 1987.

_____. "Notes on a Work of the Most Ancient Semitic Literature." *Journal of Cuneiform Studies* 41 (1989) 1–33.

_____. "Old Testament Mythology in its Ancient Near Eastern Context." Pp. 124–43 in *Congress Volume: Jerusalem, 1986.* Edited by J. A. Emerton. Vetus Testamentum Supplements 40. Leiden: Brill, 1988.

Lang, Andrew. *Myth, Ritual and Religion.* London, 1906. Reprint. New York: AMS, 1968.

Lang, Bernhard. *Monotheism and the Prophetic Minority: An Essay in Biblical History and Sociology.* The Social World of Biblical Antiquity Series 1. Sheffield: Almond, 1983.

Langdon, Stephen Herbert. *Semitic.* Mythology of All Races 5. Boston: Jones, 1931.

Langhe, R. de. "Myth, Ritual, and Kingship in the Ras Shamra Tablets." Pp. 122–48 in *Myth, Ritual, and Kingship: Essays on the Theory and Practice of Kingship in the Ancient Near East.* Edited by S. H. Hooke. Oxford: Clarendon, 1958.

Leemans, W. F. *The Old-Babylonian Merchant: His Business and His Social Position.* Studia et documenta 3. Leiden: Brill, 1950.

Lemaire, André. "Les Inscriptions sur plâtre de Deir ᶜAlla et leur signification historique et culturelle." Pp. 33–57 in *The Balaam Text from Deir ᶜAlla Re-evaluated: Proceedings of the International Symposium Held at Leiden 21–24 August 1989.* Edited by Jacob Hoftijzer and G. van der Kooij. Leiden: Brill, 1991.

Levine, Baruch A., and Jean-Michel de Tarragon. "'Shapshu Cries Out in Heaven': Dealing with Snake-Bites at Ugarit (KTU 1.100, 1.107)." *Revue Biblique* 95 (1988) 481–518.

L'Heureux, Conrad E. *Rank among the Canaanite Gods: El, Baᶜal, and the Repha²im.* Harvard Semitic Monographs 21. Missoula, Montana: Scholars Press, 1979.

Libolt, Clayton Gene. "Royal Land Grants from Ugarit." Ph.D. dissertation, University of Michigan, 1985.

Lichtheim, Miriam. *Ancient Egyptian Literature, Volume 2: The New Kingdom.* Berkeley: University of California Press, 1976.

Linder, Elisha. "Ugarit: A Canaanite Thalassocracy." Pp. 31–42 in *Ugarit in Retrospect: Fifty Years of Ugarit and Ugaritic*. Edited by Gordon Douglas Young. Winona Lake, Indiana: Eisenbrauns, 1981.

Lipiński, Edward. "Le Culte du soleil chez les Sémites Occidentaux du Ier millénaire av. J.-C." *Orientalia Lovaniensa Periodica* 22 (1991) 57–72.

———. "El's Abode: Mythological Traditions Related to Mount Hermon and to the Mountains of Armenia." *Orientalia Lovaniensia Periodica* 2 (1971) 13–69.

———. "Envoi d'un messager (V AB, F, 7–11)." *Syria* 50 (1973) 35–37.

———. "Etymological and Exegetical Notes on the Meša^c Inscription." *Orientalia* 40 (1971) 325–40.

———. "North Semitic Texts from the First Millennium BC." Pp. 227–68 in *Near Eastern Religious Texts Relating to the Old Testament*. Edited by Walter Beyerlin. Translated by John Bowden. Old Testament Library. Philadelphia: Westminster, 1978.

Liverani, Mario. "The Ideology of the Assyrian Empire." Pp. 297–317 in *Power and Propaganda: A Symposium on Ancient Empires*. Edited by Mogens Trolle Larsen. Mesopotamia 7. Copenhagen: Akademisk, 1979.

———. "ΣΥΔΥΚ e ΜΙΣΩΡ." Pp. 55–74 in *Studi in onore di Edoardo Volterra 6*. Milan: Giuffrè, 1971.

Lods, Adolphe. *Israël des origines au milieu du VIIIe siècle*. Paris: Renaissance du livre, 1930.

Loewenstamm, Samuel E. "Eine lehrhafte ugaritische Trinkburleske." *Ugarit Forschungen* 1 (1969) 71–77.

———. "The Ugaritic Fertility Myth. The Result of a Mistranslation." *Israel Exploration Journal* 12 (1962) 87–88.

Løkkegaard, F. "Some Comments on the Sanchuniaton Tradition." *Studia theologica* 7 (1954) 51–76.

Loretz, Oswald. *Ugarit und die Bibel: Kanaanäische Götter und Religion im Alten Testament*. Darmstadt: Wissenschaftliche, 1990.

McCarter, P. Kyle Jr. "Aspects of the Religion of the Israelite Monarchy: Biblical and Epigraphic Data." Pp. 137–55 in *Ancient Israelite Religion*. Edited by Patrick D. Miller Jr., Paul D. Hanson, and S. Dean McBride. Philadelphia: Fortress, 1987.

———. "The Balaam Texts from Deir ^{c}Allā: The First Combination." *Bulletin of the American Schools of Oriental Research* 239 (1980) 49–60.

———. "The Early Diffusion of the Alphabet." *Biblical Archaeologist* 37 (1974) 54–68.

Macdonald, John. "An Assembly at Ugarit?" *Ugarit Forschungen* 11 (1979) 515–26.

McEwan, G. J. P. "^{d}MUŠ and Related Matters." *Orientalia* 52 (1983) 215–29.

McKay, John W. *Religion in Judah under the Assyrians 732–609 BC*. Studies in Biblical Theology 2d series 26. Naperville, Illinois: Allenson, 1973.

MacMullen, Ramsay. *Paganism in the Roman Empire*. New Haven, Connecticut: Yale University Press, 1981.

Margalit, Baruch. *A Matter of "Life" and "Death": A Study of the Baal-Mot Epic (CTA 4-5-6)*. Alter Orient und Altes Testament 206. Kevelaer: Butzon & Bercker/Neukirchen-Vluyn: Neukirchener, 1980.

_____. "The Meaning and Significance of Asherah." *Vetus Testamentum* 40 (1990) 264–97.

_____. "The Ugaritic Creation Myth: Fact or Fiction?" *Ugarit Forschungen* 13 (1981) 137–45.

_____. "The Ugaritic Feast of the Drunken Gods: Another Look at RS 24.258 (KTU 1.114)." *MAARAV* 2 (1979–80) 65–120.

Marmorstein, Arthur. "Fallen Angels." s.v. "Angels and Angelology." Pp. 966–68 in *Encyclopedia Judaica*, volume 2. Jerusalem: Keter, 1971.

Marx, Karl. *Capital: A Critique of Political Economy.* Edited by Frederick Engels. Translated by Samuel Moore and Edward Aveling. Revised and edited by Ernest Untermann. New York: Modern Library, 1906.

Matthiae, Paolo. *Ars Syra: Contributi alla storia dell'arte figurativa siriana nella etè del medio e tardo bronzo.* Centro di studi semitici serie archeologica 4. Rome: Centro di studi semitic, 1962.

Mattingly, Gerald L. "Moabite Religion and the Mesha^c Inscription." Pp. 211–38 in *Studies in the Mesha Inscription and Moab.* Edited by Andrew Dearman. Archaeology and Biblical Studies 2. Atlanta: Scholars Press, 1989.

May, Herbert G. "Some Cosmic Connotations of *Mayim Rabbîm*: 'Many Waters.'" *Journal of Biblical Literature* 74 (1955) 9–21.

Mays, James L. "Psalm 29." *Interpretation* 39 (1985) 60–64.

Meier, Samuel A. *The Messenger in the Ancient Semitic World.* Harvard Semitic Monographs 45. Atlanta: Scholars Press, 1988.

Mendenhall, George E. "The Worship of Baal and Asherah: A Study in the Social Bonding Functions of Religious Systems." Pp. 147–58 in *Biblical and Related Studies Presented to Samuel Iwry.* Edited by Ann Kort and Scott Morschauser. Winona Lake, Indiana: Eisenbrauns, 1985.

Meshel, Ze³ev. "Did Yahweh Have a Consort? The New Religious Inscriptions from the Sinai." *Biblical Archaeology Review* (March-April 1979) 24–35.

Mettinger, Tryggve N. D. "Yʜᴡʜ Sᴀʙᴀᴏᴛʜ: The Heavenly King on the Cherubim Throne." Pp. 109–38 in *Studies in the Period of David and Solomon and Other Essays.* Edited by Tomoo Ishida. Winona Lake, Indiana: Eisenbrauns, 1982.

Meunier, Mario. *Lucian de Samosate: La Déesse syrienne: Traduction nouvelle avec prolégomènes et notes.* Paris: Éditions Janick, 1947.

Michalowski, Piotr. "Charisma and Control: On Continuity and Change in Early Mesopotamian Bureaucratic Systems." Pp. 55–68 in *The Organization of Power: Aspects of Bureaucracy in the Ancient Near East.* Edited by McGuire Gibson and Robert D. Biggs. Studies in Ancient Oriental Civilization 46. Chicago: Oriental Institute of the University of Chicago, 1987.

Milgrom, Jacob. *Numbers.* Jewish Publication Society Torah Commentary. Philadelphia: Jewish Publication Society, 1990.

Millard, Alan R., and Pierre Bordreuil. "A Statue from Syria with Assyrian and Aramaic Inscriptions." *Biblical Archaeologist* 45 (1982) 135–41.

Miller, Patrick D. Jr. "Aspects of the Religion of Ugarit." Pp. 53–66 in *Ancient Israelite Religion.* Edited by Patrick D. Miller Jr., Paul D. Hanson, and S. Dean McBride. Philadelphia: Fortress, 1987.

_____. *The Divine Warrior in Early Israel.* Harvard Semitic Monographs 5. Cambridge: Harvard University Press, 1973.

_____. "El, the Creator of Earth." *Bulletin of the American Schools of Oriental Research* 239 (1980) 43–46.

_____. "El the Warrior." *Harvard Theological Review* 60 (1967) 411–31.

_____. "Fire in the Mythology of Canaan and Israel." *Catholic Biblical Quarterly* 27 (1965) 256–61.

_____. "Ugarit and the History of Religions." *Journal of Northwest Semitic Languages* 9 (1981) 119–28.

Molin, Georg. "Die Stellung der Gᵉbira im Staate Juda." *Theologische Zeitschrift* 10 (1954) 161–75.

Montet, Pierre. *Eternal Egypt.* Translated by Doreen Weightman. New York: New American Library, 1964.

Moor, Johannes C. de. *An Anthology of Religious Texts from Ugarit.* Nisaba 16. Leiden: Brill, 1987.

_____. "The Crisis of Polytheism in Late Bronze Ugarit." *Oudtestamentische Studiën* 24 (1986) 1–20.

_____. "El the Creator." Pp. 171–87 in *The Bible World: Essays in Honor of Cyrus H. Gordon.* Edited by Gary Rendsburg et al. New York: KTAV, 1980.

_____. *New Year with Canaanites and Israelites, Part One: Description.* Kamper Cahiers 21. Kampen, Netherlands: Kok, 1972.

_____. *The Rise of Yahwism: The Roots of Israelite Monotheism.* Bibliotheca ephemeridum theologicarum lovaniensium 91. Louvain: Louvain University Press, 1990.

_____. *The Seasonal Pattern of the Ugaritic Myth of Baᶜlu according to the Version of Ilimilku.* Alter Orient und Altes Testament 16. Kevelaer: Butzon & Bercker/Neukirchen-Vluyn: Neukirchener Verlag, 1971.

_____. "The Semitic Pantheon of Ugarit." *Ugarit Forschungen* 2 (1970) 187–228.

Moor, Johannes C. de, and M. J. Mulder. "Baᶜal." Pp. 338–43 in *Theological Dictionary of the Old Testament,* volume 2. Edited by G. Johannes Botterweck and Helmer Ringgren. Translated by John T. Willis. Grand Rapids, Michigan: Eerdmans, 1975.

Moor, Johannes C. de, and Klaus Spronk. *A Cuneiform Anthology of Religious Texts from Ugarit: Autographed Texts and Glossaries.* Semitic Studies Series 6. Leiden: Brill, 1987.

Morenz, Siegfried. *Egyptian Religion.* Translated by Ann E. Keep. Ithaca, New York: Cornell University Press, 1973.

Morgenstern, Julian. "The Mythological Background of Psalm 82." *Hebrew Union College Annual* 14 (1939) 29–126.

Morony, Michael G. " 'In a City without Watchdogs the Fox Is the Overseer': Issues and Problems in the Study of Bureaucracy." Pp. 7–18 in *The Organization of Power: Aspects of Bureaucracy in the Ancient Near East.* Edited by McGuire Gibson and Robert D. Biggs. Studies in Ancient Oriental Civilization 46. Chicago: Oriental Institute of the University of Chicago, 1987.

Moscati, Sabatino. *The World of the Phoenicians.* Translated by Alastair Hamilton. New York: Praeger, 1968.

Mullen, E. Theodore Jr. *The Divine Council in Canaanite and Early Hebrew Literature*. Harvard Semitic Monographs 24. Chico, California: Scholars Press, 1980.

Murata, Sachiko. "The Angels." Pp. 324–44 in *Islamic Spirituality: Foundations*. Edited by Seyyed Hossein Nasr. World Spirituality: An Encyclopedic History of the Religious Quest 19. New York: Crossroad, 1987.

Myers, Jacob M. *I Chronicles*. Anchor Bible 12. Garden City, New York: Doubleday, 1965.

Naveh, Joseph. *Early History of the Alphabet: An Introduction to West Semitic Epigraphy and Palaeography*. Jerusalem: Magnes/Leiden: Brill, 1982.

_____. "Proto-Canaanite, Archaic Greek, and the Script of the Aramaic Text on the Tell Fakhariyah Statue." Pp. 101–13 in *Ancient Israelite Religion*. Edited by Patrick D. Miller Jr., Paul D. Hanson, and S. Dean McBride. Philadelphia: Fortress, 1987.

Negbi, Ora. *Canaanite Gods in Metal: An Archaeological Study of Ancient Syro-Palestinian Figurines*. Tel Aviv: Tel Aviv University Press, 1976.

Nielsen, Ditlef. *Ras Šamra Mythologie und biblische Theologie*. Abhandlungen für die Kunde des Morgenlands 21/4. Leipzig: Deutsche morgenländische Gesellschaft, 1936.

Nielsen, Eduard. *Oral Tradition: A Modern Problem in Old Testament Introduction*. Studies in Biblical Theology 11. London: SCM, 1954.

North, Robert. "Yahweh's Asherah." Pp. 118–37 in *To Touch the Text: Biblical and Related Studies in Honor of Joseph A. Fitzmyer, S.J.* Edited by Maurya P. Horgan and Paul J. Kobelski. New York: Crossroad, 1989.

Noth, Martin. *Exodus: A Commentary*. Translated by J. S. Bowden. Old Testament Library. Philadelphia: Westminster, 1962.

_____. *Überlieferungsgeschichtliche Studien I: Die sammelnden und bearbeitenden Geschichtswerke im Alten Testament*. Halle: Niemeyer, 1943.

Nougayrol, Jean. "Textes suméro-accadiens des archives et bibliothèques priveés d'Ugarit." *Ugaritica* 5 (1968) 1–446.

Obermann, Julian. *How Daniel Was Blessed with a Son: An Incubation Scene in Ugaritic*. Supplement to the *Journal of the American Oriental Society* 6. Baltimore: American Oriental Society, 1946.

_____. *Ugaritic Mythology: A Study of Its Leading Motifs*. New Haven, Connecticut: Yale University Press, 1948.

Oden, Robert A. Jr. "Baʿal Samem and ʾEl." *Catholic Biblical Quarterly* 39 (1977) 470–73.

_____. "The Persistence of Canaanite Religion." *Biblical Archaeologist* 39 (1976) 31–36.

_____. "Philo of Byblos and Hellenistic Historiography." *Palestine Exploration Quarterly* 110 (1978) 115–26.

_____. *Studies in Lucian's "De Syria Dea."* Harvard Semitic Monographs 15. Missoula, Montana: Scholars Press, 1977.

_____. "Theoretical Assumptions in the Study of Ugaritic Myths." *MAARAV* 2 (1979) 43–63.

Oesterley, W. O. E., and Theodore H. Robinson. *A History of Israel*. 2 volumes. Oxford: Clarendon, 1932.

Oldenburg, Ulf. "Above the Stars of El: El in Ancient South Arabic Religion." *Zeitschrift für die Alttestamentliche Wissenschaft* 82 (1970) 187–208.

_____. *The Conflict between El and Baʿal in Canaanite Religion.* Supplementa ad numen, altera series 3. Leiden: Brill, 1969.

Olmo Lete, Gregorio del. "The 'Divine' Names of the Ugaritic Kings." *Ugarit Forschungen* 18 (1986) 83–95.

_____. *Interpretación de la mitología cananea: Estudios de semántica ugarítica.* Fuentes de la ciencia bíblica 2. Valencia: San Jerónimo, 1984.

_____. "La estructura del panteón ugarítico." Pp. 267–304 in *Salvación en la palabra: Targum-Derash-Berith: En memoria del professor Alejandro Díez Macho.* Edited by Domingo Muñoz León. Madrid: Ediciones Cristiandad, 1986.

_____. *Mitos y leyendas de Canaan segun la tradicion de Ugarit: Textos, versión y estudio.* Fuentes de la ciencia bíblica 1. Madrid: Ediciones Cristiandad, 1981.

_____. "Notes on Ugaritic Semantics IV." *Ugarit Forschungen* 10 (1978) 37–46.

Olyan, Saul Mitchell. *Asherah and the Cult of Yahweh in Israel.* Society of Biblical Literature Monograph Series 34. Atlanta: Scholars Press, 1988.

_____. "Problems in the History of the Cult and Priesthood in Ancient Israel." Ph.D. dissertation, Harvard University, 1985.

_____. "Some Observations concerning the Identity of the Queen of Heaven." *Ugarit Forschungen* 19 (1987) 161–74.

_____. *A Thousand Thousands Served Him: Exegesis and the Naming of Angels in Ancient Judaism.* Texte und Studien zum Antiken Judentum 36. Tübingen: Mohr, 1993.

Otten, Heinrich. "Ein kanaanäischer Mythus aus Boğazköy." *Mitteilungen des Instituts für Orientforschung* 1 (1953) 125–50.

Ottosson, Magnus. *Temples and Cult Places in Palestine.* Boreas 12. Uppsala: University of Uppsala Press, 1980.

Pardee, Dennis. "An Evaluation of the Proper Names from Ebla from a West Semitic Perspective: Pantheon Distribution according to Genre." Pp. 119–51 in *Eblaite Personal Names and Semitic Name-Giving: Papers of a Symposium Held in Rome July 15–17, 1985.* Edited by Alfonso Archi. Archivi Reali di Ebla Studi 1. Rome: Missione Archeologica Italiana in Siria, 1988.

Patai, Raphael. *The Hebrew Goddess.* New York: Avon, 1978.

_____. *Man and Temple in Ancient Jewish Myth and Ritual.* London: Thomas Nelson, 1947.

Paton, Lewis Bayles. "Ashtart (Ashtoreth), Astarte." Pp. 115–18 in *Encyclopedia of Religion and Ethics,* volume 1. Edited by James Hastings. Edinburgh: T. & T. Clark, 1908–1922.

_____. "Baal, Beel, Bel." Pp. 283–98 in *Encyclopedia of Religion and Ethics,* volume 2. Edited by James Hastings. Edinburgh: T. & T. Clark, 1908–1922.

_____. "Canaanites." Pp. 176–88 in *Encyclopedia of Religion and Ethics,* volume 3. Edited by James Hastings. Edinburgh: T. & T. Clark, 1908–1922.

_____. "Dagan, Dagon." Pp. 386–88 in *Encyclopedia of Religion and Ethics,* volume 4. Edited by James Hastings. Edinburgh: T. & T. Clark, 1908–1922.

_____. "Sanchuniathon." Pp. 177–81 in *Encyclopedia of Religion and Ethics*, volume 11. Edited by James Hastings. Edinburgh: T. & T. Clark, 1908–1922.

Peckham, Brian. "Phoenicia and the Religion of Israel: The Epigraphic Evidence." Pp. 79–99 in *Ancient Israelite Religion*. Edited by Patrick D. Miller Jr., Paul D. Hanson, and S. Dean McBride. Philadelphia: Fortress, 1987.

Perdue, Leo G. "Cosmology and the Social Order in the Wisdom Tradition." Pp. 457–78 in *The Sage in Israel and the Ancient Near East*. Edited by John G. Gammie and Leo G. Perdue. Winona Lake, Indiana: Eisenbrauns, 1990.

Petersen, David L., and Mark Woodward. "Northwest Semitic Religion: A Study of Relational Structures." *Ugarit Forschungen* 9 (1977) 233–48.

Pettey, Richard J. "Asherah: Goddess of Israel?" Ph.D. dissertation, Marquette University, 1985.

Pettinato, Giovanni. *The Archives of Ebla: An Empire Inscribed in Clay*. Garden City, New York: Doubleday, 1981.

_____. *Ebla: Nuovi orizzonti della storia*. 2d ed. Milan: Rusconi, 1986.

Pfeiffer, Charles F. *Ras Shamra and the Bible*. Baker Studies in Biblical Archaeology 1. Grand Rapids, Michigan: Baker, 1962.

Pope, Marvin H. *El in the Ugaritic Texts*. Vetus Testamentum Supplements 2. Leiden: Brill, 1955.

_____. *Job: Introduction, Translation and Notes*. 3d ed. Anchor Bible 15. Garden City, New York: Doubleday, 1973.

_____. "The Status of El at Ugarit." *Ugarit Forschungen* 19 (1987) 219–30.

_____. "Ups and Downs in El's Amours." *Ugarit Forschungen* 11 (1979) 701–8.

Porten, Bezalel. *Archives from Elephantine: The Life of an Ancient Jewish Military Colony*. Berkeley: University of California Press, 1968.

_____. "The Identity of King Adon." *Biblical Archaeologist* 44 (1981) 36–52.

Posener, Georges. "La Légende égyptienne de la mar insatiable." *Annuaire de l'institut de philologie et d'histoire orientales et slaves* 13 (1953) 461–78.

Pritchard, James B., editor. *Ancient Near Eastern Texts Relating to the Old Testament*. 3d ed. with supp. Princeton: Princeton University Press, 1969.

_____. *The Ancient Near East in Pictures Relating to the Old Testament*. 2d ed. with supp. Princeton: Princeton University Press, 1969.

_____. *Palestinian Figurines in Relation to Certain Goddesses Known through Literature*. American Oriental Series 24. New Haven, Connecticut: American Oriental Society, 1943.

Rad, Gerhard von. *Old Testament Theology*. 2 volumes. Translated by D. M. G. Stalker. New York: Harper & Row, 1962–1965.

Rainey, Anson Frank. "The Social Stratification of Ugarit." Ph.D. dissertation, Brandeis University, 1962.

Reed, William L. *The Asherah in the Old Testament*. Fort Worth: Texas Christian University Press, 1949.

Ribichini, Sergio. *Adonis: Aspetti "orientali" di un mito greco*. Studia semitici 55. Rome: Consiglio nazionale delle ricerche, 1981.

_____. "Beliefs and Religious Life." Pp. 104–25 in *The Phoenicians*. Edited by Sabatino Moscati. Milan: Bompiani, 1988.

Ringgren, Helmer. *Israelite Religion.* Translated by David E. Green. Philadelphia: Fortress, 1966.

_____. *Religions of the Ancient Near East.* Translated by John Sturdy. Philadelphia: Westminster, 1973.

Roberts, J. J. M. *The Earliest Semitic Pantheon: A Study of the Semitic Deities Attested in Mesopotamia before Ur III.* Baltimore: Johns Hopkins University Press, 1972.

Robinson, H. Wheeler. "The Council of Yahweh." *Journal of Theological Studies* 45 (1944) 151–57.

Robinson, Joseph. *The Second Book of Kings.* The Cambridge Bible Commentary on the New English Bible. Cambridge: Cambridge University Press, 1976.

Rosenberg, Roy A. "The God Ṣedeq." *Hebrew Union College Annual* 36 (1965) 161–77.

Rowley, H. H. "Zadok and Nehushtan." *Journal of Biblical Literature* 58 (1939) 113–41.

Rudolph, Kurt. *Gnosis: The Nature and History of Gnosticism.* Translated by P. W. Coxen and K. H. Kuhn. Edited by Robert McLachlan Wilson. San Francisco: Harper & Row, 1983.

Rummel, Stan. "Narrative Structures in the Ugaritic Texts." Pp. 221–332 in *Ras Shamra Parallels: The Texts from Ugarit and the Hebrew Bible III.* Edited by Stan Rummel. Analecta orientalia 51. Rome: Pontifical Biblical Institute, 1981.

Saggs, H. W. F. *The Greatness That Was Babylon.* New York: New American Library, 1962.

Sarna, Nahum M. *Genesis.* Jewish Publication Society Torah Commentary. Philadelphia: Jewish Publication Society, 1989.

_____. "The Mythological Background of Job 18." *Journal of Biblical Literature* 82 (1963) 315–18.

Schaeffer, Claude F. A. "Les Fouilles de Ras Shamra-Ugarit quinzième, seizième et dix-septième campagnes (1951, 1952 et 1953): Rapport sommaire." *Syria* 31 (1954) 14–67.

Schmidt, Werner. *Königtum Gottes in Ugarit und Israel.* Beihefte zur Zeitschrift für die Alttestamentliche Wissenschaft 80. Berlin: Alfred Töpelmann, 1961.

Segert, Stanislav. "Die Sprache der moabitischen Königs Inschrift." *Archiv orientální* 29 (1961) 197–267.

Selms, A. van. *Marriage and Family Life in Ugaritic Literature.* Pretoria Oriental Series 1. London: Luzac, 1954.

Simpson, William Kelly. "Reshep in Egypt." *Orientalia* n.s. 29 (1960) 63–74.

Sirinelli, Jean, and Édouard des Places, editors and translators. *Eusèbe de Césarée: La Préparation évangélique, livre I: Introduction, texte grec, traduction et commentaire.* Paris: Du Cerf, 1974.

Smith, Clyde Curry. "The Birth of Bureaucracy." *Biblical Archaeologist* 40 (1977) 24–28.

Smith, Mark S. "Death in Jeremiah IX, 20." *Ugarit Forschungen* 19 (1987) 289–93.

_____. "Divine Travel as a Token of Divine Rank." *Ugarit Forschungen* 16 (1984) 359.

_____. *The Early History of God: Yahweh and the Other Deities in Ancient Israel.* San Francisco: Harper & Row, 1990.

_____. "Interpreting the Baal Cycle." *Ugarit Forschungen* 18 (1986) 313–39.

_____. "Kothar wa-Hasis, the Ugaritic Craftsman God." Ph.D. dissertation, Yale University, 1985.

_____. "The Magic of Kothar, the Ugaritic Craftsman God, in KTU 1.6 VI 49–50." *Revue biblique* 91 (1984) 377–80.

Smith, W. Robertson. *The Religion of the Semites: The Fundamental Institutions.* New York: Schocken, 1972.

Spronk, Klaas. *Beatific Afterlife in Ancient Israel and in the Ancient Near East.* Alter Orient und Altes Testament 219. Kevelaer: Butzon & Bercker/ Neukirchen-Vluyn: Neukirchener Verlag, 1986.

Stadelmann, Rainer. *Syrisch-palästinensische Gottheiten in Ägypten.* Problème der Ägyptologie 5. Leiden: Brill, 1967.

Stager, Lawrence E., and Samuel R. Wolff. "Child Sacrifice at Carthage: Religious Rite or Population Control?" *Biblical Archaeology Review* 10 (January-February 1984) 30–51.

Steinkeller, Piotr. "The Administrative and Economic Organization of the Ur III State: The Core and the Periphery." Pp. 19–41 in *The Organization of Power: Aspects of Bureaucracy in the Ancient Near East.* Edited by McGuire Gibson and Robert D. Biggs. Studies in Ancient Oriental Civilization 46. Chicago: Oriental Institute of the University of Chicago, 1987.

Sweet, Ronald F. G. "The Sage in Mesopotamian Palaces and Royal Courts." Pp. 99–107 in *The Sage in Israel and the Ancient Near East.* Edited by John G. Gammie and Leo G. Perdue. Winona Lake, Indiana: Eisenbrauns, 1990.

Tadmor, Hayim. "Autobiographical Apology in the Royal Assyrian Literature." Pp. 36–57 in *History, Historiography and Interpretation: Studies in Biblical and Cuneiform Literatures.* Edited by H. Tadmor and M. Weinfeld. Jerusalem: Magnes, 1983.

Tångberg, Arvid. "A Note on Baᶜal Zĕbūb in 2 Kings 1,2.3.6.16." *Scandinavian Journal of the Old Testament* 6 (1992) 293–96.

Tarragon, Jean-Michel de. *Le Culte à Ugarit: D'après les textes de la pratique en cunéiformes alphabétiques.* Cahiers de *Revue biblique* 19. Paris: Gabalda, 1980.

Teixidor, Javier. *The Pagan God: Popular Religion in the Greco-Roman Near East.* Princeton: Princeton University Press, 1977.

_____. *The Pantheon of Palmyra.* Études préliminaires aux religions orientales dans l'Empire Romain 79. Leiden: Brill, 1979.

Te Velde, H. *Seth, God of Confusion: A Study of His Role in Egyptian Mythology and Religion.* Problème der Ägyptologie 6. Leiden: Brill, 1967.

Thompson, Thomas L. *The Historicity of the Patriarchal Narratives: The Quest for the Historical Abraham.* Beihefte zur Zeitschrift für die Alttestamentliche Wissenschaft 133. Berlin: de Gruyter, 1974.

Tigay, Jeffrey H. *The Evolution of the Gilgamesh Epic.* Philadelphia: University of Pennsylvania Press, 1982.

_____ . *You Shall Have No Other Gods: Israelite Religion in the Light of Hebrew Inscriptions.* Harvard Semitic Studies 31. Atlanta: Scholars Press, 1986.

Townsend, Joan B. "The Goddess: Fact, Fallacy and Revitalization Movement." Pp. 179–203 in *Goddesses in Religions and Modern Debate.* Edited by Larry W. Hurtado. University of Manitoba Studies in Religion 1. Atlanta: Scholars Press, 1990.

Tsevat, Matitiahu. "A Window for Baal's House: The Maturing of a God." Pp. 151–61 in *Studies in Bible and the Ancient Near East Presented to Samuel E. Loewenstamm on his Seventieth Birthday.* Edited by Yitschak Avishur and Joshua Blau. Jerusalem: Rubinstein, 1978.

Van Buitenen, J. A. B., editor and translator. *The Mahabharata, 1: The Book of the Beginning.* Chicago: University of Chicago Press, 1973.

Van Seters, John. *In Search of History: Historiography in the Ancient World and the Origins of Biblical History.* New Haven, Connecticut: Yale University Press, 1983.

Vaux, Roland de. *The Bible and the Ancient Near East.* Translated by Damian McHugh. Garden City, New York: Doubleday, 1971.

Vawter, Bruce. "Yahweh: Lord of the Heavens and the Earth." *Catholic Biblical Quarterly* 48 (1986) 461–67.

Vincent, Albert. *La Religion des Judéo-Araméens d'Éléphantine.* Paris: Geuthner, 1937.

Virolleaud, Charles. "Le Déchiffrement des tablettes alphabétiques de Ras-Shamra." *Syria* 12 (1931) 15–23.

_____ . "Les Inscriptions cunéiformes de Ras Shamra." *Syria* 10 (1929) 304–10.

_____ . "Un Nouveau chant du poème d'Aleïn-Baal." *Syria* 13 (1932) 113–63.

_____ . "La Révolte de Košer contre Baal: Poème de Ras-Shamra (III AB, A)." *Syria* 16 (1935) 29–45.

Vriezen, T. C. *The Religion of Ancient Israel.* Translated by Hubert Hoskins. Philadelphia: Westminster, 1967.

Walker, Barbara G. *The Woman's Encyclopedia of Myths and Secrets.* San Francisco: Harper & Row, 1983.

Walls, Neal Hugh, Jr. "The Goddess Anat in Ugaritic Myth." Ph.D. dissertation, Johns Hopkins University, 1991.

Ward, William A. "La Déesse nourricière d'Ugarit." *Syria* 46 (1969) 225–39.

Ware, Timothy. *The Orthodox Church.* New York: Penguin, 1964.

Weber, Max. *The Theory of Social and Economic Organization.* Translated by A. M. Henderson and Talcott Parsons. New York: Free Press, 1947.

Weidner, Ernst. *Die Inschriften Tukulti-Ninurtas I und seiner Nachfolger. Archiv für Orientforschung* 12. Osnabrück: Biblio, 1970.

Weippert, Helga. *Palästina in vorhellenistischer Zeit.* Handbuch der Archäologie: Vorderasiaen 2/1. Munich: Beck, 1988.

Weippert, Manfred. "The Balaam Text from Deir ʿAllā and the Study of the Old Testament." Pp. 151–84 in *The Balaam Text from Deir ʿAlla Re-evaluated: Proceedings of the International Symposium Held at Leiden 21–24 August 1989.* Edited by Jacob Hoftijzer and G. van der Kooij. Leiden: Brill, 1991.

Weiser, Artur. *The Psalms: A Commentary.* Translated by Herbert Hartwell. Old Testament Library. Philadelphia: Westminster, 1962.

Wellhausen, Julius. *Prolegomena to the History of Ancient Israel.* Cleveland: World Publishing, 1957.

Wente, Edward F. Jr. "Astarte and the Insatiable Sea." Pp. 133–36 in *The Literature of Ancient Egypt: An Anthology of Stories, Instructions, and Poetry.* New ed. Edited by William Kelly Simpson. New Haven, Connecticut: Yale University Press, 1973.

Whybray, R. N. "The Sage in the Israelite Royal Court." Pp. 133–39 in *The Sage in Israel and the Ancient Near East.* Edited by John G. Gammie and Leo G. Perdue. Winona Lake, Indiana: Eisenbrauns, 1990.

Wickham, L. R. "The Sons of God and the Daughters of Men: Genesis VI 2 in Early Christian Exegesis." *Oudtestamentische Studiën* 19 (1974) 135–47.

Widengren, G. "Evolutionism and the Problem of the Origin of Religion." *Ethnos* 10 (1945) 57–96.

Wiggins, Steve A. "The Myth of Asherah: Lion Lady and Serpent Goddess." *Ugarit-Forschungen* 23 (1991) 383–94.

Wilson, John A. "The Assembly of a Phoenician City." *Journal of Near Eastern Studies* 4 (1945) 245.

_____. "Egyptian Myths, Tales, and Mortuary Texts." Pp. 3–36 in *Ancient Near Eastern Texts Relating to the Old Testament.* 3d ed. Edited by James B. Pritchard. Princeton: Princeton University Press, 1969.

Wilson, Robert R. "The Death of the King of Tyre: The Editorial History of Ezekiel 28." Pp. 211–18 in *Love and Death in the Ancient Near East: Essays in Honor of Marvin H. Pope.* Edited by John H. Marks and Robert M. Good. Guilford, Connecticut: Four Quarters, 1987.

Wintermute, O. S. "Jubilees (Second Century B.C.)." Pp. 35–142 in *The Old Testament Pseudepigrapha,* volume 2. Edited by James H. Charlesworth. Garden City, New York: Doubleday, 1985.

Wolfe, Rolland Emerson. "The Editing of the Book of the Twelve." *Zeitschrift für die Alttestamentliche Wissenschaft* 53 (1935) 90–129.

Wood, W. Carleton. *The Religion of Canaan: From the Earliest Times to the Hebrew Conquest.* Ontario: Newmarket, 1916.

Wyatt, Nicolas. "Cosmic Entropy in Ugaritic Religious Thought." *Ugarit Forschungen* 17 (1985) 383–86.

_____. "The Hollow Crown: Ambivalent Elements in West Semitic Royal Ideology." *Ugarit Forschungen* 18 (1986) 421–36.

_____. "Quaternities in the Mythology of Ba^c^al." *Ugarit Forschungen* 21 (1989) 451–59.

Xella, Paolo. "Aspekte religiöser Vorstellungen in Syrien nach den Ebla- und Ugarit-Texten." *Ugarit Forschungen* 15 (1983) 279–90.

_____. *Gli antenati di Dio: Divinità e miti della tradizione di Canaan.* Verona: Essedue, 1981.

_____. *Il mito di ŠḤR e ŠLM: Saggio sulla mitologia ugaritica.* Studia semitici 44. Rome: Istituto di studi del vicino oriente, 1973.

_____. *I testi rituali di Ugarit, Testi.* Studia semitici 54. Rome: Consiglio nazionale delle ricerche, 1981.

Yaron, Kalmon. "The Dirge over the King of Tyre." *Annual of the Swedish Theological Institute* 3 (1964) 28–57.

Yon, Marguerite, and Jacqueline Gachet. "Une Statuette du dieu El à Ougarit." *Syria* 66 (1989) 349.

Zevit, Ziony. "The Khirbet el-Qôm Inscription Mentioning a Goddess." *Bulletin of the American Schools of Oriental Research* 255 (1984) 39–47.

Zijl, Peter J. van. *Baal: A Study of Texts in Connexion with Baal in the Ugaritic Epics.* Alter Orient und Altes Testament 10. Kevelaer: Butzon & Bercker/Neukirchen-Vluyn: Neukirchener Verlag, 1972.

Index of Deity Names

205

Index of Authors

207

Index of Scripture References

213

Index of Ancient Sources